The Masque
of Stuart Culture

The Masque of Stuart Culture

Jerzy Limon

DELAWARE

Newark: University of Delaware Press
London and Toronto: Associated University Presses

© 1990 by Associated University Presses, Inc.

All rights reserved. Authorization to photocopy items for internal or personal use, or the internal or personal use of specific clients, is granted by the copyright owner, provided that a base fee of $10.00, plus eight cents per page, per copy is paid directly to the Copyright Clearance Center, 27 Congress Street, Salem, Massachusetts 01970. [0-87413-396-3/90 $10.00+8¢ pp, pc.]

Associated University Presses
440 Forsgate Drive
Cranbury, NJ 08512

Associated University Presses
25 Sicilian Avenue
London WC1A 2QH, England

Associated University Presses
P.O. Box 488, Port Credit
Mississauga, Ontario
Canada L5G 4M2

The paper used in this publication meets the requirements of the American National Standard for Permanence of Paper for Printed Library Materials Z39.48-1984.

Library of Congress Cataloging-in-Publication Data

Limon, Jerzy, 1950–
   The masque of Stuart culture / Jerzy Limon.
   p. cm.
   Includes bibliographical references.
   ISBN 0-87413-396-3 (alk. paper)
   1. Masques—History and criticism. 2. English drama—17th century—History and criticism. 3. Theater—England—History—17th century. 4. Great Britain—Court and courtiers—History—17th century. 5. Stuart, House of. I. Title.
PR678.M3L56   1990
822'.05—dc20   89-40475
                                                                 CIP

PRINTED IN THE UNITED STATES OF AMERICA

Contents

Preface	7
Acknowledgments	11

Part 1

1	The Literary Masque	17
2	The Emblematic Masque	52
3	The Masque of Behavior	92

Part 2

4	Masque Cycles and Courtly "Festivals"	107
5	Masque Cycle I	125
6	Masque Cycle II	170

Conclusion	198
Notes	201
Bibliography	217
Index	231

Preface

Recent masque criticism has been dominated by the tendency to see the masque in its immediate political context and to read the extant texts as deeply involved in current politics. This trend in criticism results in works frequently entitled "The Politics of . . ." or "The Occasion of . . . ," followed by the masque title. Critics who admire this trend usually believe that a literary work has one invariant meaning and that the role of literary studies is to elucidate this meaning by reconstructing the contemporary connotations of a given work. Thus it is indirectly implied that an understanding of a given work should rely on the current reception of the work. Consequently a critic following this trend is more interested in what went on "behind the scenes" than in the text itself, and focuses on patronage and factions at court. He or she sees the masque as an important tool in the political struggle of the time, used either to support or undermine the interests of those in power.

An approach of the kind described above has primarily a historical and sociological focus, and the analysis of a literary text is used to corroborate certain ideological views of the period under discussion, views of history, and, generally, a critic's world view. In other words, literary texts are instrumental in the discussion of issues other than literature; literature becomes only a pretext to talk about history, politics, and so forth. At times it is impossible to distinguish whether a given work was written by a literary scholar or by a historian. It is true that literature does not exist in isolation, but if the study of literature is to remain a distinct discipline of scholarship, then at least its areas of interest should be made distinct from those of other disciplines. In the "literary" studies concerned predominantly with patronage, for instance, one can see no difference in the approach of either a political or cultural historian. This is what makes it possible for historians, as Kevin Sharpe has recently shown, to enter into what seems to be the study of literature but in fact is the study of history with the use of specific sources—namely literary texts. However, the use of literary sources does not necessarily guarantee the literary nature of a given scholarly work.

For literary historians, it seems, the matter of patronage and political topicality should be of secondary importance. Not that one should neglect them, but both of these factors do not really describe a literary work: they reveal the function of the text in its social circulation. This function is not an invariant feature of the text: it changes in time. What was true, say, in 1600 was not true a year later, or in 1620. "Political" texts of the past always lose their original political character as time goes on. Actually, any discussion of "meaning" is confounded by temporal barriers. Meaning is not an invariant feature of a literary work. It changes in time, as the history of reception proves. Rather a literary historian should ask questions concerning how a literary work creates meaning, whether political or not. What is in a literary text that makes it distinct from all other types of texts?

In this book I shall concentrate on a group of seventeenth-century texts, called masques, in an attempt to distinguish their common and characteristic features. What exactly is it that enables one to classify them as a genre, and what genre is it? Are masques a minor dramatic form or are they journalistic narratives? Are they, perhaps, an example of occasional poetry? How did masques create meaning in their own time, and how can they be related to the courtly culture that produced them? How are they related to other court entertainments? All of these questions will be dealt with, not necessarily in this order, in an attempt to see masques as the fullest manifestation of the culture of the early Stuart court.

By the term *masque* I mean two different phenomena. The first is the literary masque as a type of text that has survived in print or manuscript to the twentieth century. The second is the masque-in-performance, a theatrical text that can only be reconstructed on the basis of surviving contemporary sources. Both of these types will be taken into account in this book. The opposition of a "literary" and a "theatrical" text derives from my conviction that theater is not literature: these are in fact two distinct systems, governed by their intrinsic rules. A literary text, like a piece of drama, may become a part of a theatrical text, where it may (but often does not) play a dominant role. In this way, by becoming one of many elements of a theatrical production (along with music, choreography, acting, lighting, scenography, and so forth) a literary text loses its generic autonomy and should only be treated as a significant part of the whole. Theater uses its own

Preface

system of signs, which is different from the literary sign-system, and when a literary text is transformed into the sign-system of the theater it creates meanings peculiar to theater and not to literature. A transformation of this kind is always connected with interpretation: every production that adapts a literary text is somebody's (usually the director's) interpretation of this text.

The distinction between theater and literature is very helpful here for it allows discussion about two separate phenomena: the masque-in-performance and the literary text preserved in print or in manuscript. The distinction enables one to avoid some of the recurrent critical controversies connected with the masque's "meaning." One of the aims of this book is to show that the two types of masque texts not only belong to different systems (theater and literature) and therefore create meanings in a different way, but also that these meanings are essentially different.

The aim of this book is not to give a final answer to the critical problem that the masque creates; it only attempts to show several possible approaches to these highly complex and "hieroglyphic" texts. First, I discuss the literary masque as a group of texts that share certain common and distinctive features that allow their treatment as a discrete literary genre. One of the suggestions I make in the following chapter is that the masque-in-performance can be viewed as a theatrical, three-dimensional emblem in which the stage-picture (designed with the use of illusionistic perspective) functions as the emblem's icon, while the verses and lyrics function as the emblem's motto. For this reason the Jacobean masques may be seen as a theatrical emblem book of the early Stuart courtly culture in general and King James's *Basilikon Doron* in particular. In a later chapter I discuss the masque as an example of a text that shows a tendency to join into cycles with other masques and into sequences with other texts of courtly culture. The masque may also be seen as a peculiar form of courtly behavior, which often reveals the distinctive features of a ritual.

Part 2 is devoted to one of the most fascinating features of masques: their almost magnetic tendency to form cycles with each other and to acquire textual significance within larger sequences of courtly events. The latter could include public shows of various kinds such as sea battles, fireworks, parades, and knightly challenges and tournaments; it could also include courtly ceremonies connected with such events as the election of the Knights of the Garter, noble marriages, princely investitures, and the like. Being a part of a sequence, the masque develops its fullest meanings in relation (and only in this relation) to other concomitant events.

There is considerable evidence that the order and subject matter of particular events was at least in some cases programmed; through its structural features a sequence of that sort reveals the characteristics of an artistic text and may therefore be analyzed as such. Detailed discussions of two complex sequences of courtly events provide an illustration of this phenomenon.

Acknowledgments

I wish to thank the Folger Shakespeare Library for a senior fellowship in 1987–88 and the Huntington Library for a short-term grant in the summer of 1988, which enabled me to compile materials necessary for this book. Parts of the manuscript have been read by Barbara Mowat, David Loewenstein, Linda Levy Peck, Jerry M. Pinciss, Frank Cioffi, and Colin Campbell, who have smoothed the rough style of the original, with the final polish given by Elizabeth Reynolds. All of these people, along with the libraries' ever-helpful staffs, deserve the author's deepest gratitude. The faults that remain are his own.

The Masque
of Stuart Culture

Part 1

1
The Literary Masque

The task of defining the masque is not easy, for a great variety of definitions exist, a number of which lack precision. Most of these definitions, however, have one element in common: they are theater-oriented and they deal with the masques as courtly spectacles that originated in the late sixteenth century and fully developed during the reigns of James I and Charles I. The Civil War in England brought an abrupt end to the flourishing form (for many reasons the "masques" staged during Restoration have to be excluded from consideration). Following the British tradition of labeling literary periods by the names of monarchs or dynasties (which in itself assumes a direct relationship between the two historical phenomena),[1] the masque is often referred to as the Stuart masque, and because a number of these pieces were written by Ben Jonson, one of the literary giants of the period, one frequently encounters yet another name—the Jonsonian masque. The latter notion implies, of course, that the masque as a whole may be divided into at least two generic subgroups, the Jonsonian and the "non-Jonsonian" masque, and in fact a number of critics have been at pains to prove that the one group includes distinctive features that are absent from the other one. According to these studies (and to Ben Jonson himself), the Jonsonian masque is more authentic than those written by other poets; it is "truer" to the "essence" of the form. Inigo Jones, as the chief designer of masques, has also evoked much critical interest. Consequently, the study of masques concentrates predominantly on Ben Jonson and Inigo Jones, and not much critical attention is paid to other poets.

Although the masque has almost always been the object of theater studies, as exemplified by Allardyce Nicoll's book,[2] it has evoked considerable interest from historians of literature, who—generally speaking—tend to treat the masque as a minor dramatic form, inferior to serious drama, and who usually do not distinguish between extant texts and their past theatrical realizations at court, treating both distinct phenomena as inseparable. In a recent book on the masque, David Lindley observes that "Confronted by a few pages of text which is often chiefly concerned to describe scenery and costume, contains lyrics that have no music, and is frequently opaquely allegorical or nakedly flattering, the commentator is bewildered. It is not surprising, therefore, that despite a thin trickle of significant scholarly studies, the masque should have been largely neglected or lightly dismissed."[3] The difficulties connected with defining the masque were recognized long ago; George F. Reynolds, among other critics, wrote that "As literature it [the masque] is not to be regarded primarily as narrative or play, but rather, with its inevitable compliments and explanations, as expository dialogue and set speeches interspersed with lyrics. As such it is a unique form of art."[4] In what follows I will attempt to distinguish not only the extant text from its past staging (as belonging to two different systems, literature and theater), but also to bring some order into the general classification of the masque as a textual phenomenon.

We know the titles of about ninety court masques, of which more than half have been preserved, either in print, or—on a few occasions—in manuscript. Strictly speaking, there are two distinct types of manuscript—one written by the poet before the performance and another written by the author of the text prepared for publication. These two writers are in most cases one person, but there are some intriguing exceptions to this rule. The extant texts have to be distinguished from the past spectacles they were part of, for these theatrical performances were the creation of several authors, of whom the poet was not necessarily the most important one. The fact that in the seventeenth century the masques were printed, very often in separate quarto editions, means that contemporaries thought they were worth preserving. Ben Jonson included masques in the carefully prepared 1616 folio edition of his *Workes*, which means that he treated them seriously. The more striking, then, is the lack of distinction, both in specialized dictionaries and in criticism, between the two distinct phenomena in this case: a theater spectacle on the one hand and an extant literary text on the other. To read the latter through what is known about the actual performance is only one of the possible critical approaches: it reconstructs the most likely meanings the text may have created during its first appearance. However, if the extant texts belong to literature they should be able to create meanings independent of their past realizations on stage. If they do not create these meanings, they do not belong to literature. At

The Literary Masque

first sight the distinction seems to be of the same nature as the one between drama and theater, but this turns out to be a false analogy, as I will demonstrate below.

One of the early attempts to treat the masque as a literary form was Dolora Cunningham's article "The Jonsonian Masque as a Literary Form."[5] Quite contrary to the title, throughout her essay Cunningham talks predominantly about the masque-in-performance and does not recognize the transformation that a literary (dramatic) text undergoes on stage. This transformation is caused by the fact that a given text is taken from one system (literature), where it exists as an independent work of art, and is incorporated into a different system (theater), where it loses its independence to become one of several major elements of the production (along with music, scenography, choreography, acting, and so on). For instance, when she talks about Jonson's own concept of the masque, she writes: "The nature of the device [of a masque] is explained by language at times dramatic and at times narrative, and the whole is further illustrated by music, spectacle, and symbolic characters in a sequence of dances."[6] Now in a literary text there is no "music," there is no "spectacle," nor can there possibly be "dances." All of these belong to a different system, not to literature. A literary text can only have a description of the performance and its particular elements, and can only have a projection of a performance that might but does not have to take place in the future.

In his influential book, *The Jonsonian Masque* (1965), Stephen Orgel made a serious attempt to discuss the masque as a literary genre. However, the book does not go far enough in its basically original and often illuminating arguments. At one point, for instance, Orgel writes: "In considering the Jonsonian masque as a literary form, on the one hand, and as an occasional entertainment, on the other, we are not dealing with two independent things, but only with two aspects of the same thing."[7]

One of my arguments in this book is that these are, in fact, two independent things. As I already mentioned, in critical writings the printed masque is usually treated as a minor and somewhat inferior generic offspring of drama, or as a sort of "scenario," a script, or even a "libretto" for a theatrical performance. Again, Stephen Orgel is an honorable exception here, for he tends to treat some of the masques as a specific form of didactic poetry. At the same time not much attention has been paid to the fact that, without a serious violation of the text, not a single one of the printed masques could, for reasons that will be discussed shortly, be staged in theater or at court. Of course, the lack of stage "realization," or production, does not determine whether a given text is drama or a "scenario." But in the case of printed masques, with possibly one exception, none of the texts known to me "foresees" its own staging. The above observation may be received with some scepticism, for the custom of staging masques at court has already been mentioned. But the poet's text that was used for particular performances was at times drastically different from the one that has been preserved in the printed form.

We are actually dealing with three different texts, which belong not only to different genres but also to different systems. Thus, if one takes into account their succession in time, the first text one could distinguish would be some "Ur-masque," a "pre-text," a part of a syncretic scenario for the performance—"syncretic" because it was composed of verbal elements (stage directions, lyrics, dialogues) and nonverbal elements (stage design, costume design, technical drawings and plans for stage machinery, sheet music, some idea of choreography). This pre-text, one has to remember, was not the creation of one person and did not have to be written down as one script; rather it was a sum of texts prepared by the poet, stage designer, stage engineer, composer of music and choreographer. It could exist as a whole, for example, only in the mind of the person or persons responsible for a particular production, somebody today called the director. Stephen Orgel and Roy Strong believe that "there is considerable evidence that [Inigo] Jones was responsible for the direction of the masques."[8]

Most interesting to my purpose is the poetic or literary pre-text, which obviously did fulfill the function of one of the elements of the scenario, by which it projected its transposition to a different system, such as a stage production. By doing so, the text projected its own staging, which allows one to treat it as a text linked to drama. It may therefore be distinguished from its later versions by the term *dramatic masque*. One of the rare preperformance manuscripts of this kind is Ben Jonson's *Christmas his Show*—in the collection of the Folger Shakespeare Library[9]—in which we do not have the usual descriptions of stage design, where entrances of particular characters are not marked at all and the brief stage directions are in the imperative, as "singe." In its first printed version, in the second folio of Jonson's *Workes,* lengthy descriptions of costumes are added and all references to stage action are in the past tense (as is always the case in the printed masques). A manuscript of lyrics for Thomas Campion's *Lord Hayes Masque* has

The Literary Masque

also been preserved among the Robert Cecil papers, and this also is a preperformance text, for the brief stage directions are in the future tense, as "The full song to be songe while the trees are transformed and to be repeated thrice."[10]

In the extant manuscript of Ben Jonson's *The Masque of Blackness* are stage directions that are not included in its first quarto edition of 1608.[11] On the other hand, the printed text of this masque includes lengthy descriptions of scenery and stage action that are not to be found in the preperformance manuscript. Table 1 illustrates some of the conspicuous changes made by Jonson while preparing the manuscript for the press.

It may be added that some of the elements of the performance, such as changes of scenery (as the one following the appearance of the masquers) are not even mentioned or alluded to in the manuscript, which means that they were not foreseen by the author of the dramatic masque. A number of changes, cuts, and additions undoubtedly were made during the rehearsals.

In the manuscript of Jonson's *Pleasure Reconciled to Virtue* (1618) all the stage directions are in the present tense, all of which are altered to the past tense in the printed version (F2). The only exception from the use of the past tense in printed masques is Sir Aston Cohayne's *Bretbie Masque,* originally staged in 1639 and published in his *Chaine of Golden Poems* (1658), where a preperformance text is reproduced. This is proven by the use of the future tense, as in instructions like "To be spoken by whom the Masquers shall appoint," or "Satyrs . . . come in, and dance as many several Anticks . . . as shall be necessary." This feature seems to indicate that the printed version was not prepared for the press by the author. Otherwise, the printed texts, written by professional masque-writers, are always different from the extant preperformance manuscripts.

The second type of manuscript that has been preserved to the twentieth century is that written after the performance, when a given text was prepared for print or presentation. An example of this kind would be Jonson's *The Masque of Queens* (1609), preserved in the British Library (Royal MS.18.A. XLIII). The manuscript does not differ greatly from the quarto edition of this masque, and it includes elaborate descriptions of scenery and a number of learned marginal notes.

During its staging the dramatic text transposed into a different system of signs—that is, into a masque spectacle. One may treat the latter as a theatrical text. This particular text, which is usually defined in specialized dictionaries and has traditionally been the

Table 1
The Masque of Blackness

The Quarto Edition of 1608	The Manuscript (Royal MS. 17.B.XXXI)
The *Masquers* were placed in a great concaue shell, like mother of pearle curiously made to moue on those waters, and rise with the billow; the top thereof was stuck with a *cheu'-ron* of lights, which, intended to the proportion of the shell, strooke a glorious beame vpon them, as they were seated, one aboue another: so that they were all seene, but in an extrauagant order.	The *Masquers* are placed in an entire concave shell of mother of pearle, curiously made to move on those waters, and
On sides of the shell did swim sixe huge *Sea-monsters,* varyed in their shapes, and dispositions, bearing on their backs the twelve *torch-bearers*; who were planted there in seuerall greces; so as the backs of some were seene; some in *purfle,* or side; others in face; and all hauing their light burning out of *whelles,* or *murex* shells.	guarded (for more ornament) wth *Dolphins,* and sea-monsters of different shapes: on wch in payres their light-bearers are wth their lights burninge out of *Murex* shells, advanced. . . . .
At this the Moone *was discovered in the upper part of the house, triumphant in a Siluer throne, made in figure of a Pyramis. Her garments White, and, Siluer, the dressing of her head antique; & crown'd with a Luminarie, or Sphere of light: which striking on the clouds, and heightned with Siluer, reflected as natural clouds doe by the splendour of the Moone. The heaven, about her, was vaulted with blue silke, and set with starres of Siluer which had in them their seuerall lights burning. The suddaine sight of which made NIGER to interrupt OCEANUS with this present passion.*	At this the *Moone* is discovered in ye vpper pte of the house, triumphant, in a chariot, hir garments white, and siluer, the dressinge of hir head antique, and crowned wth lights. To hir *Niger.*

The Literary Masque

object of critical writings, may be called the *masque-in-performance*. The irony is that it does not exist and can never be retrieved. We can only try to reconstruct it, an attempt comparable to describing today's musicals without the use of audiovisual aids, which is virtually impossible. How does one describe choreography? Or music? Jonson himself acknowledged a literary text's inability to describe the dances: "Here, they danc'd a third most elegant, and curious dance, and not to be describ'd againe, by any art, but that of their owne footing."[12] And, in another place, Jonson—who fully recognized the ephemeral character of a spectacle—stressed the impossibility of reconstructing the actual performance either by imagination or a description:

> Such was the exquisit Performance, as . . . that alone (had all else beene absent) was of power to surprize with Delight, and steale the *Spectators* from themselves. . . . Only the Envie was, that it lasted not still, or (now it is past) cannot by Imagination, much less Description, be recover'd to a part of that *Spirit*, it had in the gliding by.[13]

Consequently, in comparing the masque-in-performance with the extant printed text, one will notice a striking reversal of the proportion of the structural elements of the form. What dominated the masque-in-performance were the dances, which were able to create meanings other than aesthetic, which means that they were given text-significance. These are reduced to one or two sentences of description in the printed text, if mentioned at all. On several occasions, however, instead of descriptions of the dances in the masques, one finds authorial interpretations of their "meaning." One ought to remember that dances were much more "meaningful" than they are today; in other words, they were significant and were analyzed as a text. Francis Bacon mentions dances to music as the most prominent feature of the masque. Sir Thomas Elyot remarked in his *Boke, Named the Governor* (1580) that "The interpretours of Plato doe thynke, that the wonderfull and incomprehensible order of the celestiall bodyes . . . and their mocions harmonycall, gaue to them . . . a fourme of imitation of a semblable mocion which they called dauncing";[14] he then provides many ancient examples to prove his point. Sir Thomas included even a whole chapter on "How dauncing may be an introduction vnto the first vertue called Prudence."[15] What dominated in the masque-in-performance, however, is reduced in the printed text to a small fraction of the whole work. The same rule applies to music, which—as is well known—played a very important role in actual performances, whereas in the printed texts it is reduced to brief descriptions. On the other hand, what was perceived with other senses—vision in particular—during the spectacle and did not have any influence on the length of the actual performance (scenery or costumes, for instance), here occupies a substantial portion of the text in the form of lengthy narrative descriptions.

The third type is the text of the masque that has been preserved until this century in printed form. For many reasons this type may not be treated as a dramatic text. To make it distinguishable from the dramatic masque, it might be convenient to label it a *literary masque*. This does not mean that "dramatic" is not "literary," but rather that the latter is "nondramatic." It would be tempting to label this masque "poetic" instead of "literary," but the problem is that a number of masques are dominated by the narrative and cannot be classified as "poetic," even though they include poetic elements. This suggested division of masques has, of course, to be corroborated by other reasons than one's conviction. It is, for instance, supported by the fact that the three types of texts described above were by different authors, although they usually carried similar titles.

The scenario, or the pre-text, was the creation of at least four people: the poet who provided the dramatic masque, the stage designer, the composer of music, and the choreographer—a fact that was generally acknowledged by contemporaries. The contributions of the poet and the stage designer, although not necessarily in that order, were considered the most important. The dramatic masque had usually one author, although there are conspicuous exceptions. The authorship of masques presents a problem and is therefore worth a more careful consideration. The problem appears as early as in Gascoigne's *The Masque at Kenilworth*, first published in 1576; in the printed version, all the narrative bits and comments were actually written by the printer, one Richard Jones, who also compiled the whole. Consequently the printed text has two authors. A similar problem appears in the first text that resembles a fully developed masque, Francis Davison's *The Mask of Proteus and the Adamantine Rock*. This appeared in print as part of *Gesta Grayorum* (1595), which narrates all the entertainments of the Gray's Inn in 1594/95. The anonymous author (who is not Davison) concludes his description of the festivities with *The Mask of Proteus* without mentioning the author of the speeches (i.e., the author of the dramatic masque). Thus the narrator is a coauthor since he provides the descriptive part to

The Literary Masque

Davison's dramatic part. To make matters even more complicated, the verse sections of the masque have in fact two authors, for the opening hymn was written not by Davison, but by Thomas Campion (whose name does not appear in the text, but when the same hymn was published several years later by Davison, he attributed the authorship to Campion). Thus, in what is sometimes considered the first masque there are three authors of the printed, postperformance text (i.e., the literary masque) and two authors of the preperformance dramatic masque. And naturally, when the latter was incorporated into a different system, it became a part of the masque-in-performance, which had even more authors (as actors, musicians, director, and the like).

For contemporaries, the most important category linked with authorship was that of invention, or the discovery of a main idea and its attendant images. It was not important to know who actually wrote the dialogues or lyrics or who actually designed the emblematic scenery; what really counted was who invented them. Sometimes the subtle distinctions made by contemporaries as to who invented what seem pedantic and utterly unnecessary. But they were important to those who created the masques, as it was for Ben Jonson, who stated in one of his masques that although the actors' costumes were the "deuice" of Inigo Jones, the "properties" (or the attributes) of Witches, such as "vipers, snakes, bones, herbs, rootes, and other ensignes of theyr *Magick*, out of the authority of ancient & late *Writers*" were all his invention.[16] The title page of George Chapman's *Memorable Masque* (1613) states that the masque, or the spectacle, was "Invented, and fashioned, with the ground, and special structure of the whole work, By our Kingdomes most Artfull and Ingenious Architect Innigo Jones"; the printed, postperformance text, however, was "Supplied, Aplied, Digested, and written, By Geo: Chapman." From the printed version of *Tempe Restord* (1631) we learn that "All the Verses were written by M. *Aurelian Townshend*. The subiect and Allegory of the Masque, with the descriptions, and Apparatus of the Sceanes were invented by *Inigo Iones*, Surveyor of his Maiesties worke."[17] Thus Inigo Jones was not only the main inventor of the masque-in-performance, but he was also a coauthor of the printed version.

The introductory comments to *Luminalia* (1638) state that

> the Queene commanded Inigo Iones . . . to make a new subject of a Masque for her selfe, that with high and hearty invention, might give occasion for variety of Scenes, strange aparitions, songs, Musick and

dancing of severall kinds . . . This being suddainly done and shewed her Majestie, and she approving it, the work was set in hand, and with all cele[b]rity performed in shorter time, than any thing here hath bene done in this kind.[18]

Thus, Inigo Jones was the chief author of the masque-in-performance, to which D'Avenant provided the verbal part. On the other hand, D'Avenant is the only author of the printed postperformance text, or of the literary masque. And on the title page of *Britannia Triumphs* (1638), the authorship is revealed in the following order: "By Inigo Iones . . . and William Davenant." Jones also appears as the first "inventor" of *Pans Anniversarie* (1620), and his name is followed by that of Ben Jonson's. It is, of course, possible to argue that the order was alphabetical, but it cannot be a matter of mere coincidence that—as in the previous example—Jones's name precedes that of Davenant. Consequently, in discussing both the masque-in-performance and the literary masque, one should treat *Pans Anniversarie* as (primarily) Inigo Jones's. Ben Jonson's role was to provide the verses for somebody else's invention.

Similarly James Shirley "invented" and "wrote" *The Triumph of Peace* (1633), and Thomas Campion "invented and set forth" *Lord Hayes Masque* (1607). Aurelian Townshend and Inigo Jones were the joint inventors of *Albions Triumph* (1631), but Townshend was the sole author of the printed text. In the quarto edition of *The Masque of Augurs* is a final note (missing in the second folio of 1640) signed "B[en]. J[onson]":

> For the expression of this, I must stand, The inuention was diuided betwixt Mr. Iones, and mee. The Scene, which your eye iudges, was wholly his, and worthy his place of the Kings Surueyour, and Architect, full of noble obseruation of Antiquitie, and high Presentment. The Musique compos'd by that excellent paire of Kinsemen, Mr Alphonso Ferrabosco, and Mr. Nicholas Lanier.[19]

As we read in the printed masque by Davenant *Salmacida Spolia* (1640), "the invention, ornament scenes, and apparitions with their descriptions, were made by Inigo Jones. What was spoken or sung, by William Davenant. . . . The subject was set down by them both." Thus the poet is only a coauthor of the printed postperformance version, which includes "descriptions" written by Jones, whereas he undoubtedly was the sole author of dialogues and lyrics of the preperformance part of the scenario, or the dramatic masque. The multiple authorship of the masque-in-performance was often acknowledged by contemporaries, and the printed versions occasionally give names of the collaborators. For instance, in *The Masque of Queens* (1609) Ben Jonson gives a detailed description of a "magical dance," mentioning that "all which were excellently imitated by the maker of the dance, Mr Hierome Herne, whose right it is here to be named." James Shirley in *The Triumph of Peace* (1634) explained that "the scene and ornament [i.e., the proscenium arch] was the act of Inigo Jones. . . . The composition of music was performed by Mr William Lawes and Mr Simen Ives, whose art gave an harmonious soul to the otherwise languishing numbers." And Samuel Daniel, in the preface to *Tethys Festival* (1610), openly admitted the secondary role of the poet:

> . . . in these things wherin the only life consists in show, the art and invention of the architect gives the greatest grace, and is of most importance: ours [i.e., the poet's], the least part and of least note *in the time of the performance thereof;* and therefore I have interseded the description of the artificial part, which only speaks M. Inigo Jones. (Emphasis added.)

It is worth noting that Daniel clearly distinguishes the masque-in-performance, which has several authors, of whom the stage designer was the most important, from the printed text that has only one author: the narrative "I" of the quoted fragment. What was clear to contemporaries became confused in twentieth-century criticism. Owing to the fact that the bulk of the latter has been written by historians of literature, the question of authorship often is not even disputed: it is always the poet who is treated as the first author. This remains a rule even when the focus is placed on the masque-in-performance. As Roy Strong points out, "we are so used to approaching the masque by means of the literary text that we forget that it was Jones who actually devised the plots and allegories of virtually all of them after 1630."[20] The problem of course is of a different nature when one makes a distinction between the literary masque and the masque-in-performance, something that Strong apparently does not do; instead, he defends one form against the other as if they were in opposition. Another example of a similar confusion in criticism is Graham Parry's comment, "Since the music of almost all the masques is lost, and the dances are irretrievable, modern attention concentrates *excessively* on the documented contributions of Jonson and Jones, with the result that we give *too much prominence* to the intellectual [sic] element of the genre . . . [and] since we tend to read the masques from the standpoint of Ben Jonson, who was only one of a group of collaborators, we exaggerate the importance of his images and learning in the total effect of the revels"[21] (emphasis added). Parry obviously confuses the masque-in-performance with the literary type. Once the distinction is made, the problem he raises ceases to exist. At any rate, the entire question of masque authorship needs a thorough revision. It is impossible to speak about the "Jonsonian" masque when one has the actual production in mind.

From the evidence provided above it seems clear that the masque-in-performance and the printed literary masque not only belong to different systems, but also that their authorship is not the same. The first type of masque always has several authors (not to mention all those who actually performed), the second is the creation, with few exceptions, of an individual. They also differ in length, for in a number of printed texts elaborate notes are added, along with dedications, "arguments," addresses, and the like. In other words, the text that has come down in print did not exist before the performance. What did exist was a pre-text, or dramatic masque, that was also a part of a larger scenario for the performance, and which, for many reasons, cannot be identified with the printed, or literary masque.

The authorial dramatic text, when adapted for the stage, was often altered beyond the author's control during the actual performance, at times by the king himself. Both kings, James I and Charles I, played the roles of censors for the masques (since the latter did not need a license from the Master of the Revels) and were responsible for the deletion of whole passages that they found unpalatable to their tastes or incompatible with the "present occasion." Sometimes political cuts were made to not offend foreign ambassadors, who were customarily invited to court masques. King James, for instance, personally censored Ben Jonson's *Neptune's Triumph* in 1624.[22] At times the king's intervention led to the cancelation of a masque, as was the case with *The Masque of Amazons*, scheduled for 6 January 1618. As John Chamberlain writes in a letter of 3 January of that year, "There was a masque of nine Ladies in hand at their own cost, whereof the principal was the Lady Hay, as the Queen of the Amazons . . . but whatsoever the cause was, neither the Queen nor King did like it or allow of it,—and so all is dashed."

Moreover, the unpredictability of the king's reactions and behavior during the performance, James's in particular, made it impossible to foresee and include in the preperformance scenario

The Literary Masque

everything that actually happened. King James could, for instance, get bored with the masque, as during the performance of Ben Jonson's *Pleasure Reconciled to Virtue* (1618), which he interrupted in the middle with a shout, "What did they make me come here for? Devil take you, all dance."[23] Of course, the printed text includes the dialogues the spectators did not hear and does not include any indication of the king's behavior. As an account of the actual performance it fails in its accuracy and shows its independence as an artistic text. This was a feature that Jonson insisted upon in his later masques, when he had turned away from what initially was a narration of the actual performance, with the poetic parts appended to the dominating narrative text, to literary masques that are independent of their past staging. Sometimes these texts even pretend to have been staged when in fact they were not. All of these tendencies will be discussed below in detail.

From the *Masque of the Inner Temple* (1613) by Francis Beaumont we learn that during the performance the king liked one of the dances so much that "it pleased him to call for it at the end, as he did likewise for the first anti-masque, but one of the Statues by that time was undressed." This masque followed the first unsuccessful attempt to stage it: the earlier performance, which was to follow the progress by the Thames that did actually take place, was called off because the king was "so wearied and sleepie . . . that he had no edge to yt." Similarly, in Ben Jonson's *Masque of Beauty* (1609) some dances were repeated on James's request: "they danced forth their second dance, more subtle, and full of change, then the former; as the Kings maiestie incited first (by his owne liking, to that whill all others, there present wish'd) requir'd them both againe, after some time dancing with the Lords. Which time, to giue them respite, was intermitted with song. . . ." Ben Jonson's *Pleasure Reconciled to Virtue* ends with the following comment: "This pleas'd the KING so well, as he would see it againe, when it was presented with these additions [being the sequel masque, *For the Honour of Wales*]." As one can see, King James did not believe in the finite state of a work of art.

And when a masque was staged in honor of the King of Denmark in 1606, the performance could not be predicted by either the authors or the spectators. A contemporary report says that, first, the woman who played the Queen's part tripped and fell at the Dane's feet; then the King of Denmark got up, but being intoxicated fell down and "humbled himself." The show went on, however, with the guest of honor carried away to an inner chamber. Unfortunately, as Sir John Harrington writes, "most of the presenters went backward and fell down—wine did so occupy their upper chambers. Now did appear, in rich dress, Hope, Faith, and Charity: Hope did assay to speak, but wine rendered her endevours so feeble that she withdrew. . . . Charity came to the king's feet . . . she then turned to Hope and Faith, who were both sick and spewing in the lower hall."[24] One detail certainly not included in the scenario for the masque was a woman who, as a contemporary source notes, "lost her honesty, for which she was carried to the porters lodge being surprised at her busines on the top of the Taras."[25]

Sometimes the stage machinery failed, destroying the development of stage action. The printed version of Thomas Campion's *Lord Hayes Masque* (1607) describes a change of scenery that actually did not take place. A marginal note informs that "Either by the simplicity, negligence, or conspiracy of the painter, the passing away of the trees was somewhat hazarded the patterne of them the same day hauing bene showne with much admiration, and the 9 trees beeing left vnsett together euen to the same night."[26] This implies that the description in the main text is inaccurate, for it describes the change of scenery that should have taken place but in fact did not. The printed masques often treat the actual performance as they ought to have been staged but not as they really were.

It is worthwhile to analyze Andrzej Zgorzelski's concept that the basic distinctive feature of drama as a genre is its "double nature"[27] from the standpoint that on one hand a dramatic text functions as an autonomous literary text, and may be analyzed as such, and on the other it projects its own staging. These two functions stand in opposition to each other and thus generate a tension peculiar to all dramatic texts. However, in the case of the printed texts of masques there is no opposition of this kind, no "double nature" in the text. Nearly all the printed texts do not foresee their staging. In other words, a theatrical production at court brings an end to the dramatic masque: it ceases to exist once the production had ended. Because of its peculiar features, it cannot be repeated without substantial changes in the text: the meanings generated during the particular performance are unique for the particular occasion and cannot be retrieved. On the other hand, the meanings created by the printed text are never the same as those of the spectacle. These are two different texts, each belonging to a different system. The fact that the masques might be staged in a theater even today does not impair the validity of this assertion because a performance of that kind would be an adaptation. It is, after all, possible to adapt for stage a short story, a novella, or even a cycle of sonnets. That the printed masques have hitherto been treated by a number of critics as a minor dramatic form has partly been caused by the typographical similarity of the extant texts to printed drama. There are dialogues, lyrics, and something that at first sight looks like stage directions but in fact is not.

However, in the vast majority of printed masques there also are—as pointed out above—prefaces, addresses, introductions, dedications, plot summaries, and even elaborate footnotes and marginal notes; sometimes there are also digressions or even replies to criticism. A good example of the latter may be found in Ben Jonson's *Masque of Queens* (1609), where at one point, following a lengthy description, the author makes this statement:

> But here, I discerne a possible obiection, arising against me; to which I must turne: As, *How I can bring* Persons *of so different Ages, to appeare properly together? or, why (which is more unnaturall) with* Virgil's *Mezentius, I ioyne the liuing with the dead?* I answere to both these, at once. . . .

And in George Chapman's *Memorable Masque* (1613) is the author's reply to "certaine insolent obiections made against the length of my speeches and narrations." All of this causes a conspicuous distortion of the proportion of dialogues and the subordinate text: in drama, almost without exception, dialogue dominates; here dialogues and songs often constitute less than half of the whole text. In addition, stage directions are a very important element in a play's construction: they project theatrical realization of the text and provide people responsible for the production with various pieces of information concerning stage business, acting, scenery, music, and so on. In the printed, or literary, masques there are no stage directions; instead of the projected staging are *descriptions* of performances that have already taken place. These are not just any performances but ones that took place on the night and in the place revealed in the title.

I have already pointed out that in most cases the grammatical tense used in the descriptions in the masques is the simple past, which never happens in dramatic stage directions. Even when the present tense is used occasionally, it is what we call "presens historicum." Let me give several examples from a typical text, such as Ben Jonson's *Pleasure Reconciled to Virtue* (1618). Some "stage directions" read as follows: "The scene was the mountain Atlas"; "At this the whole grove vanished, and the whole Music was discovered"; "Here the whole Choir of music called the masquers forth"; "Hence they danced with the ladies." With few exceptions, which are discussed below, this is the feature of all extant texts. They do not project their own staging and they are in fact narrative relations about a single performance that had already taken place. Ben Jonson is the only masque writer who tried at one point to abandon the narrative character of printed masques in order to create a new literary form that would be autonomous, or independent from the past theater realization. This resulted in amalgamated works composed of poetic, dramatic, and narrative elements.

The narrative character of most of the extant texts is additionally confirmed by the appearance of a first-person narrator who often reminds the reader that he is not omniscient and that he describes the performance in the best way he can. The narration is always selective, and it may be treated as the author's subjective account of what had actually happened during the performance. For instance, in Thomas Campion's *Lord Hayes Masque* (1607) is a typical example of the narrator's skipping over some of his material: ". . . about it [the stage] were plac't on wyer artificial Battes, and Owles, continually mouing: with many other inuentions, the which for breuitie sake I passe by with silence."[28] Does this ever happen in drama? The selective character of the printed texts is also proven by omissions. For instance, one of the characters, Antaeus, does not appear in the printed text of Jonson's *Pleasure Reconciled to Virtue*, although his battle with Hercules evidently was a part of the masque-in-performance, for it is mentioned by an eye-witness in his description of the spectacle and is also alluded to in a sequel masque, *For the Honour of Wales*. In most masques the descriptions of dances and music are very brief, if included at all. Descriptions of costumes may be very elaborate, or—as in most Jonsonian masques—costumes are almost totally ignored.

By and large the narrative descriptions are often very lengthy and elaborate, for they tend to include the miracles of changing scenery, the wonders of costumes, stage action, and, occasionally, dances and music. This narrative part dominates the dialogues and lyrics in a number of printed texts, and it seems that the poetic bits function as "quotations" or illustrations of the narrative. A good example may be found in Inigo Jones's and James Shirley's *The Triumph of Peace* (1633):

The Literary Masque

> After him rode Opinion and Confidence together; Opinion in an old-fashioned doublet of black velvet and trunk hose, a short cloak of the same with an antique cape, a black velvet cap pinched up, with a white fall, and a staff in his hand; Confidence in a slashed doublet parti-coloured, breeches suitable with points at knees, favours upon his breast and arm; a broad-brimmed hat, tied up on one side, banded with a feather; a long lock of hair, trimmed with several-coloured ribbons; wide boots, and great spurs with bells for rowels.

There would perhaps be nothing curious or extraordinary in the quoted passage if it were not merely an excerpt from a lengthy description of more than twenty stage characters. Similarly, the fourteen printed pages of *Tethys Festival* have only 159 lines of verse (and no dialogues at all). Nearly half of the entire length of Daniel's *Vision of the Twelve Goddesses* (1604) is a prose introduction. In early masques by Jonson, the elaborate marginal and footnotes extend from the left to the right margins; that is, they are often fully justified and occupy most of the space on a printed page.[29]

There is little doubt that the first printed masques were treated by their authors purely as descriptions of memorable court entertainments. This is confirmed, for instance, by the full titles of the printed texts, which almost always differ from the titles of the spectacles they describe, and also from the titles attributed to them by later editors and critics. So, for instance, the masque usually referred to by critics as *Vision of the Twelve Goddesses* by Samuel Daniel carries the following title in the original edition of 1604: *The True Description of a Royal Masque presented at Hampton Court upon Sunday night being the eighth of January 1604 and personated by the Queen's most excellent Majesty, attended by eleven Ladies of Honour*. Thus it is obvious that Daniel draws the distinction between the spectacle and its printed description. And in his dedication to the Countess of Bedford, he confesses that he had "thought not amiss . . . to describe the whole form [which he defines as "the masque and the invention"] thereof in all points as it was then performed." It is worth noting that the narrative dominates in Daniel's text: it contains more than twice as many words as the dialogues and lyrics; furthermore, the latter are in fact relegated to the end of the text and thus function as a sort of appendix to the main text, which is the narrative. What actually appears in this first printed masque is a fusion of a preperformance text with a later description of the spectacle, printed in reversed order. Daniel did not even try to arrange his material in any logical or chronological order, and as a result a lengthy and detailed description of the whole masque precedes the dialogues and songs. Later printed masques have a tendency to insert dialogues and lyrics into appropriate places in the narration.

Similarly, Chapman's *Memorable Masque*, mentioned above, begins with a two-page dedication. This is followed by a description of the procession to the palace and a brief account of the performance—twelve pages altogether. Next is Chapman's reply to criticism—another two pages, after which is something that the author calls "The aplicable argument of the Maske," followed by "Errata" and the cast list. Only after all of this are the dialogues, which, as in the case of Daniel's text, function as an illustration of or an appendix to the main narrative part. Daniel himself, in *Tethys Festival*, declared that:

> For so much as shewes and spectacles of this nature, are vsually registred, among the memorable acts of the time, beeing Complements of state, both to shew magnificence and to celebrate the feasts to our greatest respects: it is expected (*according now fo* [=of] *the custome*) that I, beeing imployed in the busines, should publish a *description and forme* of the late Mask wherewithall it pleased the Queenes most excellent Maiestie to solemnize the creation of the high and mightie Prince Henry, Prince of Wales, in regard to preserue the memorie thereof, and to satisfie their desires, who could haue no other notice, but by others report of what was done. . . .[30]

Thus the text defines itself not as a masque but as a "description and forme" of a masque. Consequently, when a critic talks about the printed text, he or she talks about something substantially different from the masque-in-performance.

There is also no doubt that following the performance, the texts were especially prepared for publication. In other words, they were written in their final form after the performance. This is especially the case with all those texts in which the narrative elements dominate. The twelve masques printed in Ben Jonson's first folio edition of his *Workes* (1616) may be roughly divided into two groups: one, which includes masques with very elaborate descriptions of scenery, costumes, and stage action, and fully annotated with notes (or basically narrative in character), and the second, which includes masques with dominating dramatic elements with no descriptions at all, and with not a single note. The first group belongs to the early phase, or to the years 1605–9, the second to 1610–15. Significantly, all the masques belonging to the first group were first published in quarto editions, a feature that is

The Literary Masque

not shared by any of the masques belonging to the second group. This means that Jonson prepared the fully annotated descriptive masques only when they were to be published as separate editions, and not—as some critics suggest—for the monumental edition of his *Workes* in 1616. This is additionally proven by the curious example of *Oberon* (1611), where there are elaborate notes, common for earlier texts, that appear only in the beginning of the text: it seems as if Jonson, having started preparing the text for print, stopped halfway through and left the work unfinished. And *Oberon* was not published separately before its first appearance in the Folio of 1616.

It seems that this evidence allows the conclusion that in a number of cases the reader is dealing with a description of a single performance, and not a dramatic text that would foresee its own staging. In other words, these texts are basically journalistic in character, a feature that makes a number of printed masques strikingly similar to the descriptions of other courtly or civic events. Even their typographical layout is similar.[31] Dolora Cunningham went so far as to say that

> literature alone can keep the masque alive. The description of the spectacle and the explanation of the various devices are important, also, because they make it possible for posterity to reconstruct the actual performance, to reproduce those elements of scenery, dance, and music which make a direct appeal to the senses and are in large measure responsible for the desired effect of magnificence.[32]

Of course, only some of the masques had this ambition of being a precise "recording" of a performance. In spite of this, many critics and editors found this peculiar feature of masques hard to digest, so the former often neglected the narrative parts, concentrating on dialogues and lyrics, whereas the latter "improved" the text by relegating the descriptive parts and the notes to the appendices or notes of their own editions.[33]

However, it was Ben Jonson who first noticed the potential of these journalistic narratives to become a new literary form, or even a new genre. For this new genre, a description of the actual or even fictitious[34] performance would be its distinctive feature, would be the element modeling the created world, space, characters, action; the description would also play an important role in allegorizing the created world, which, in turn, creates several layers of meaning. In point of fact, it took some time before Jonson found the required results. Stephen Orgel has noted,

> Just as it is clear that Jonson alone conceived of the masque as literature, so it is equally clear that this was his primary concern for it. . . . Nevertheless, there is a curious uncertainty in his theorizing, as if he did not know quite when to begin to establish his new literary form. In the learned footnotes and prefaces we sense that Jonson somehow felt a need to vindicate his attempt to treat the masques as significant didactic poetry.[35]

Treating a description of the actual or fictitious theatrical performance, however brief this description may be, as the most conspicuous feature of this literary genre will enable us to distinguish the literary masque from minor dramatic forms, such as, for instance, Thomas Heywood's *Pleasant Dialogues and Drammas*. . . .[36] These are usually as long as the masques, four hundred to one thousand lines of verse; present allegorical or mythological characters (two to six in number); are often preceded by an "Argument"; sometimes include stage directions (as *Apollo and Daphne*); and are annotated at the end of the volume, where the allegory and mythology are explained. What Heywood's *Dialogues and Drammas* lack, however, are the descriptions of the actual or fictitious performances; this makes them minor dramatic forms (like today's one-act plays) and makes it impossible to treat them as masques, even if the texts claimed this in their titles.

As is apparent from the often-quoted passage, Ben Jonson distinguished two basic elements of the masque-in-performance: "the outward celebration or show," or what is termed today the nonverbal means of communication, and "the most high and hearty inventions to furnish the inward part (and those grounded upon antiquity and solid learning) which, though their voice be taught to sound to present occasions, their sense or doth or should always lay hold on more removed mysteries,"[37] by which he means the verbal elements of the spectacle. Attention should be drawn to the opposition of what Jonson calls "outward celebration or show" and "the inward parts." He does not insist on subordinating one to another, but rather on the coexistence of these elements in a performance. However, as critics have often noticed, Jonson fully realized that spectacle is a transitory art form, something that could not possibly be preserved in time. But the literary element of the performance, although often topical, dealing with the "present occasion" (the referential function of a text), should always be grounded on the several layers of meaning: in other words, it should reveal a poetic function. In this

The Literary Masque 37

Jonson saw the sense of writing and printing masques; he understood masques not only as journalistic descriptions or commentaries on the spectacle, but as autonomous texts creating their worlds according to the rules of literature. This is a conscious creative act that will be revealed, among other things, in the development tendencies of the literary masque. For instance, there will be a tendency to minimize the length and to conventionalize the descriptive part, and also to subordinate it to the rules of literature. This will lead to the creation of what appears to have been a new literary genre, in which one of the constructive elements (apart from mottos, footnotes, marginal notes, quotations, and so forth) will occasionally be a description of a fictitious performance.

It may be useful to recall Roman Jakobson's category of transmutation, or intersemiotic translation.[38] For example, when a text created within one system (in this case theater) is reconstructed with materials of another system (in this case a literary work), it loses its specific theatrical qualities and gains specific literary ones. This is exactly what happens, for instance, in poetry dealing with painting, sculpture, architecture, or music. A good example would be Sir John Davies's *Orchestra, or a Poem of Dancing*,[39] in which the author reconstructs the characteristics of dancing with materials of poetry. The effect of this can be illustrated by stanza 70 of Davies's poem:

> Yet is there one, the most delightful kind,
> A lofty jumping, or a leaping round,
> When arm in arm two dancers are entwin'd,
> And with themsellves with strict embracements bound,
> And still their feet an anapest do sound;
> An anapest is all their music's song,
> Whose first two feet are short and third is long.

Even if a rhythmical analogy is achieved, this will always remain an analogy. Poetry cannot reconstruct any dance, even the simplest one; in spite of all the similarities, poetry will never become music nor painting, and vice versa. As Timothy Murray rightly observed, "The aim of the Jonsonian printed masque is not, then, to recapture and codify the revels, their dances, music, and machines. Rather, Jonson developed a descriptive poetry to be reproduced imaginatively and differently through reading."[40]

In this sense one may define the literary masque as a form dealing with a spectacle, specifically with the court spectacle of the early Stuart epoch. The literary masque reconstructs but at the same time postulates specific attitudes to court performances. It intervenes in the process of perception, by explaining, for instance, the complex symbolism of the nonverbal spectacle signs. This is done through either direct explanation leading to a thorough elucidation of the "difficult bits" or by referring the implied reader to other literary texts through mottos, notes, quotations, sententiae, and the like. All references to other literary works play an additional function of setting the masque within a specific intellectual tradition. At the same time, qualitative comments on particular elements of the spectacle are often inserted. Thus, in what is sometimes considered the first Stuart masque, in Samuel Daniel's *Vision of the Twelve Goddesses* (1604), detailed descriptions of scenery and stage action are accompanied by lengthy explanations of the allegory, as the following passage illustrates:

> . . . in this proiect of ours, *Night & Sleepe* were to produce a Vision, an effect proper to their power, and fit to shadow our purpose, for that these apparitions & shewes are but as imaginations, and dreams that protend our affections, and dreams are neuer in all points agreeing right with waking actions. . . . And therefore was *Sleepe* . . . apparelled in a white thin Vesture cast ouer a blacke, to signifie both the day and the night . . . hee was shewed bearing a blacke Wand in the left hand, and a white in the other, to effect either confused or significant dreames. . . . And in this action did he here vse his white Wand, as to infuse significant Visions to entertaine the Spectators, and so made them seeme to see there a Temple, with a *Sybilla* therein attending the Sacrifices. . . .[41]

The emblematic and allegorical character of masques-in-performance was sometimes very complex indeed, and much contemporary evidence indicates that many spectators did not understand the meaning of the stage design. This could be one of the reasons why the printed texts elucidate meaning that was not at all that clear during the performance. The same Samuel Daniel in his *Tethys Festival* (1610) explained the allegory of the stage design, as in comments such as:

> First on eyther side stood a great statue of twelue foot high, representing *Neptune* and *Nereus*. *Neptune* holding a Trident, with an Anchor made to it, and his Mot[to] His artibus: that is, Regendo, & retinendo, alluding to this verse of *Virgill, Hae tibi erunt artes, & c. Nereus* holding out a golden fish in a net, with this word *Industria*: the reason whereof is deliuered after, in the speech vttered by *Triton*. (E2v–E3)

The Literary Masque

In *Cupid's Banishment* (1617), in turn, the allegorical significance of costumes is explained, as in the following passage:

> Fortune, at the bottom of the Mount, in a rich mantle wrought with changeable colour to expresse hir incertainty, with a vaile before hir face to shew hir blindness . . . her wheele in hir hand to signify hir momentary favor.[42]

Sometimes the "meaning" of music was also explained, as in Ben Jonson's *The Masque of Queens*, where loud and triumphant music wins over "strange" music, to which the hags dance wildly; and the author of the printed text explains to the reader that the meaning of this was "that the sounde of a virtuous fame is able to scatter and affright all that threaten yt." Jonson was often concerned—at least in his early masques—with minutest detail, as in *Hymenaei*, where in one of many marginal notes he explains why the four Humours had been impersonated by men on stage:

> That they were personated in men, hath (already) come vnder some *Gramatical* exception. But there is more than *Gramar* to release it. For, besides that *Humores*, and *Affectus* are both *Masculine in Genere*, not one of the *Specialls*, but in some Language is knowne by a *Masculine* word. Againe, when their *Influences* are common to both *Sexes*, and more generally impetuous in the *Male*, I see not, why they should not, so, be more properly presented. And, for the *Allegory*, though here it be very cleare, and such as might well escape a Candle, yet because there are some, must complain of Darknes, that have but thick Eies, I am contented to hold them this Light. . . .[43]

In all of his masques Jonson quotes (or refers to) over seventy authors, which makes him exceptional among masque writers.

That these comments were addressed to a reader, and not to a spectator, is proven by Jonson himself in asides like "Yet, that I may not vtterly defraud the *Reader of his Hope* [to learn about scenery, costumes and the like], *I am drawne to give it these brief touches, which may leave behind some shadow of what it was: And first the Attires.* . . ."[44] Sometimes passages in dialogues are additionally explained by notes, as if they were not self-explanatory. This is the case, for instance, in Jonson's *Love Freed From Ignorance and Folly* (1611), where at one point Sphinx orders the Follies to catch Love and "beare him / To the cliffe," and a footnote explains that "This shewes, that *Loues* expositions are not always serious, till it be diuinely instructed; and that sometimes it may be in the danger of Ignorance and Folly, who are the mother, and issue: for no folly but is borne of ignorance."[45] Thomas Campion, in turn, in his *Lord Hayes Masque* (1607) found it necessary to explain the significance of the number 9:

> Their [the masquers'] number nine, the best and amplest of numbers, for as in Musicke seuen notes containe all varietie, the eigth being in nature the same with the first, so in numbering after the ninth we begin againe, the tenth beeing as it were the Diappason in Arithmetick. The number of 9. is famed by the muses, and Worthies, and it is of all most apt for chaunge, and diuersitie of proportion.[46]

In most masques the identity of allegorical characters, or the "hieroglyphics" (the "hidden meaning") of the scenery is fully revealed. In Ben Jonson's and Inigo Jones's *Chloridia* (1631), the four persons seated on the hill were "Poesie, History, Architecture, and Sculpture." The five persons sitting on a bright cloud in Aurelian Townshend's and Inigo Jones's *Albions Triumph* (1632) turn out to be—as the authors state—"Innocency, Iustice, Religion, Affection . . . & Concord." In the same masque the significance of names is expounded: "Names [used in the masque, are] not improper, eyther for the Place, or for the Persons: ALBION being (as it once was) taken for England; ALBANACTVS, for the King, *Quasi in Albania natus: Borne in Scotland*. And ALBA, for the Queene. . . ." Townshend's and Jones's *Tempe Restord* (1632) includes a separate "chapter" entitled "The Allegory," in which the latter is fully revealed in several pages of print.[47] Shirley's and Jones's *The Triumph of Peace* (1634) has a description of scenery, the elements of which are said to be the "Hieroglyphics" of Peace, Justice, and Law.

Practically every description of scenery in printed masques elucidates—in one way or another—the significance of particular elements (always involving a selection), which during the performance was the task of spectators themselves. The choice of elements to be described varies in number and in detail. The general rule for this seems to have been that the more influential Inigo Jones was at court, the more descriptions, full of detail and paraphernalia, one finds in the printed texts. Most of Caroline masques include very technical descriptive parts, and there is evidence that at least some of them (if not all) were written by Jones himself. At any rate, the examples above make it clear that every description is an interpretation of the particular elements of the actual performance. Paradoxically, the lack of description is also an interpretation, for it eliminates those elements of the production that, from the writer's point of view, are not significant

The Literary Masque

to his literary purpose. If one treats the postperformance text as an accurate account of the spectacle, then it is natural to make the descriptive parts longer and more detailed, often to the point where they dominate the whole text. If, on the other hand, one treats this text as an autonomous literary work, then the tendency is to select only those elements of the spectacle that are useful materials for the construction of a literary work. If this work is to retain its initially poetic character, it is natural to keep down the length of prose descriptions. The first tendency will lead to basically journalistic accounts (and there is no reason why the masques belonging to this category should not be treated as such); the second may lead to the creation of literary works. In the first type the allegorical, or symbolical, meanings will be expounded, which to a large extent deprives the text of its many layers of meaning, that is of its poetic function; in the other type the poetic function will be preserved, which allows one to treat these texts as literary works in their own right.

The shift from the fully annotated and narrative text to a poetic text is well illustrated by the development of Ben Jonson's masques. In his intriguing study of Ben Jonson's *Workes*, Timothy Murray discusses at length the masques included in the first volume.[48] Among other things, Murray noted that "long and detailed descriptions of masquers and machines often dominate the space and figure of the poetry, performing visually and linguistically as the dominant element of spectacle." Pointing to the digressive character of Jonson's descriptions, he concludes that

> Jonson's frequent digressions distinguish his masques printed in the folio of 1616 from other printed accounts of spectacles and masques. Printed descriptions of masques normally focus on loyal reports of the events, costumes, and scenery without lapsing into interpretation or discussion of historical precedents. While most descriptive reports call attention to the figure of the prince, Jonson's annotative accounts display the presence of the author.[49]

However, as shown above, only half of the masques included in the first folio are annotated, and these have been prepared for print in earlier quarto editions. Moreover, all of them were written in the early phase of Jonson's career as a writer of masques. None of the masques written after 1610 and printed in the first folio, and very few added to the second folio of 1640, include elaborate descriptions or notes. Moreover, it seems that all masques written by other poets are selective interpretations of actual performances, so this feature does not make Jonson distinct. But Murray draws attention to the importance of the

> visually striking layouts of text in which mechanical form functions to embody authorial mind. The elaborate marginalia and footnotes accompanying many of Jonson's printed masques tend to distract the reader from concentrating on an imaginative reconstruction of the revel itself. . . . In addition to provoking the readers to reflect on their reproduction of the ideology of the masque, Jonson's typographical disruptions of text display the author's own attitude vis-à-vis his role. His technique of marginal interruption often serves as a method of authorial commentary.[50]

But again this is true for only a handful of masques, for most Jonsonian texts do not have any "typographical disruptions," and may in fact be treated as literary works about court revels that are composed of poetic, dramatic, and narrative elements.

One of the distinctive features of these works is the fact that they function to a great extent as a commentary on the actual (or fictitious) performance, especially as these texts recall the contemporary stage conventions. They assume that the reader is well acquainted with theater and with, broadly speaking, the court culture of the epoch. On the one hand, the literary masque directs the reader to a specific cultural event that has already taken place (or in some cases that might have taken place); on the other, it creates autonomous meanings that may be considered irrespective of the performance. This leads to at least two possible critical approaches to the literary masque: one, treating the extant text in relation to the actual performance and to its cultural and political milieu, and the second, seeing the masque as a literary genre. In the history of masque criticism the first trend dominates, with topicality, patronage, and the "present occasion" being the critics' favorite areas of investigation. A large part of critical controversy is caused by the fact that the above distinctions are not even acknowledged. What is true for the masque-in-performance does not have to be, and usually is not, true for the literary masque. And vice versa.

As pointed out above, the literary masque assumes a reader who is well acquainted with theater. To comprehend the meanings that the text creates, the reader is expected to know the stage conventions of the time, including the most recent developments in technical innovations of the stage, which apparently made their way to England through the masques. After all, the laws that govern the literary masque are to a large extent the laws of the

The Literary Masque

stage, of the constantly improved illusionistic stage, where more than ever before "anything was possible"; where, quite contrary to the laws of the empirical reality, stars can sing and dance; islands can float like sailboats; huge rocks can open and close, disclosing beautiful palaces; where the bottom of the ocean will uncover mysterious worlds and people will undergo miraculous transformations and metamorphoses, as in Ovid or in Kafka, turning into animals, plants, beasts, and when need be, into bottles; where mythological gods descend to earth; where one can overcome the laws of gravitation; and where it is possible to stop time.

One has to remember that the illusionistic stage was not at all easy for contemporaries to comprehend. Every now and then uninitiated spectators complained that, for instance, on the stage "there were fish but no water."[51] For the knowledgeable reader the laws that govern the literary masque are not the creation of a flamboyant imagination but refer to a specific stage tradition and to artistic reality, where they can actually operate. The created world of a literary text is thus created on the basis of rules taken from a different system—that of the theater. However, they come not only from that system, for with the tendency to pare the descriptive part down to a minimum, poetry becomes the major constructive element in the literary masque, at least in Ben Jonson's. This in turn refers to the tradition of dramatic and other literary forms. Thus, for instance, the antimasque has a conspicuous link with popular tradition, even with the carnival tradition. Very often the antimasque is in fact a short piece of folk drama: during the performance it functions as a dramatic induction to what basically is a ritualistic, emblematic, and poetic spectacle of the masque; in the postperformance literary masque it functions as a prose juxtaposition of the poetic part of the text and marks the inner structural division of the created world.

The principal masque draws from the tradition of allegorical, mythological, and pastoral drama. It also draws from the rich tradition of courtly entertainments and from civic pageantry. The dialogue and speeches in the literary masque also borrow from the tradition of allegorical and pastoral poetry, from satirical and epideictic poetry, and even from medieval forms such as romances, dialogues, disputes, or even riddles. The anonymous *Masque of Flowers* (1614), for instance, contains a typical dispute on the superiority of wine over tobacco, and in Jonson's *Love Freed From Ignorance and Folly* (1611) Cupid's attempt to solve the riddle of Sphinx forms the major plot of this piece. Different literary traditions lie behind mottos, quotations, and explanatory notes. These range from the Bible and ancient Roman and Greek authors through medieval theologians to contemporary commentators on these authors. Contemporary emblem books are also a very important, if not essential, source for practically all the masques (and especially for the masques-in-performance, to the extent that makes it possible to see the latter as three-dimensional "theatrical emblems"). One may thus conclude that the literary masque creates its meanings on the basis of two major codes deriving from two different systems and traditions, from the spectacle and from literature. The major task of this book is to show exactly how these meanings are created.

The fact that a literary text draws from both spectacle and literature may also be attributed to drama. But for reasons presented above, the literary masque is not drama. It does not foresee its own staging; on the contrary, it is a single courtly spectacle that is translated, or "transmuted," into the language of literature. In other words, unlike drama, the literary masque refuses to be incorporated into a different system. As a matter of fact it cannot be staged, but can only provide material for an attempt to reconstruct the performance it describes. For instance, the physical presence of the monarch is almost without exception a condition *sine qua non* for the masque to create meaning during its performance. The king is incorporated into the masque world, and without his presence the masque cannot even begin. To have an actor impersonating James or Charles would change the essential nature of the original spectacle and would in fact be a dramatic reconstruction of a courtly ritual.

In the early phase the relationship between the printed masque and the actual performance seems "real"; in other words, without the performance the literary masque would not be created. Later, in some conspicuous cases, this relationship becomes irrelevant and one can only talk about a literary convention. To illustrate the latter phenomenon, it is useful to discuss briefly two printed texts that define themselves as masques and yet are not based on any actual performance. These are Jonson's *Neptune's Triumph* (1624) and Thomas Nabbes's *The Spring's Glory* (1637/8). The staging of the former had been planned for 6 January 1624, but owing to a diplomatic quarrel it was called off. Nabbes's text, in turn, was never staged; it was not written on the order of the court, but for the public stage.[52]

The comparison is quite interesting: there are two texts, both of which define themselves in the subtitles as masques, and yet they

The Literary Masque

obviously belong to two different genres. Nabbes's text belongs to drama, because his text, even in its printed version, does not describe any earlier performance and moreover it projects its own staging. Jonson's text is not drama because it pretends to have been staged and as such is a description of a fictional performance, and it does not foresee its own staging. What Jonson did here is of great significance: he consciously created a text that has been defined as a literary masque by including in the created world a description of a court performance that never took place. Thus his text pretends to have been staged. Interestingly, following the rules of the convention, Jonson gives fictitious details concerning the time and place of the performance on the title page. Furthermore, he even includes King James in his text and describes the monarch as taking part in the performance, which he never did. In the descriptive part, James's entrance is mentioned as being (as in practically all Jacobean masques) the signal for the beginning of stage action, in which James plays the mute part of the Spectator and the title protagonist, Neptune. Therefore this is a text that relates a fictitious event in exactly the same way that other literary masques describe actual performances.

The above example shows that it was in fact possible to create a literary masque without the spectacle. This could suggest a further evolution of the genre in the direction of full autonomy, all in accordance with Jonson's views on the masque and his deep conviction that real values are unnecessarily suppressed by the dominance of the spectacle. To preserve these values he turned to strictly literary means of expression, for which the performance was not relevant at all. The case is different with Nabbes's text: there is no descriptive part in it, and instead there are conventional stage directions. It is drama, a play that "pretends" to be a literary masque, and to include it in the relatively recent *Book of Masques* was a mistake.

There are several other plays, some of which are full-length five-act pieces, that use the word *masque* in the title (or subtitle), but this does not determine their generic affiliation.[53] A good example of this is Thomas Heywood's *Loves Mistress: or The Queenes Masque* (1636) which—contrary to the title—is a full-length play. What links the play with the masque is the use during its actual production of changeable scenery.[54]

It is therefore possible to analyze the extant printed texts as works of literature, and without taking into account their actual performances. As indicated above, not all of these texts may be treated as literature; some are basically journalistic in character, being narrative accounts of a performance. It seems to have been Ben Jonson's original idea to create the literary masque, where the narrative part is reduced to a minimum and is used as one of many elements in the construction of the fictional world. He also realized the possibility of creating new meanings by consciously using a new medium, print. He could and did, for instance, arrange his works in such a way as to show their relatedness. This is done through the violation of the actual chronology of the performances. The best-known example is that of *The Queens Masque*, which consists of two parts, known as *The Masque of Blackness* and *The Masque of Beauty;* the first of these parts was staged in 1605, the second three years later. In print, however, they appear one after the other, in spite of the fact that between them another masque was staged. The original title in the Folio of 1616 is significant: *The Queenes Masque. The first of Blacknesse . . . ;* when this part ends it is separated from the second one by a lace ornament that is smaller than the head ornament of the other masque. The latter begins on the same page as the first ends, and its title begins with *The Second Masque Which was of Beautie.* All of this implies that there are two sequel parts that should be treated as one text. What was impossible to achieve during the spectacle was achieved in print. As Stephen Orgel put it,

> . . . it is a measure of the immaturity of the work that the two parts do not coincide and that . . . there is no stage action corresponding to the real point of the masque. At the theatrical climax of *Blacknesse,* nothing really happens; and the significant action, the metamorphosis of blackness to beauty, takes place between the masque and its sequel, *The Masque of Beautie,* in which the nymphs are already white when they appear. Indeed, if we recall that not only three years but two other Twelfth-Night masques intervened between the production of *Blacknesse* and *Beauty,* we shall perceive that the only place these two bear the proper relationship to each other is in the printed text, where they stand side by side and appear at last as antimasque and masque. Only as literature, that is, do these works achieve their full intended meaning.[55]

The latter statement is of course only partly true, because during the performance the second masque "reminded" the spectators of the plot details of the first one; those who had seen it would certainly interpret the second masque as a sequel to the first one.

As he experimented with the new form, Ben Jonson went even further. *The Masque of Augurs* (1622) is a good example of the poet's conscious handling of the text while preparing it for the press.

The Literary Masque

The "device" of this piece focuses on the interpretation of the world. Two spheres are presented and contrasted with one another. The first sphere is chaotic and not organized, or anti-aesthetic and nonsignifying; the second is highly organized (structured), harmonious, and therefore aesthetic and signifying. The first sphere does not create meanings other than what is presented, and it therefore does not need to be interpreted. The second sphere creates several layers of meanings, through which it reveals its poetic function; it creates a meaningful world that may be (and is) analyzed philologically.

The masque proper is preceded by two antimasques, the first of which is basically a dramatic dialogue and occupies one-half of the printed text, whereas the second, a dance, is described in only several lines. In this way the dance that was a more significant part of the masque-in-performance is here reduced to mark the transition from the antimasque sphere to the sphere of the court. It also divides the printed text into two equal parts. The first of these spheres is governed by different rules than for the second one since it takes place outside the court and slightly "before" the spectacle began. "The first Antimasque had for the Scene the Court Buttry-hatch," the reader is informed. The buttery was a place for storing liquor, which makes the setting quite appropriate for an antimasque. The dialogue reveals that the several characters that appear on the stage—Notch, Slug, and Van-Goose—are on their way to the Banqueting House to present a masque they had prepared for the king. The reason for this performance is that they had heard that neither the king's poet nor his architect had any new and interesting concepts for the masque. Consequently, in the first part of *The Masque of Augurs* the spatio-temporal boundary between the actors and the spectators is clearly marked, which is a common feature of dramatic texts.

In the second part, however, when the buttery is replaced by the mythological sphere, from which gods descend to the court, the spatio-temporal distance is completely abolished. The actors perform in the here-and-now of the Banqueting House. In this way the second antimasque dance marks the transition from one sphere to the other. During the dance a light above "opened" and Apollo appeared, frightening away all the antimasquers. His entrance suspends the mimetic rules of the antimasque world. This is the only world the antimasquers can inhabit: there is no place for them in the courtly-mythological sphere. Thus the two spheres of the fictional world are separate in spatial and temporal terms. They are also distinct in class terms. This juxtaposition is deepened further by the contrast of qualities characterizing each sphere.

This contrast is not difficult to detect, because the basic activity of the characters in each sphere is practically of the same nature: they must prepare a court entertainment in the form of a dance; only on the axiological level is this given a different treatment. The first sphere is qualified negatively, the second positively; the first one fails to create meaning (as the dance of "straying and deform'd Pilgrims") and therefore does not have to, and is not interpreted; the second one does (being the dances of Augurs) and is given an interpretation. Parallel to this is yet another division of the printed text. This time it is a division possible to achieve only in print: the first part, qualified negatively, is without a single note, whereas the second part, from its very beginning, has a great abundance of elaborate and detailed notes. In this way the "significant" part of the actual performance is interpreted by Jonson; the "insignificant" part does not need a critical or scholarly interpretation. It may be added that the notes are set in smaller type and are fully justified, meaning that they extend from one side of the page to the other. The notes are set up as footnotes to each "scene," and thus in the printed text serve the additional function of marking the inner division of the text into a sequence of "scenes." Moreover, the dialogue in the first part is in prose, in the second in verse, manifesting one more contrast between the two worlds.

From their first appearance it is apparent that Notch, Slug, and Van-Goose belong to a different world. This is their first visit to the court, and they do not know their way around there. They are referred to by the Groom of the Revels, when he first sees them, as "gamesters." "What's this?" he exclaims, "A hogshead of beere broake out of the Kings buttery, or some Dutch Hulke!" He also complains that they stink. Another distinctive feature of these antimasque characters is their language: with the exception of Van-Goose, they all speak lower-class English, full of colloquialisms. Van-Goose, in turn, speaks with a distinct foreign accent, but he is not a foreigner. As Notch tells the Groom, Van-Goose is "a Brittaine borne, but hath learn'd to misuse his owne tongue in travell, and now speakes all languages in ill English; a rare Artist he is sir, and a Projector of Masques."[56] He is the "inventor" of the entertainment brought by the merry companions.

Van-Goose presents an entertainment that is in direct contrast to the central masque that follows. First, this "rare artist" brings

The Literary Masque

three bears on stage; then another character appears, John Urson, who sings a drinking ballad. Apparently the ballad was added to the text after the performance, which means that it never had been a part of the masque-in-performance.[57] This is further proof of the printed text's autonomy. The ballad ended, Van-Goose promises more: "Tis noting, tis noting; vill you see someting? Ick sall bring in de Turkschen, met all zin Baschawes, and zin dirty towsand Yanitsaries, met all zin Whooren, Eunuken, all met an auder, de Sofie van Persia, de Tartar Cham met de groat Kind of Mogull. . . . And all dis met de Ars van Catropricks, by de refleskie van de glassen" (85).

"Catoptrics" are the phenomena of reflection, or the formation of images by mirrors. Public presentation of this art was known in England. On 14 August 1624, for instance, a license was granted to one Edward James "to sett forth a Showing Glass, called the World's Wonder." His accent notwithstanding, Van-Goose is made additionally ridiculous by his mispronunciation of words like "Catopricks" for Catoptrics, "dirty" for "thirty," "ars" for "art," and so on. The whole group functions as a comical negation of the classical and learned topic suggested by the title. This serious topic is fully developed in the following masque.

There is also one more feature of the printed text that enables it to create meanings peculiar to this medium. As I have already mentioned, Van-Goose is presented as the masque writer; he is the inventor and a boastful artist. However, everything he says is contradicted either by the quality of his invention or by the distinctive type with which his utterances are printed—namely, in the so-called black letter. This makes him distinct from all other characters. At that time black letter was considered appropriate for "low" characters; moreover, ballads were most frequently printed in black letter.[58] It was considered an "easier" type, so that even less educated people could read it. In this way, Van-Goose's boastfulness and his pretense to high art are negated in print (and this can be achieved only in print).

This masque is also a good example of the development of Jonson's treatment of the masque dance. The earlier masques rarely have descriptions of the dances, and at best, Jonson acknowledges his inability as a poet to express the dance in literary terms. Discussing the *Masque of Blackness*, Stephen Orgel observes that

> As the dramatic action yields to the dance, so does the text, which at this point pauses to give the names of the masquers and to enumerate

their symbols. For while the drama of the masque properly employs the devices of theater as a means of expression, Jonson has yet found no way to unite the text with choreography, and thus to make the verse underlie the revels as it had the spectacle. . . .[59]

In *The Masque of Augurs*, however, the dances are analyzed as signs, or as one is tempted to say, semiotically. Following the dance of the Augurs, Apollo interprets it, beginning his speech with "The Signes are luckie all. . . ." The dance itself is relevant in this masque because it can be interpreted (as opposed to dances that cannot be interpreted and therefore cannot play any significant role in a literary text). Thus the dance reveals, and strictly speaking its semiotic interpretation reveals, that the King's peace will increase, that he will "control / The course of things" and live free from "hatred, faction, or the feare." This first interpretation, of course, originally belongs to the spectacle, but is given yet another interpretation in print (in the footnotes), and Jonson leaves to the reader the interpretation of the whole. This is a rule for all other masques: dances play a significant role in the composition of the printed text only when they can be described philologically; otherwise, they are either totally neglected or passed over in asides telling the reader that they were beautiful or harmonious. For instance, all that remains from the spectacle dances in the printed text of *Cupid's Banishment* (1617) is their philological "meaning": in the first dance they "daunce ANNA REGINA in letters; their second masking-daunce JACOBUS REX; their departing daunce CAROLUS P."[60] The same rule may be applied to the general treatment of scenery and costumes in the literary masques.

To sum up, let me point out again that the printed texts of masques reveal a tendency to evolve from basically journalistic forms to the literary ones. The first are characterized by the dominance of the narrative, whereas in the second group poetry dominates, often preceded by the prose drama of the antimasques. In its developed form, the literary masque is a conglomerate form composed of elements of poetry (didactic, epideictic, pastoral, and so forth), drama, and whatever is left of the narrative. The latter, however, always plays the very important function of referring the reader to the actual or fictitious theatrical performance that had already taken place. This is achieved through direct information about the place and date of the performance included in the title, or in dedications, addresses, and the like. Also, the brief narrative parts, scattered throughout the text, provide de-

The Literary Masque

tails concerning the actual (or fictitious) staging and strongly rely on the readers' knowledge of current theater conventions and techniques. The created space of the literary masque reconstructs the actual space of court theater. Thus the narrative part plays an important role in the construction of the fictive world and in its allegorization. The allegory is often achieved through references to the realm of emblems. The reader is asked to "recreate" in his or her imagination those elements of the performance that the author considers significant to his artistic purpose. The material for "reconstruction" provided is always selective and often does not include a number of details relevant to the actual production. The author controls the reader's response through footnotes, marginalia, digressions, allusions, quotations, and the like. As the above example has shown, even the typeface itself is capable of creating meaning. Once it frees itself from the actual performance, the literary masque attempts to create meaning through a reader's "reconstruction" of an imaginary performance of a masque. In this sense the masque may be treated as an ephemeral genre dealing with theater.

2
The Emblematic Masque

In one of the most recent definitions of the masque, David Lindley states that the heart of the masque "is the appearance of a group of noble personages dressed in elaborate disguise to celebrate a particular occasion and to honour their monarch. They perform some specially designed . . . masque dances, and then take out the members of the court audience in the communal dance of the revels. The fundamental job of the masque writer is to provide a fiction to explain the disguised arrival."[1] Because this fiction, surviving in several pages of printed texts, is based on long-forgotten Renaissance codes of meaning and makes little sense to today's uninitiated reader, the fundamental job of a critic is to elucidate its "hidden meanings."

Practically all the printed texts of masques, their topicality notwithstanding, direct the implied reader to other systems, without which the masque text cannot be decoded. One of these systems is ancient Greek and Roman mythology (and Renaissance mythographies); others are the contemporary emblem book (like Ripa's *Iconologia*) and the Bible. Ritualistic and theatrical courtly behavior may also be treated as a system of signs that is always manifested during the masque spectacle, and yet another is the Stuart ideology, as expressed, for instance, by King James in his own writings. Last but not least are the conventions and mechanistic and illusionistic stage of the court theater.

Without the knowledge of the latter, a reader will be baffled—to say the least—by the extraordinary events that occur within the created worlds: gods may ride chariots across the sky, mountains can rise and disappear, underwater palaces can open their interiors, and the whole world is governed by fairy-tale laws that are at best similar to Hollywood interpretations of myths or biblical stories. Moreover, without the knowledge of the rules by which the masque world was originally created in actual performances, a reader may well miss the nature of this peculiar model of the universe that the masque-in-performance reveals. One ought to

The Emblematic Masque

remember, though, that the masque-in-performance is a different text—in the semiotic sense of the word—from the surviving, printed texts that may be called the literary masque, for they belong to two different systems, theater and literature, and employ different modes of expression.

This chapter concentrates on the masque-in-performance, and because space limitations do not allow me to dwell on any one text in great detail, I will attempt to single out common features of all masques staged at the Stuart court. These features are also essential to an understanding of the literary masque and are relevant to any discussion of Stuart culture in general.

Theater historians emphasize that the masque is important because their productions first introduced illusionistic scenery to England. What this means is that in an enclosed space, essentially a cube open only towards the audience, objects are displayed according to a specific set of geometric and mathematical rules, which creates an illusion of depth greater than that of the actual cube, and—strictly speaking—of an infinite space. This is called the perspective stage, and its appearance follows the Renaissance discoveries in other fields such as optics and astronomy. Nicolas Cusanus and Giordano Bruno defined space as endless and geometric, and Erwin Panofsky strongly insists in his controversial essay that only after space was conceived of as continuous, endless, and geometric was it possible for the artist to show space projecting into the depth of the picture.[2] It was, in fact, Cusanus's revolutionary idea that one might consider space from any point that marks the turn from the theocentric to the homocentric view of the world and space. What this meant was that there was now a multitude of possible viewpoints.

Furthermore, turning away from the Middle Age philosophy that only God was infinite, Cusanus claimed that both God and the world are infinite spheres whose boundaries and centers were everywhere and nowhere. Thus, presenting an infinite human world on canvas or on stage would be congruous with this new philosophical concept, and linear perspective, with its vanishing point, would serve as the most appropriate convention for the pictorial representation of "truth." To understand the mathematics and geometry of space and the physical laws of optics meant that one might gain insight into the very nature of the universe and of God.[3] In this way art could gain a scientific dimension.

The importance attached to mathematics, geometry, and optics in the Renaissance is well recognized in specialized studies. All of these areas of human knowledge must be taken into account when discussing the nature of the masque-in-performance. The Renaissance habit of thinking in terms of universal analogy is also quite well known.[4] Simply put, the basic correspondence was seen between man's body and the body of the universe, between man's soul and the soul of the universe, between the microcosm of man and the macrocosm of the world. This was the inevitable pattern of the universe, in which the small body of man corresponded exactly to a larger body of the universe, and this design was everywhere present. Thus the laws that govern this universe could be discovered in plants, in animals, or in people; all could serve as a model of the world. Works of art could visually present a model of that kind. "I am a little world made cunningly of elements," wrote John Donne in his *Holy Sonnets* (V); "thou seemst a world in thyself, containing heaven, stars, earth, floods, mountains, forests and all that lives," states Drummond of Hawthornden in *A Cypress Grove*;[5] and Thomas Nabbes wrote *Microcosm: A Moral Maske* (1637), which—as the title suggests—combines morality and masque traditions, and where the dramatic conflict is caused by misbehaving Elements that refuse to succumb to the rules of the "harmony of parts."

Henry Peacham, in his *Minerva Britanna, or a Garden of Heroical Deuises*, which was a popular and widely known book of emblems, reproduced an emblem showing a globe amid clouds; within the circle there was a nude male figure with a raised right hand and the sun, the moon, and the stars on either side. It was entitled "Homo Microcosmus"; in the motto is the following:

> Heare what's the reason why a man we call
>   A little world? and what the wiser ment
> By this new name? two lights Coelestiall
> Art in his head, as in the Element:
> Eke as the wearied Sunne at night is spent,
>   So seemeth the life of man a day,
>   At morne hee's borne, at night he flits away.
>
> Of heate and cold as is the Aire composed,
> So likewise man we see breeth's hot and cold,
> His bodie's earthly: in his lunges inclosed,
> Remaines the Aire: his braine doth moisture hold,
> His heart and liver, doe the heate infold:
>   Of Earth, Fire, Water, Man thus framed is,
>   Of Elements the threefold Qualities. . . .[6]

Ernst Cassirer remarked that one of the characteristics of Renaissance philosophy is the reluctance shown by its philosophers to

The Emblematic Masque

express themselves in abstract terms; instead, through analogy they expressed themselves largely in linguistic terms stylized with "poetic" diction, mythological parallels, and symbols rich in imaginative elements. This metaphorical mode of expression led, of course, to a lack of precision and to conspicuous ambiguities. Furthermore, their idea of the truth or falsity of a statement seems to have been linked to the degree of richness in "poetic" elements. The more metaphorical the language of discourse, the closer to the truth it led. And, of importance here, in the Renaissance it was not only the philosopher and scientist studying the nature of the universe but the poet as well who, by universal analogy, discovered and expressed the common pattern in the world created by God. Thus, as observed by Joseph A. Mazzeo, "the principle of universal analogy or universal correspondences provides the basis for a unified theory of the imagination which joins the philosopher or investigator of nature and the poet."[7] Cassirer also advances a link between the Renaissance mathematical physicist and the artist sharing an equal interest in measurement and proportion, which were considered the foundation of all knowledge.

Since the individual experience of a philosopher, an artist, or a poet could provide insight into the nature of the universe, there is no reason why one should not treat the court masque as a model of this universe, created by an educated poet, an artist designing scenery, a composer of music, and a choreographer. Instruction of the rational faculties of humanity was considered the most important purpose of art, but at the same time, art—in whatever form—should always be harmoniously well proportioned, "reflecting," as Jensen writes, "in its own order and harmony the harmony God created in the universe. In this way, a work of art, the microcosmic reflection of the macrocosm, expresses and appeals to the most rational part of the mind, as well as to the highest emotions."[8] This, of course—as is frequently noted—is linked to the Neoplatonic conception of art and artists.

Generally speaking, Neoplatonists believed that divine reality—of which this world is a poor imitation—consisted of perfect harmony, proportion, goodness, virtue, and so forth; that divine reality could be envisioned by the artist through his or her imagination as a part of his highest soul; and that in art the artist as a creator attempted to communicate divine reality to the recipients of his art.[9] The artist's or the poet's inspiration was of divine origin (often referred to as "furor divinus"), and in his creation he was analogous to God. The most important part of the process of artistic creation was the invention, or discovery of a main idea and its attendant images. Invention could draw from other works (as masques often did), but it could also be imagination in its highest form (as masques often were), when the artist or the poet (or both) conceived of a vision identical or close to a Platonic absolute: the imaginative vision as a glimpse of an absolute reality.[10] This explains why the printed texts of masques always stressed who was responsible for their "invention," since the person involved was not necessarily the one who actually wrote the printed text.[11] This is discussed in detail elsewhere in this book, and now just one example will suffice. Aurelian Townshend's *Tempe Restord* (1632) ends with the following comment: "All the verses were written by Mr *Aurelian Townshend*. The subiect and Allegory of the Masque, with the descriptions, and Apparatus of the Sceanes were invented by *Inigo Iones*, Surveyor of his Maiesties worke." The poet provided only the verses and the masque was "invented" by the artist, who should therefore be treated as the principal author.

Thus there were sundry reasons why the court spectacles, being highly imaginative "inventions," could be treated as unique insights into not only courtly matters ("the present occasion") but into the nature of the universe, revealing the laws that govern it. As Roy Strong has stated in his excellent book on Renaissance festivals, court spectacles presented an ideal world "in which nature, ordered and controlled, has all dangerous potentialities removed. In the court festival, the Renaissance belief in man's ability to control his own destiny and harness the natural resources of the universe find their most extreme assertion. In their astounding transformations, which defeat magic, defy time and gravity, evoke and dispel the seasons, banish darkness and summon light, draw down the very comprehension of the laws of nature . . . in its fulness of artistic creation [this] was a ritual in which society affirmed its wisdom and asserted its control over the world and its destiny."[12] With minor reservations these words could apply to the Stuart masques. In the latter case, however, it was not society's wisdom but the king's that—with the support of his superhuman powers—controlled the harmony and order of the world and its destiny.

Let us, then, have a closer look at this truly bizarre world of the masque in which, quite contrary to the laws of empirical reality, everything is possible; where, among other miraculous effects, even the stage set can instantly change from a castle to a landscape or a seascape or a moonscape, or to an allegorical or emblematic composition. However, the laws that govern this highly imaginative world are not accidental or merely designed to evoke

The Emblematic Masque

wonder: they are a part of the created model of the universe, which ought to reveal its true nature during the actual performance of a masque.

Even a brief glance at the surviving texts of the masques will show that the created or artistic world is basically divided into three spheres: the divine or metaphysical, the sphere of the court, and the noncourt world. The metaphysical sphere is inhabited by mythological gods who rule over the whole universe and also by a number of allegorical characters that usually stand for the virtues that mortals should follow. The supreme power in this model of the universe rests in Jove, or Saturne. Sometimes they appear to the mortals. In Ben Jonson's *Masque of Augurs* (1622) at one point "the heaven opened, and *Jove*, with the Senate of the Gods were discovered." In his *Time Vindicated* (1623), "the whole Scene [i.e., the stage] opens, where Saturne sitting with Venus is discover'd above." The gods above are careful observers of everything that takes place on the earth, and they always, in practically every masque, send down their messengers to convey various messages to the king and his court.

The court sphere is inhabited by select human and superhuman beings ruled by a monarch whose power and authority comes from the first sphere. The king and his court are often presented as an almost ideal reflection of the divine order. For instance, in *Time Vindicated*, King James is addressed directly and learns that the "glories of the Time," imprisoned by Hecate, are to be freed "by Loue's suit" and are just about to come to James's court, because they are

> . . . fitter to adorne the age,
> By you restor'd on earth, most like his [Saturne's] owne:
> And fill this world of beauties here, your Court.

Contrasted with the court is the outer sphere, inhabited by ordinary humans and all sorts of vices, who occasionally enter the sphere of the court but take part only in the "antimasques." They are never fully admitted to the court sphere. This tripartite structure of the created universe is vertical, of course: the gods and allegories always descend from the divine sphere to the world of the court (and never to the "lower" sphere). The existence of heavens is additionally confirmed in dialogue, songs, and speeches and is visually presented on stage, as the above examples illustrate. The illusionistic stage functions here as a sort of magical box, or perhaps as a new scientific instrument, which allows for encounters between divine beings and the court. The latter is naturally located in the middle, between the metaphysical sphere and the mundane, noncourt world. The very structure of this universe is significant: communication between the ordinary, human world and the representatives of the divine sphere is possible only through the mediation of the court; this model of the universe makes no provision for any link between the "commons" and divinity. And this rudimentary law operates in other ways, too: divine messages of various kind (provided to applaud the king's reign) are conveyed only to the court, and only through this medium can they be transmitted further down.

The boundaries between the three spheres are clearly marked by the organization of space in the masque-in-performance. It is possible to distinguish two basic types of organization of space in theaters. One, composed of two "open" spaces, forms one space of the theater; the other consists of two "enclosed" spaces. The first type, familiar to all students of ancient Greek or Elizabethan theater, is characterized by an open stage surrounded on at least three sides by an amphitheatrical auditorium. A theater of this type provides a multitude of possible viewpoints and "perspectives"; furthermore, this stage does not "hide" anything from the spectators, nor does it create any physical or optical illusion as far as its dimensions and shape are concerned. It does not "pretend" to be anything else, and a convention has to be employed to transform this stage space into, say, the space of a hall or a street (this phenomenon is sometimes referred to as "verbal scenography"). The two spaces are divided only by the difference in their ontological status: one is the created, artistic reality; the other is the empirical reality of the spectators. However, the openness of space in this kind of theater is in fact of a double nature: the stage not only opens out toward the auditorium, but the auditorium opens out toward the stage.[13] This leads to an illusionary reduction of the boundary and distance between these two spaces and two groups of people: the actors and the spectators. The latter phenomenon in turn leads to the well-known illusion of communal participation in the performance. Thus the theater world is created by two open spaces and is distinct from the nontheater outside this world.

The second type of space organization in theater is based on a different concept: a closed stage, hiding a number of its features, is rigidly separated from the auditorium that forms the second closed space in this theater. The stage is a cube open on one side only to the auditorium. With the help of stage design it presents

The Emblematic Masque

an illusionistic space that seems infinite when viewed from the right station point (as it is called in descriptive geometry) and is also similar to a painting framed in a proscenium arch. This type of space and its inner organization by the rules of linear perspective determines the single best location for the spectator. A stage of this sort is always equipped with a large area invisible to spectators, where all stage machinery is concealed, a factor that additionally stresses the isolation of the stage world from the auditorium. In other words, the stage tells the spectator where he or she is "allowed" to sit or stand and what he or she is allowed to see. I will argue later that the court theater created for the staging of masques is basically a transitional fusion of the two types of space organization described above.

Most critics tend to treat the masque-in-performance as a spectacle staged in a nineteenth-century theater, where the boundary between the fictitious and empirical realities are clearly marked by a raised stage, by the curtain, by proscenium and proscenium arch. Since elaborate illusionistic scenery was used in masques, a number of critics assume that the action of these spectacles, including speeches and songs, took place within the stage set and on the proscenium. However, there is much evidence—and this has been noticed by others—that the most important acting area was not what we would normally call the stage but rather the "dancing place"; this is true not only because dances occupied most of the time of the masque-in-performance, but also because a number (if not most) of the important speeches and songs were actually presented in the area below the perspective stage and close to the king, who was seated in a throne on a raised platform, directly opposite the center of the stage. This is often referred to as the "state." The surviving text of *The Masque of Twelve Months* (1612?) for instance, states that in the opening scene "the Heart opens, and Bewty issues . . . the two Pulses beating before them towards ye King. Beinge neare, Beauty speaks. . . ."[14] In the *Masque at Coleoverton*, the masquers descend and pass directly to the "dancing place." Similarly, in practically all other masques there are characters descending from above or entering from the sides or from below, taking steps down to the dancing floor in order to address the king or to present songs and dialogues immediately in front of him.[15] Sometimes precious or allegorical gifts are presented to members of the royal family. And one must not forget that with few exceptions all the speaking parts were played by professional actors and songs were sung by musicians; the most important roles in these spectacles, those of the masquers, were always mute. Moreover, most of the dialogues belong to antimasques that were usually presented in other acting areas than the stage proper.

For this reason one should not forget that most of what happened in the masque-in-performance took place not within the illusionistic stage but immediately in front of it, on the narrow proscenium[16] and on the dancing floor, which was a large rectangular area in the middle of the hall, surrounded on three sides by spectators and backed with the stage picture. Allardyce Nicoll, in his influential *Stuart Masque and the Renaissance Stage*, observed long ago that the masquers habitually descended upon the "dancing place," "while frequently, in the very course of the masque action, characters were made to move downward and approach the royal throne."[17] Stephen Orgel and Roy Strong also point out that

> during the production of masques the centre of the hall had to be left clear for dancing, and this meant that the audience was seated not across the width of the room, but around the walls on three sides of the dancing area. Since Jones's theatre relied heavily on perspective, the seating arrangement meant that much of the audience missed a good deal of the point of the spectacle. . . . By modern standards the stage was unusually shallow. This will be less difficult to understand if we remember that most of the action of the masque took place not on the stage but in front of it, on the dancing floor. The area behind the proscenium was essentially a scenic machine, and Jones devised its proportions primarily to suit his settings.[18]

Allardyce Nicoll further notes that occasionally "dispersed scenery" was employed on the dancing place, as in *Tethys Festival*, which had a "tree of victory" represented by a "bay at the right side of the state, upon a little mount there raised."[19] One should therefore treat the dancing floor as an important acting area in the productions of masques. Since the perspective stage was raised (one of the two stages used in actual productions), most of the action and all of the dances took place on a level below the stage, or below the stage picture. To a certain extent the perspective stage was predominantly "mute" and basically pictorial in character, providing an illusionistic space from which mythological and allegorical characters descended to "earth."

This organization of the acting space is similar to the typographical layout of printed emblems, where the poetic or narrative part is always set below the engraving, which is the illustration of a given emblem. In addition, the perspective of the illusionistic stage picture could not possibly include the characters or stage properties on the dancing floor. The optical laws that govern the illusionistic stage are based on distortion (by which the illusion is created), whereas they are natural or "real" outside that space. If both acting areas were treated as one, the discrepancy between the natural and distorted optic laws would become apparent. Whatever or whoever appears on the dancing floor is not distorted by the stage designer in order to create an illusion of depth. Since the spectators are seated on three sides of this acting area, there is a multitude of possible "perspectives," and not a single one is privileged.

The natural optic laws characterize the first type of theater, discussed above. In this sense, the hall floor, between the "state" and the raised stage picture, forms an open stage that is familiar to all frequenters of public theaters. This means that the stage picture and frame do not mark the boundary between the fictitious, or artistic, and "real" worlds: they mark instead the inner division of the created world, which is composed of two visible spheres linked physically by the magical powers of the stage box. The heavenly sphere is brought closer—as if viewed through a telescope—to the world of the court, and it is presented basically as a three-dimensional picture, governed by the rules of linear theater perspective. These rules stress the Platonic ideal revealed in this geometric, perfectly proportioned world, the harmony of which is additionally corroborated by "divine" music. It was of course an aesthetic principle of the Renaissance that beauty is harmony of the parts in relation to the whole and a mathematically correct system of relationships. In this sense, as was the case with painting, the perspective stage, which presented a geometric and harmonious world, brought the art of stage design closer to the *artes liberales*.[20]

Opposed to this "artificial" (in what was then the meaning of the word) sphere is the court, which is "real" only in the sense that the laws that govern this world are similar to empirical reality. I should add that there is also a third sphere—the implied earthly noncourt world, from which either antimasque or ordinary human characters enter into the court world from the sides, which mark its physical boundaries, or from below the stage, which stresses even more strongly the vertical hierarchy of the created universe. The noncourt world is also separated from the other two spheres by its most conspicuous feature—a lack of harmony. This is manifested by, among other things, the often "deformed" shape and character of the antimasquers, and by the "wild" music and chaotic dances intrinsic to this world.

Music is one of the devices constantly used to stress the separation of the two spheres: it is the "divine" courtly sphere from the mundane world outside. The first sphere is always "modeled" by harmonious music, which by analogy implies the ideal harmony of the entire sphere, including its inhabitants. The source of this harmony is of course King James, who in several masques is referred to in musical terms. In Jonson's and Jones's *Pans Anniversarie,* for instance, which was staged on James's birthday, Pan's or James's "loud Musicke" is mentioned as making the masquers' "Common-wealth a harmonie." On the other hand, the antimasque world is always filled with "wild" music. In Thomas Campion's *The Lords Masque,* for instance, twelve "Franticks" appear on stage to "the sound of strange musicke." This "strange" music is often accompanied by "wild" dances.

Many examples of this significant use of music may be found in the extant masques. Music's function is quite obvious: it marks the boundary between the chaotic world of the noncourt sphere and the harmonious sphere, which includes both the court and metaphysical space. A secondary function of music is to demonstrate how harmony wins over chaos (which by analogy stresses the role of King James in the human world). A good example of this is Jonson's *Masque of Queenes,* where "loud triumphant musicke" serves to chase away the hags who had been dancing to "strange and sodayne Musicke." The "allegory" is explained by the author himself: this use of music shows "that the sounde of a virtuous fame is able to scatter and affright all that threaten yt."

I stress again that the separation between the fictitious world and the spectators' reality does not apply to the masque-in-performance. In other words, the masque spectacle is not autonomous after the fashion of a self-contained fiction performed before spectators who "belong" to a different reality, but is, rather, an institutionally autonomous performance of a ritual in which all present take part.[21] The masque, in fact, may be seen as a peculiar manifestation of courtly behavior, of which the ceremonial and the ritual were important components. Theatricality of behavior inevitably leads to theatrical means of artistic expression. It may also be seen as—to use Roy Strong's phrase—a "liturgy of state," which assumes particular importance in Protestant countries, where the Reformed church does not make extensive use of elaborate ceremonials involving images, paintings, and sculpture. In this sense the masque-in-performance filled the obvious gap in Stuart iconography and propaganda. As David Norbrook observes, "the increasingly elaborate concluding scenes of Jacobean and Caroline masques, in which Jones's scenery transformed courtiers into images of transcendent truths, formed a secular counterpart to the cult of religious images."[22] Jonas A. Barish points out that the "frequency of prayer as a rhetorical mode is . . . not accidental."[23] Nor is it accidental that some of the songs sung in praise of James or Charles are similar to hymns (in, for instance, Ben Jonson's *Pans Anniversarie*). In this way the masque becomes a useful medium for Stuart ideology in general, and it frequently comments on current political issues in particular. It is not surprising that the most important guests in these spectacles were foreign ambassadors. From the point of view of Stuart interests, the perspective setting added not only the third but also a divine dimension to their ideology.[24]

It has been noticed by scholars and theater practitioners that dramatic or artistic worlds are immediately recognized by the audience as counterfactual but that they exist simultaneously as if in progress in the actual here and now. Any other approach or misunderstanding of this convention will result in mistaking the stage for actuality (an error made by children and other uninitiated spectators). The separation of the two worlds is stressed additionally by their asymmetrical character, which means that their relationship of accessibility is one-way: it is the spectators who can see into the created world on stage, follow the events presented, overhear even the most personal confessions, witness embarrassing scenes, and so forth, but the spectators' world is not visible—or even noticed—by the characters on the stage.[25] This convention makes the two realities conspicuously distinct. However, modern theater practice often tries to violate this rule of asymetry, and actors will sometimes interact directly with spectators. But this is, in fact, yet another convention, the creation of another illusion: the auditorium is simply incorporated into the artistic reality of the performance and thus tricks the spectator—to use Keir Elam's expression—into believing that it is really his or her own world.[26] In the masque this convention, or "trick," is used constantly: spectators are led to believe that their world is the "real" world and appears in opposition to the superfluous world of the stage. But in fact they are incorporated into this fictitious reality, as is always the case in a ritual. In this way the masque audience is transformed into a stage character who "impersonates," for instance, the court hierarchy of importance (the closer one sits to the king, the higher one's court position) or represents the earthly instrument of king's power. The king, of course, is also a stage character who plays the triple role of the spectator, the implied author of the "magic" and harmony at court, and a "little god" equipped with superhuman wisdom and power.

I have indicated the ritualistic quality of the masque-in-performance on several occasions in this chapter. At this point I should perhaps explain the ritual further. Victor Turner, in his *From Ritual to Theatre: The Human Seriousness of Play*, outlines several features that make ritual distinct from theater:

> Ritual, unlike theater, does not distinguish between audience and performers. Instead, there is a congregation whose leaders may be priests, party officials, or other religious or secular ritual specialists, but all share formally and substantially the same set of beliefs and accept the same system of practices, the same set of rituals or liturgical actions. A congregation is there to affirm the theological or cosmological order, explicit or implicit, which all hold in common, to actualize it periodically for themselves and inculcate the basic tenents of that order into their younger members, often in a graded series of life-crisis rituals, passages from birth to death, through puberty, marriage. . . .[27]

The masque, however, only partly reveals the features of a ritual; when it affirms the political, theological, and cosmological order, it actualizes ritualization periodically and does not distinguish between audience and performers. As noted by Stephen Orgel, it is only "the characters in Jonsonian antimasques, played by professional actors [who] are nearly always unaware that there are spectators" (the only exception to be found in *Love Restored*).[28] In other words, only in the antimasque is the asymmetry rule fully applied: the two worlds of the stage and the auditorium are clearly distinct.[29] For this reason ritual is not appropriate here; in most instances, the antimasque-in-performance is a theatrical spectacle. Of course, in this way the differences between particular spheres of the masque world are clearly marked. The relationship between the court and the antimasque is that of an audience and actors in the theater, whereas the relationship between the court and the masque reveals all the features of a ritual. The congregation is formed by the courtiers and by the gods and allegories of the masque world. This was expressed in similar terms by Mary Chan:

The Emblematic Masque

> [At a later phase of Jonson's masques] The link between antimasque and masque was no longer presented as a change in scene but rather as a recognition of the audience so that the audience could become an integral part of the masque proper. This allowed the antimasque to develop itself as *a little drama,* for part of its meaning lay precisely in the fact that it *was* separate from the audience, the court and the values for which it stood.[30] (Emphasis added.)

Furthermore, the antimasque characters cannot really communicate with characters from the masque proper: they are usually scared or chased away by the appearance of the latter, and consequently the chaos or the evil of the antimasque is brought to order or otherwise neutralized. The only communication possible in this tripartite world is between the court sphere and the metaphysical sphere, and between the court and the noncourt. Thus, for instance, when Iris appears "above" in the *Masque* staged at Coleoverton in 1618(?), all the antimasque characters "run out distractlie."[31] Similarly, in the *Masque of Augurs* (1622) the antimasque characters are "frightened away" by the appearance of Apollo, which is a sign for the main masque to begin.[32] In the earlier *Masque of Queens* (1609), during a wild dance of the Witches, "on the sodayne, was heard a sound of loud music, as if many Instruments had given one blast. Wth wch, not only the *Hagges* themselves, but their *Hell,* into wch they ranne, quite vanishd; and the whole face of the *Scene* alterd," by which twelve masquers were discovered in the House of Fame.[33] In *Pleasure Reconciled to Virtue* the Pigmees of the second antimasque dance around a sleeping Hercules "at ye end whereof they think to surprize him: when sodainly, being wak'd by the *Musique,* and rowsinge himself, they all run into holes."[34]

As Francis Bacon observed in his essay "Of Masques and Triumphs," "*Angels* . . . [are] not Comical enough, to put them inn *Anti-Masques;* And any Thing that is hideous, as Deuils, Giants, is in the other side vnfit."[35] The transition from the antimasque to the masque world plays an important function. Kevin Sharpe's comment on the Caroline masques applies just as well to masques in general:

> Neoplatonic philosophy postulates an ascent of cognition from the plane of senses and material objects to a loftier stratum of knowledge of forms and ideas, of which objects were but an imperfect material expression. The Caroline masque enacted that philosophy in the transition from antimasque to masque. The world of sense and appetite

A conjectural reconstruction of a performance of a masque in the Banqueting Hall. Drawing by Andrzej Markowicz.

The Emblematic Masque

was represented in the masque by images of nature as an ungoverned wilderness, threatening, violent, ignorant and anarchic; the sphere of soul was depicted as nature ordered and governed by the patterns of the forms. So in the Caroline masque the transcendence is most often a transformation of nature—from chaos to order and from disjuncture to harmony.[36]

I would add that the transition from the antimasque to the masque is also a transition from theater to ritual. This is in fact the most distinctive feature of the masque-in-performance.

Only one sphere and only one acting area of the created world of the masque is organized according to the rules of linear perspective—the three-dimensional stage picture. In early masques this is exclusively a divine sphere, presented as a harmonious, proportioned, geometric, and infinite space. The importance of geometry was widely acknowledged in the Renaissance. Sir Thomas Elyot, for instance, in his *The Boke, Named the Governor* (1580), insisted that "Musicke and Geometrie" exemplify "a perfect harmonie."[37] Taking into account the enormous role of music in the masque-in-performance and the seemingly perfect geometry of the perspective stage, the world within was indeed ideal harmony. Linked to this was the world of the court, which was finite, enclosed by the walls of the hall, the floor and the ceiling; it was equipped, however, with one open wall, through which, as if through a window, it was possible to see the metaphysical order of this universe. This presented the court as the seer of truth. As an acting area, the "divine" sphere (which in later masques will alternate with human worlds presented within the illusionistic stage) was used primarily for discoveries (of gods and masquers) and for descents from the "heavens" or from any other allegorical location (in the *Masque of Beauty*, Reason descends from the top of "microcosm").

With hardly any exceptions, the movement of characters in this highly structured (hence signifying) space was two-dimensional: up and down and to the sides, as if on a flat surface of a painting on canvas. Except for possibly one instance,[38] not a single character entered or exited through the back of the perspective stage. Doing so would ruin the artistic concept of the organization of the stage space. Since the stage was relatively shallow, the actors could not act anywhere near the back of the stage because they would then expose the optical illusion and reveal the distorted proportion of "diminishing" set elements: that is, the last columns in a colonnade or the last houses in a street or trees in a landscape would all appear disproportionally small or low when compared to the height of an actor standing beside the set. Only the very front of the stage design—the vertical plane framed by the proscenium-arch, could be proportioned in accordance with the natural dimensions of the nonstage world. One has to remember that whenever the stage space is organized by the rules of perspective, all shapes and figures, hence dimensions, are distorted. For example, the common illusion of the great depth of the stage box is caused by a floor that gradually rises towards the back wall, a ceiling that gradually slopes downward, and side walls that tend to "come together"; this means that what seems to us—by optical illusion—a perspective view of a square (the floor, for instance) or a rectangle is in fact a perspective view of a trapezoid.

Understandably, the introduction of the perspective stage required an audience that would know how to "read" the perspective, something that is not at all obvious, or innate, to human beings. One has to learn how to perceive the artistic perspective. As Orgel and Strong have pointed out, "straight lines on a page moving upward and converging will appear to recede to a vanishing point only if we have learned the rules for translating three-dimensional images into two dimensions and back again; otherwise the lines will simply appear to move upward and converge. The evidence indicates that Jones had to deal with an untrained audience who were not, moreover, quick learners."[39]

As mentioned above, no action was possible towards the back of the perspective stage. The proscenium, in turn, was too narrow—as surviving designs indicate—to accommodate any major stage action.[40] This leaves the "dancing space" as the main acting area; characteristically the second general movement in the masque-in-performance went outwards from the stage picture towards the court's center—the king. This movement occurs in practically all masques. The central position of the monarch was also marked by the laws of perspective, a fact noticed by a number of critics who have written about masques. The king's eye is directly opposite the vanishing point and on the same level as the illusionary horizon. Thus the space between the king and the stage picture was the main acting area, surrounded on three sides by spectators. It is also worth mentioning here that only the king and those select few surrounding the monarch actually faced the stage picture; the vast majority of spectators were seated with their sides to the stage picture and were in fact facing the dancing floor.

However, as indicated above, the boundary between this stage

The Emblematic Masque

and the auditorium was an illusionistic artistic device—a trick, because in fact the entire hall was incorporated into the created world, along with the spectators. This hall always appeared as "here" in masques, as opposed to the implied "there" of the stage picture or of the noncourt. The court as a whole may, in addition, be given an explicit allegorical meaning, as in *Love's Triumph Through Callipolis* (1631), where it stands for the title Callipolis, a city that is in fact the only invariable element of the overall stage design; it cannot "disappear," because it is the here and now of the court, and all other elements of the setting in the stage picture are always presented in relation to Callipolis, or to the court. Fama in *Time Vindicated* (1623) praises the king directly for restoring the divine age on earth and promises to "fill this world of beautie here, your Court";[41] similarly, Cupid addresses the king:

> You, Sir, that are the Lord of Time,
> Receive not as my crime
> 'Gainst Majesty, that Love and Sport
> To night have entred in your Court.[42]

And in *The Masque of Augurs*, Apollo calls the king with the familiar

> Prince of thy Peace, see what it is to Love
> The Powers above
> Jove hath commanded me
> To visit thee.[43]

What has misled some critics is that in all the masques the court seems to be only the court and the king and his courtiers seem to be only themselves. This creates the illusion of a "real" world. However, taking into account the laws that govern this sphere of the created world, one immediately notices that they are substantially different from the physical laws that govern empirical reality. To begin, all the people of the court world have a miraculous insight into the metaphysical sphere: they can see mythological heavens inhabited by gods, floating islands approaching English shores, the underwater kingdoms of Neptune and Oceanos. The entire celestial world that is said to govern the universe, is brought—as if through a magical and powerful telescope—close, enabling them to see with their own eyes what is happening on the moon or to learn what is new on the Olympus or to watch the stars dancing. All of this could also occur in a public theater, but there these visions would not be distinctive for any particular

Antimasque characters. Drawing by Andrzej Markowicz.

The Emblematic Masque

group of people; anyone could come and watch the spectacle. The case is totally different in masques-in-performance: they were staged by the court for the court; no one else, with the exception of honored guests, was admitted. The masque could be "experienced" only by those who were the closest to the monarch.

Another characteristic that distinguishes the masque-in-performance from other types of theatrical spectacles is that the masque never reenacts a historical moment: it is a historical moment happening here and now, a fact stressed by the temporal and spatial unity of the entire hall space. In drama time is always compressed (even if the classical unities are observed) or stretched or cut, and on those occasions when it seems to coincide with the empirical time of the spectators, it is in fact a reconstruction of a different time (past or future). In the masque-in-performance (as in a ritual) there is only one temporal dimension joining the two spheres of the created world, the court and the metaphysical sphere. As indicated above, however, there appear "scenes," especially in antimasques, that take place somewhere else, such as outside the court hall, and at a different time. In all these cases (few as they are) one may talk of elements of drama that are soon replaced by what basically is a ritualistic courtly event. The antimasques that take place in the here and now of the court may also be treated as theatrical performances, for in them the boundary between the spectators and the actors is marked. However, we should not forget that in length antimasques dominate only in the printed texts: in the actual performance they were brief episodes.

Moreover, allegorical and mythological characters (and sometimes even the souls of the blessed) may enter into the court world with ease, by simply descending from their heavens. This feature is asymmetrical: none of the mortals, not even the king, has the ability to enter the divine sphere, which can happen only after death. Similarly, the metaphysical characters communicate various messages to the king and to the other courtiers present, often praising, for example, the beauty of the ladies. This, again, does not work the other way around: neither the king nor any of his courtiers ever say anything to their visitors from outer space. The next difference between the "real" court and the masque court is that the masque king is equipped with superhuman qualities and powers that one can see in operation in the created world (and only during the actual performance). For example, in many masques the king is said to be the source of light and harmony; this should not be taken as a metaphor because many of the newcomers to the court are literally "blinded" or "stunned" by this light. Even if the individual and skeptical courtiers did not actually see the fluorescent monarch, they are after all only mortals and it is only divine beings that can fully see into his true nature. Furthermore, it is the king's mere presence (who by laws of divine geometry is placed in the center of the court world) that brings order and (literally and physically) governs this world. It is the king's very presence that enables flowers to be transformed into human beings or brings spring in winter. Many masques stress that the source of the king's superhuman power lies in the divine sphere; this is corroborated by the laws of perspective that link the monarch, and only him, with divinity.

At this point one ought to consider also the function of the masquers. Critics have often observed that their discovery and descent was the most important moment in the whole spectacle; in fact, the whole masque may have been written to provide an explanation for the appearance of the masked nobles. Surprisingly, hardly any space has been devoted to the function of the masquers within the created world. Who were they, anyway? Obviously they are a part of the metaphysical sphere, and by entering the court with hidden identities, they could not be treated as individuals (the Prince, the Queen, or Lord so-and-so), but rather as paragons representing the courtly virtues. To follow these virtues was a way to secure one's passage to the divine sphere. Thomas Middleton's *The Masque of Heroes* announces that the Masquers are, in fact, "Heroes deified for their virtues."[44] They descend in order to show others an example to follow: "They all descend to have their worth / Shine in imitation forth." In James Shirley's *The Triumph of Peace* the masquers are called "the sons of Peace, Law and Justice" and the "children" of the king's "reign." In this sense the masquers function as mirror reflections of the king's virtues. They are said to be the offspring of the king's wisdom, a quality that enables them to perform an important function within the created world. It is through them that the king's superhuman powers can be seen in operation. This is especially evident when the masquers undergo, as they often do, a transformation from a state of chaos or imprisonment to harmony and freedom that is made possible only by the godlike powers of the king.

The appearance of the masquers, made possible only because of the king's presence, literally brings harmony and order and objectively reveals the divine origin of royalty. After their dances with

The Emblematic Masque

the ladies of the court, the masquers usually return to where they came from and disappear with the closing of the scene. Whenever the masquers do not return to the metaphysical world, they take off their masks, thus marking the end of the spectacle and their becoming mortal, identifiable individuals again who simply join the others at the following banquet. This was the case in *Lord Hayes Masque,* where "at the end whereof the Maskers putting off their visards, & helmets, made a low honour to the King, and attended his Ma: to the banquetting place." However, the world they return to is not substantially different from the world of the masque. Changing the space means moving from one genre of behavior to another. The "real" boundary is that between the court and the noncourt worlds. As Stephen Orgel observes,

> A masquer's disguise is a representation of the courtier beneath. He retains his personality and hence his position in the social hierarchy. His audience affirms his equality with them by consenting to join the dance. This is the climax of the Jacobean masque, and dramatically equivalent to the Tudor unmasking, whereby the symbol opens and reveals reality. But a professional dancer is like an actor; he plays any part; he can assume all personalities because he has none of his own. Like the courtly masquer, he is identical with his mask, but for a different reason: his persona is not a *representation* of the reality beneath, but the reality itself. When an actor unmasks, the revelation is trivial. We see a person who is no person, who may be anybody, who has been performing an *impersonation.* Whereas the courtier's unmasking is the point of the masque, through which its significance is extended out beyond the boundary of the stage into the real world, the actor's unmasking is the destruction of the dramatic illusion.[45]

Thus, through the king's wisdom and virtue, a place among gods is secured for the most noble courtiers. At the very end of the Middleton masque quoted above, Time, one of the characters, "makes his honour to the Ladies":

> Line long the Miracles of Times and Yeeres,
> Till with those Heroes, You sit fixt in Spheres.[46]

In *Love Restored,* the masquers are referred to as "The spirits of the Court, and flower of men" and are led by Cupid to a dance so that they can "figure the ten ornaments / That doe each courtly presence grace." In a dance that follows the masquers impersonate virtues like honor, courtesy, valor, confidence, industry, and so on (all of these "ornaments" are mentioned by Cupid). In William Browne's *Circe and Ulysses* (1615) the masquers are called "worthy knights" and are asked to dance and imitate the sun.

Very often the masquers are contrasted with antimasquers. The latter, in Jonson's *Mercury Vindicated* (1616), for instance, are described as "imperfect creatures" and are chased away by Mercury. The "creatures" are the product of Vulcan's experiments that went astray: he has been trying to produce "artificial men," which explains why they appear with alembics on their heads (and could perhaps be considered as antecedents of Frankenstein's monster!). They are contrasted with "the creatures of the Sun," the masquers, who are said to be perfect creations of Mother Nature. The antimasquers in Jonson's *Pans Anniversarie* (1620), in turn, are contrasted with the masquers who are "prime Arcadians" (the masque takes place in "Arcadia," or Britain), who have been taught by Pan (King James) "the rites of true society."

In spite of all its seemingly mimetic qualities, then, the court of the masque cannot be treated as an empirical reality opposed to the fictional world on stage. Both of these spheres are parts of the created model of the universe, and it is a critic's task to describe the laws that govern this universe. This will, one may hope, explain why Ben Jonson considered these highly illusionistic and certainly nonmimetic spectacles "mirrors of man's life."[47] What he actually means is that the laws that govern this artistic reality are by analogy the same as those governing the microcosm of man (who governs his body in the same way as the king his nation), the geocosm of earth, and the macrocosm of the universe. With the closing of the scene, after the final dance and speeches, with the disappearance of the stage picture, the court goes through the final transformation: it instantaneously returns to its "real" ontological status, or to empirical reality. The ritual is over.

Another important element joining the two spheres of the court and divinity is light, which makes the stage picture visible to the onlookers. In many masques, the source of light was concealed, hence the initial effect of a magical self-illuminated reality. However, many texts state that the king himself is the source of light: after all, he is the sun. In *The Masque of Blackness* Jonson talks of Britain "Rul'd by a SUN . . . Whose beames shine day, and night." In a marginal note in *Love Freed From Ignorance and Folly* (1611), Jonson explains the allegory: "The meaning of this is, that these Ladies being the perfect issue of Beautie, and all worldly grace, were carried by *Loue* to celebrate the Maiestie, and wisdome of the King, figur'd in the Sunne. . . ."[48] In Robert White's *Cupid's Ban-*

The Emblematic Masque

ishment (1617) the king is addressed directly, and his most conspicuous feature is mentioned: "bright Spheare of Greatnes, thy faire beames, / Which shoote with splendour from thy Majesty."[49] In *Pleasure Reconciled to Virtue,* King James is called

>   the glory of ye West,
> the brighter star, yt from his burning Crest
> lights all on this side ye *Atlanticke seas*
> . . . .
> Se[e] where He shines: *Justice, & Wisdome* plac'd
> about his *Throne.*

And *News From the New World* (1620) has a characteristic reference to the king:

> Now looke and see in yonder throne,
> How all those beames are cast from one.
>   This is that Orbe so bright,
> Has kept your wonder so awake;
> Whence you as from a mirrour take
>   The Suns reflected light.

Light, as is well known, played an important role in most cosmologies of natural philosophers of the Renaissance, and the identification of space with light was common because light was considered the all-pervading, all-preserving medium of three dimensions. The three-dimensional space, made visible by self-emanating light, the entity that is neither corporeal nor immaterial, serves as the intermediary between the corporeal, concrete world of nature and the incorporeal world of spirits. As Max Jammer observed, "Indeed, it [light] was created by God for the fulfillment of this function . . . and it is also metaphysically the way to God." John C. Meagher also noted in his excellent *Method and Meaning in Jonson's Masques,*

> Through the visible light of the masque and through the poetic image of light which defines and sustains its implications, the masques not only allege but demonstrate that one becomes splendid by relating oneself properly with the powers of heaven, with nature, with virtue, with wisdom, with love, with the divinely instituted and perfecting order of the king. And through the light thus acquired, men may, as the masquers do, resemble the heavens. . . .[50]

It is therefore significant that the major source of light in the masque world is the king himself. It is through this light that the way to the divine sphere is visualized in ritualistic spectacle.

When discussing the similarity of early nineteenth-century Russian theater to painting, Yuri Lotman noted that "The analogy between painting and theatre was manifested above all in the organization of the spectacle through conspicuously pictorial means of artistic modelling, in that the stage text tended to unfold not as a continuous flux . . . imitating the passage of time in the extra-artistic world, but as a whole, clearly broken up into single 'stills' organized synchronically, each of which is set within the decor like a picture in a frame."[51] This description may just as well be applied to the masques-in-performance, which consist of a series of changes of scene in which each stage picture is not only similar to painting in general but reminiscent of the graphic arts and emblem books in particular. It is not surprising that the masque has been labeled a "speaking picture." There is more to this simile than one may suppose. In what follows I attempt to show that the masque-in-performance may be seen in fact as a theatrical "equivalent" of an emblem book.[52]

It will be useful at this point to introduce the category of ostension to this discussion, by which semioticians such as Elam mean an action in which "in order to refer to, indicate or define a given object [instead of describing it], one simply picks it up and shows it to the receiver of the message in question."[53] Umberto Eco has argued that this is "the most basic instance of performance: semiotization involves the *showing* of objects and events . . . to the audience, rather than describing, explaining or defining them. This ostensive aspect of the stage 'show' distinguishes it, for example, from narrative, where persons, objects and events are necessarily described and recounted."[54] The masque-in-performance, however, besides being a courtly theatrical spectacle, also borrows from the tradition of courtly ritual in which the basic formula remains the same and is repeated in every masque but details of the "invention" are variable and often have to be "supported" by words that describe and explain the "hidden meanings"; this explains the double nature—dramatic and narrative—of the masque.

This double nature is fully revealed in most of the masques: their performances have both elements—the theatrical ostension, by which "living emblems" and the "mechanics of the world" are presented to spectators by predominantly pictorial means and that may be decoded without description,[55] and the verbal element, which in numerous speeches, dialogues, and songs is in fact narrative in character and describes the events, people, allegories, and visual images that they accompany. This double

The Emblematic Masque

nature of the masque has intrigued and often irritated scholars, causing them to complain about the "nondramatic" quality of these texts. The list of complaints is actually impressive and even includes accusations that "the theatrical machine has a life of its own, and one that is . . . quite *separate* [emphasis added] from the life of Jonson's text" and that "the scene, whether symbolic or realistic, was related to the text but not integrated with it."[56] Perhaps the above statements would be true if one treated the masque as a minor form of drama. But drama it is not; it is basically a courtly ritual (with elements of drama) that is constantly being rewritten but invariably deals with the infinite depth of the king's divine wisdom. Victor Turner writes that "few rituals are so completely stereotyped that every word, every gesture, every scene is authoritatively prescribed. Most often, invariant phases and episodes are interdigitated with variable passages. . . ."[57]

In speaking about the similarity between the masque-in-performance and pictorial arts, one must not forget basic differences. To begin, following the rules of perspective and optics in general, a stage picture creates an illusion by which a three-dimensional setting "pretends" to be a two-dimensional painting, or engraving, disguised as a three-dimensional space.[58] In other words, the stage picture wants to be seen as a two-dimensional painting constructed in accordance with the rules of linear perspective. In contrast to this, a perspective painting not only creates the illusion of three dimensions, but also re-creates a perspective view "seen" or imagined by the painter some time in the historical past. The painter, who is usually not seen within the frame but who is implied by the painting itself, functions as a "witness" to the historically true or fictitious scene that is represented. The ideal viewpoint for an onlooker, determined by the laws of perspective, is in fact the very point from which the painter viewed (or imagined) the scene. Thus, anyone looking correctly at the actual painting sees everything presented on canvas through "the painter's eye." Yet it is quite obvious that the viewer and the painting (or rather the scene it represents) belong to different temporal realities. In the masque-in-performance, however, the perspective scenes are located *hic et nunc* and are not re-creations of anyone's view or vision that occurred in the historical past. The king is not seated in the place from which somebody earlier saw the unfolding stage pictures. The temporal unity of the perspective stage and the court has already been discussed. The magical box generates pictures that do not "bring to life" past events but constitute entirely new events in the "now" of the temporal dimension of the court.

It is useful to recall once again Roman Jakobson's category of transmutation, or intersemiotic translation.[59] For example, when a text created within one system (say an emblem book, which in fact would be a fusion of the graphic arts and literature systems) is reconstructed with materials of another system (in this case theater art), it loses its specific literary qualities and gains specific theatrical ones. Thus a painting, when "translated" (or rather "transmuted") into the language of poetry, loses its painting-specific qualities and gains literary-specific ones. In the case of masque-in-performance, the perspective three-dimensional stage is in most cases an example of transmutation of an emblem-book picture (either actual or invented *ad hoc*) into the "language," or system of theater. The illusionistic stage picture may therefore be treated as a scenographic transmutation of a two-dimensional emblem icon, and the dialogues, speeches, and songs may consequently be treated as theatrical transmutations of the emblem mottos. The basically literary origin of this transmutation explains why both pictorial and verbal components of the masque may with ease be analyzed philologically. From this point of view, the masque-in-performance is to a great extent a text about another text (being "the book of the king's wisdom"); it is the theatrical equivalent of an emblem book.

Take as an example a scene from Ben Jonson's *Hymenaei* (1607), where a new emblematic scene is discovered with Juno sitting in her throne, Jupiter above, the Rainbow or Iris below, and eight "ladies" on the sides; the printed text says that "All which, upon discovery, REASON made *narration of*" (emphasis added).[60] And in what follows, Reason in a lengthy speech in verse actually describes what is seen in the "picture" and elucidates the significance of its particular elements. Thus a theatrical equivalent of an emblem from a book is created. In this respect one may agree with Roy Strong's comment that "Jones's scenery was essentially the action of the masque with its dialogues, songs and dances elucidated and moralised. . . . Every stage picture he presented was a symbol composed of a composite series of hieroglyphs."[61] And long ago Allardyce Nicoll observed that "the audience gathered at Whitehall, trained in the study of emblems and *impresa* . . . can have looked upon the masques as nothing but a series of living emblems or have listened to their verses as ought else than a string of mottos."[62] Both of these comments apply of course only to the masque-in-performance.

The Emblematic Masque

Even the dances were often "emblematic" in character, as when the dancers formed certain geometric figures such as a circle, a "chain," or an initial of somebody's name. Their painterly quality is sometimes stressed in descriptions in the printed texts. In Jonson's *Pleasure Reconciled to Virtue,* for instance, the dancers are asked to "put all the aptness on / Of figure that proportion / Or colour can disclose"; the reader is told that even if the rules of painting were lost, they could be reconstructed on the basis of the dance (which implies that that particular dance was an ideal transmutation of a painting):

> That if those silent arts were lost,
> Design, and picture, they might boast
>   From you a newer ground
> Instructed by the height'ning sense
> Of dignity and reverence
>   In you true motions found.

The picturelike character of the stage and its "bookish" origins are additionally stressed by its frame—what later became known as the proscenium arch. As Richard Southern writes, "for the first time in history a *frontispiece* was made to frame-in the stage picture. One saw the show *through* it. This frontispiece was, in Jones's hands, an emblematic decoration at the front of the stage, designed separately for each show [which makes it a part of the stage text] and consisting of two side pieces adjoining the walls of the hall and flanking the scene, with a cross-piece connecting their tops and reaching up to the ceiling."[63] What is striking in this description, and in the surviving designs, is the close similarity of this concept of framing the stage picture to the contemporary framing borders or architectural designs of graphic (and often emblematic) frontispieces in printed books.

Rosemary Freeman in her *English Emblem Book* notes in passing that "emblems entered the masques in ways other than through personifications. The scene was often painted with small emblematic designs arranged in much the same fashion as they were in the engraved frontispieces of books."[64] It is well known that in the Renaissance the most popular frame for title pages was the classical recess flanked by architectural wings, standing on a base and surmounted by a pediment. The title was often enclosed in a cartouche or frame, and generally hung from the overall architectural frame or was affixed to it at the top.[65] Similarly, in a number of masques the title appears within the architectural frame. In

Tempe Restord (1632), for instance, the description of the "ornament"—as the proscenium arch was then called—reads: "In the vpper part of the border serving for ornament to the SCENE, was painted a faire compartment of scrowles and quadratures, in which was written TEMPE RESTAVRATVM" (A2V). Thomas Carew's and Inigo Jones's *Coelum Britanicum* (1634) has a "frontispiece" with a compartment and the title inscribed in it. The same arrangement appears in *The Triumphs of the Prince D'Amour* and in a number of other masques that include descriptions of the proscenium arch. The reason for doing so on title pages was to create a front or façade to the book. In the later sixteenth and seventeenth centuries these were often enriched with allegorical figures, emblematic attributes, symbols, and so on. Similarly, in at least those masques-in-performance where evidence remains, allegorical and mythological figures appear in the designs for the proscenium arch, as do other basically graphic elements. As specialized studies have shown, the title page always maintains its character as graphic art.

The two-dimensional graphic character of the "frontispiece" in the masque was additionally stressed by the introduction of a flat curtain that was separately designed for each spectacle. The painted curtain, framed by an architectural "arch," must be treated as part of the design. The existing meager evidence on the use of curtains in masques proves that at least sometimes they were pictures in themselves. Orgel and Strong observe that "in a sense, the curtain itself was announcing a programme."[66] In the *Masque of Flowers*, for instance, there "appeared a *Travers* painted in *Perspective*, like a wall of a Cittie with battlements, over which were seene the Tops of houses. In the middle whereof was a great gate and on either side a Temple . . . in either of which opened a little gate."[67] Clouds were painted on the curtain used for *Lord Hayes Masque* in 1607, and the one used for *The Masque of Beauty* represented "Night." The curtain in *Oberon* presented a map of the kingdom, quite appropriate for the circumstances of that production.

The architectural inventions of title pages often employ fantastic, highly ornamental forms, as do the designs for the frontispieces in masques. The surviving designs, published by Orgel and Strong, provide considerable evidence for this. Traditionally, inventions of this kind are often loosely called portals and triumphal arches. Thus the triumphal arch set on the title page may symbolize the formal entrance to the work within,[68] whereas in the case of the masques-in-performance the proscenium arch and

The Emblematic Masque

the curtain would create a theatrical equivalent or transmutation of a title page, being a formal entry to the worlds within. It is perhaps not without significance that the stage frame in printed masques is usually called "Arch Triumphal," as in *Somerset's Masque* or in *Lovers Made Men*.

However, this was not the only possible meaning of a title page. Towards the end of the sixteenth century, emblematic title pages began to appear in England that were always closely connected with the contents of the book for which they were made.[69] As authorities on the subject have observed:

> Generally the design was not confined to the expression of one idea or one theme. It was the vehicle for the thoughts of the author on his work, but might also give indication of its scope, and include pictorial representations which should be understood only by perceiving the book, thus stimulating the reader's curiosity. All the themes were carefully interwoven into the set patterns for the design of title-pages, according to an inner logic, to make up the meaning of the whole.[70]

The same description could in fact be applied to the frontispieces in masques, for they were meaningful introductions to the worlds within. Even the scarce evidence available for the actual stage frontispiece designs reveals that at least sometimes these designs repeated certain motifs from the rich interior decorations of the Banqueting House, thus identifying particular stage texts with the iconographical and ideological program of the entire space of the hall.[71] Ben Jonson considered the frontispiece design for his *Lord Haye's Masque*—to give just one example—important enough to have its description included in the printed text:

> The Front before the Scene, was an Arch-Triumphall. On the top of which, Humanitie placed in figure, sate with her lap full of flowers . . . holding a golden chaine in her left hand: to shew both the freedome, and the bond of courtesie, with this inscription.
>
> SVPER OMNIA VVLTVS.
>
> On the two sides of the Arch Cheerefulnes, and Readines, } her servants
>
> Cheerefulnes, in a loose flowing garment, filling out wine from an antique piece of plate; with this word
>
> Readines, a winged Mayd, with two flaming bright lights in her bands, and her word,
>
> Amor addidit alas.

Adsit laetitiae dator [Let the giver   [Love gave wings]
of joy be present][72]

The emblematic character of title pages led to the appearance of explanatory verses, which first occurred in England during the reign of James.[73] Similarly, in those printed masques in which the frontispiece is described, the description usually includes explanatory comments, as the example given above illustrates.[74]

Aurelian Townshend's and Inigo Jones's *Albions Triumph* (1632) is a good case for a discussion of the significance of the stage design (and the proscenium arch in particular) in the masque-in-performance. This will naturally lead to the realization of the deep differences in the meanings created by the former and the printed masque. Even though the printed version of *Albion's Triumph* includes lengthy descriptions of the scenography, if it had not been for the actual designs that have been preserved, one would not have been able to grasp all the semantic richness of the stage text. Consider first the description of the "frontispiece":

> The first thing that presented it self to the eye, was the Ornament [the proscenium arch] that went about the Scene: in the middest of which was placed a great Armes of the Kings, with Angels holding an Emperiall Crowne, from which hung a Drapery, of crimson Velvet, fringed with gold, tackt in severall knotts, that on each-side, with many folds, was wound about a Pillaster; in the freeze, were festones of severall fruites in their naturall colours, on which, in gratious postures lay Children sleeping; at each end was a double sheild, with a Gorgons head, and at the foot of the pillasters, on each side, stood two Women, the one young, in a watchet Robe looking vpwards, and on her head, a paire of Compasses of gold, the poynts standing towards Heaven: the other more ancient, and of a venerable aspect, apparreled in tawney, looking downewards; in the one hand a long ruler, and in the other, a great paire of iron Compasses, one poynt whereof, stood on the ground, and the other touched part of the ruler. Above their heads, were fixt, compartiments of a new [?] composition, and in that over the first, was written *Theorica*, and over the second *Practica*, shewing that these two, all works of Architecture, and Inginiring have their perfection. The Curtaine being suddenly drawne vp, the first Sceane appeared, which represented a *Romane Atrium* . . . and beyond these, were other pieces of Architecture of a Pallace royall.[75]

In his well-known essay D. J. Gordon claims that the figures of "Theorica" and "Practica" "have no relevance to the special glorification of the king and queen which is the burden of the masque. But perhaps they have another relevance, they and the architectural settings of the masque. The triumphs of Roman architecture which lead up to the palace of Whitehall (and one would like to know whether the view showed the Banqueting House, or perhaps part of the projected palace), do they not celebrate the glory of the architect as well as of the king?"[76]

A close reading of Townshend's description leads to the discovery that the entire design has relevance to the special glorification of the king and queen, which is the burden of the masque. The central element, and the one first described, is the royal coat of arms, adorned with an imperial crown, which immediately suggests the imperial/Roman heritage of King Charles. This is held by two angels, which stresses the divine patronage and origin of Charles's kingship. In the design the angels blow on trumpets, announcing to the world the king's glory of triumph (note the title). The groupings of fruit on the frieze are inhabited by two sleeping children: they can sleep in peace, being born to the world of plenty, where the calamities of war are not known. The frieze is supported by two pilasters; at the points where they meet, at both ends of the frieze, are double shields with a Gorgon's head on each—an allegorical representation of the king's victories over the forces of evil (Medusa's head is nonliving). At the foot of the pilasters (and on the bases of the extant designs) stand two allegorical figures, one of "Theorica," the other of "Practica." Their attributes leave no doubt that they represent the theory (which is inspired by heaven) and practice of architecture.

Thus the sign of the royal power (the crowned coat of arms), a part of the architectural element, "the frieze of royalty," is supported physically by another architectural element, the pilasters. In this way, a parallel is drawn between the royal power, which rests on the divine order of this universe, and architecture, which is a material and artistic manifestation of that order.[77] The divine origin applies both to kings and to architecture; the royal crown is held by the angels, and *Theorica* is looking up to heaven, the compass on her head pointing in the same direction. One has to remember that a compass is an instrument of precision. *Practica*, in turn, is looking down, with her instruments pointing to the ground. The practice of architecture is realized by the very design, but what about the "practice" of kingship?

When the scene opens, the first plan reveals a Roman "atrium" (forum), where apart from architectural buildings, are golden statues; beyond these there were "other pieces of Architecture of a Pallace royall." The latter does not necessarily have to be an ancient emperor's palace. It is very likely, as Gordon has suggested, that this represented a part of Whitehall, which would draw an architectural link between ancient Rome and the England of the 1630s. The function of the forum, then, is to link the ancient past to the royal palace, thereby stressing the classical roots and heritage of Charles's kingship. The passage of time is presented through purely architectural (and, of course, theatrical) means, and the history of architecture parallels the history of kingship. Later in the masque the scene is changed again, and a "Landscipt" is presented, with "a prospect of the Kings Pallace of *Whitehall,* and part of the Citie of *London."* Suddenly, heaven above "opened" and "in a bright cloud were seen sitting fiue persons, representing *Innocency, Iustice, Religion, Affection to the Countrey & Concord,* being all Companions of *Peace."* Thus, a part of an ancient city of Rome, with its symbolic virtues, finds a modern equivalent in the panorama of London. Even if the opening scene presented an ancient palace, its parallel to Whitehall would be preserved. Most important is the fact that the entire stage design and the stage text create meanings in relation to the emblematic proscenium arch. It is "read" through the proscenium arch.

The printed text, or the literary masque, creates the parallel between ancient Rome and present-day London through purely literary means. For instance, there is a surprising disregard for spatial and temporal distances in the masque. Early in the text the king is identified with the Emperor "Albanactus" who rules "Albipolis" and is married to Queen "Alba," but the action is set—through design and dialogue—in ancient times. The function of this has been discussed above. However, following the antimasque, the king appears as one of the masquers; after their dance, he retires, "taking his seat by the Queene." Only after this does the scene change to show a part of London and a view of Whitehall. The allegories that appear above descend and proceed to the throne, praising the king and queen and presenting them several gifts. The suspension of mimetic rules such as the principles of the space-time continuum characterizes all masques and allows the characters to move instantaneously in both space and time. Since the two spheres of the fictional world are not separate in spatial and temporal terms, an equivalence is created by which the ancient Albipolis becomes the London of 1632. The proscenium arch does not change, for there is no need for change: the peace, glory, and plenty of the past have not changed in the present. It may be said that the emblematic proscenium arch

The Emblematic Masque

provides an axiological fusion of the two spatio-temporal spheres in the masque. It equates and qualifies both the spheres.

Thus, to sum up, the emblematic frontispiece in the masque-in-performance is reminiscent of emblematic title pages in printed books. In this particular case the theatrical "title page" is iconographically (and through inscriptions) closely linked with the contents of the "theatrical book of emblems." As the curtain is dropped, or drawn to the sides, one passes over the title page and is presented with several three-dimensional pages of this "book," a sequence of living emblems accompanied by living mottos. The book, owing to the miraculous powers of the magical box of the stage, reveals itself to the spectators and allegorical and mythological characters step down from its pages onto the court floor and interact with the courtiers.[78] This marks the union or fusion of the two spheres. Naturally the book needs an author (as magic needs its source), and he is here implied by the rules of perspective: it is the king's eye or his mind that is equipped with supernatural powers that enable the contents of his "book" to appear in the magical box. Thus the model of the universe created in the masque—leaving aside its immediate political implications—is based on the concept of the world as a book, or a text, being a projection of the king's mind. This also implies that the masque is a theatrical transmutation of a book and may therefore be treated as a text about a text. In another attempt of this kind Henry Peacham "translated" James's *Basilikon Doron* into an emblem book, three manuscripts of which have survived to the present day. These were originally presented to the king and Prince Henry. The emblems are in Latin, and each accompanying picture is based upon some part of the king's instructions and supported by quotations from the classics.[79] Roy Strong has convincingly argued that *Basilikon Doron* was the key source book for the iconography of the Rubens ceiling in the Banqueting House, being "James's own exposition of monarchy by Divine Right."[80] In this way, the Banqueting House itself is a "book" that on special occasions "comes alive" and reveals its content to the court and through foreign ambassadors to the world.

In this sense all the masques presented at the Stuart court may, and perhaps should be treated as one text, being a projection of royal wisdom. Again, their apparent political connotations are not my concern here. Their emblematic interrelationship has not been sufficiently studied and is certainly worth a closer scrutiny. For instance, in Jonson's *Hymenaei*, Atlas and Hercules appear, supporting the heavens; the extant text of this particular masque does not really explain why Atlas and Hercules have been brought together, and one needs to read the later *Pleasure Reconciled to Virtue* to discover that traditionally Atlas is associated with Wisdom and Hercules with Virtue. Thus the firmament of the masque world in *Hymenaei* is supported by Wisdom and Virtue, the union of which is a recurrent motif in other masques as well and is epitomized in King James himself. Another familiar emblem closely associated with Wisdom and Virtue is that of a king holding a book and sword in his hands.[81]

Since the masque is based on the concept of the world as a book, it may be philologically analyzed as a book. This is in fact proven by numerous printed texts of masques that include entire *apparatuses critici* with elaborate marginal notes, footnotes, lengthy quotations, and references to dozens of ancient and contemporary sources. The latter occasionally include direct references to King James's works. For instance, an obvious allusion to the instructions for the Prince as they are laid out in *Basilikon Doron* may be found in Ben Jonson's *Haddington Masque*:

> A Prince, that draws
> By 'example more, than others do by laws:
> That is so just to his great act, and thought,
> To do, not what Kings may, but what Kings ought.
> Who, out of piety, unto peace, is vow'd;
> To *spare his subjects*, yet to quell the proud,
> And dares esteem it the first fortitude,
> To have his passions, foes at home, subdued.
>   (Emphasis added.)

It may be pointed out, as D. J. Gordon has first noticed, that the Virgilian "Parcere subiectis" is the last line in *Basilikon Doron*. Similarly, as observed by Ernest William Talbert, in *The Masque of Augurs* "the statement that Prince Charles does, 'by his Fathers light his courses run' and the final conception of the relationship between Jove and Apollo express the same ideas, the ideas implicit in James's writing *Basilikon Doron*. . . . In fact, he who reads the *Basilikon Doron* and Jonson's masques will notice similarities in sentiment and in emphasis."[82] And one can agree with Allen H. Gilbert that "the masques constitute almost a King's Mirror, echoing precepts familiar to James in the volumes he turned over when composing his own book."[83]

The world-as-book concept was in fact quite common in Renais-

The Emblematic Masque

sance literature and thought. Man himself wás a book, the Book of Nature or the Book of God.[84] In one of his sermons John Donne wrote that "The World is a great Volume, and man an Index to that Book; Even in the Body of Man, you may turne to the whole world."[85] In this case the king's wisdom found an appropriate reflection as a living emblem book, for remember that contemporaries considered emblem books as epitomes of wisdom of almost divine dimension. As Francis Quarles writes in the introduction to his book of emblems, "An Emblem is but a silent Parable. . . . Before the Knowledge of Letters, God was known by *Hieroglyphics*. And, indeed, what are the Heavens, the Earth, nay every Creature, but *Hieroglyphics* and *Emblems* of His Glory?"[86] And as pointed out by Peter M. Daly, in the seventeenth century "both the poet and the emblematist look upon nature as God's second book, which reveals much of God's intentions."[87]

Samuel Daniel explains in his *Vision of the Twelve Goddesses* that the goddesses of his invention will appear in human shapes, so that it would be easier to "read" their "mysticall Ideas, dispersed in that wide, and incomprehensible *volume of Nature* [emphasis added]." And Ben Jonson in *Newes From the New World Discover'd in the Moone* draws the readers' attention to the king, whose greatness can be "read" (his word) "as you would doe the booke / Of all perfection. . . ." In Jonson's *Pleasure Reconciled to Virtue*, the first living emblem opening the masque is "the mountain Atlas, who had his top ending in the figure of an old Man, his head and beard all hoary and frost. . . ." The text states that this mountain is the "hill of knowledge," the epitome of wisdom, where twelve princes "have been bred" ("near Atlas' head"). One of the princes is the offspring of Hesperus, by which name King James appears in the text. In this way a significant equivalence is created between the mountain of wisdom (and its ancient head), where the fictitious prince has been educated, and the royal court of Britain and its head—King James—where the real prince has been brought up, nourished with the fruits of his father's wisdom. And all this was presented in a hall that had its own elaborate and sophisticated ideological program, that of the Temple of Solomon.[88] In the same masque the masquers are discovered on the "lap of the mountain" and a choir asks them to descend to earth, pointing to the allegorical significance of Atlas:

> Ope, aged Atlas, open then thy lap,
> And from thy beamy bosom strike a light,
> That men may *read* in thy mysterious map

> All lines
> All signes
> Of royal education, and the right . . .
>
> (Emphasis added.)

Thus one is asked to read from the "mysterious map" of royal wisdom. Everything that the masquers do is meaningful, as opposed to the "actions of mankind" that are "but a labyrinth or maze." Even the masquers' dance is full of wisdom:

> [*Dedalus.*] So let your dances be entwin'd,
>   Yet not perplex men unto gaze;
>   As men may *read* each act you do;
>   And when they see the graces meet,
>   Admire the wisdom of your feet:
>   For dancing is an exercise
>   Not only shows the mover's wit,
>   But maketh the beholder wise,
>   As he hath power to rise to it.
>
> (Emphasis added.)

Similarly, readers of emblem books were expected not merely to look at the pictures and learn; they were also asked to imitate what they saw when the emblem represented an exemplar.[89] Thus, when a courtier was invited to dance with the masquers, he imitated the divine perfection of the latter's movements.[90]

While "reading" the book of royal wisdom during the masque performance, spectators became in fact incorporated into it, for they constituted a significant part of the projected model of the world. As Orgel and Strong put it, the perspective scenery (actually more than just this) transformed "audiences into spectators, fixing the viewer, and directing the theatrical experience toward the single point in the hall from which the perspective achieved its fullest effect, the royal throne. . . . Jones's theatre transformed its audience into a living and visible emblem of the aristocratic hierarchy: the closer one sat to the King, the 'better' one's place was, and only the King's seat was perfect. It is no accident that perspective stages flourished at court and only at court, and that their appearance there coincided with the reappearance in England of the Divine Right of Kings as a serious political philosophy."[91] The masque, I should add, proves the validity of this philosophy, reveals its "objective" power, and stamps it with a divine seal of *nihil obstat*.

But there is even deeper significance in the concept of the world

The Emblematic Masque 89

as a book, for this concept is in fact congruous with one of the distinctive features of the type of culture developed in Renaissance England. The importance attached in the masques to minute and seemingly trifling details, their enormously rich and elaborate iconography, is a good starting point for a larger chapter on the subject, or for the conclusion of this one. From the semiotic point of view, the masque-in-performance may be treated as a peculiar form of courtly behavior or as a ritualistic spectacle capable of generating content, and not as a symbolic one, for a symbol usually presupposes an external, relatively arbitrary expression of some content.[92] Yuri Lotman and Boris Uspensky observe, "To a culture directed towards expression that is founded on the notion of *correct* designation and, in particular, correct naming, the entire world can appear as a sort of text consisting of various kinds of signs, where content is predetermined and it is only necessary to know the language; that is to know the relation between the elements of expression and content. In other words, cognition of the world is equivalent to philological analysis."[93]

The masques hardly say anything "new." Stephen Orgel is certainly right when he remarks that "the masque world, in fact, is a world of self-evident truths, such as that whiteness is better than blackness or good better than evil."[94] Their content is predetermined by the objectively existing Stuart ideology, and what counts is the level of expression: how the book of royal wisdom is translated into the system of signs of theater. What counts is the "invention" because the content is known and readily available in other texts. Even the "present occasion" (one of the favorite topics in masque criticism) is only a pretext to present the recurrent motif of the king's wisdom which, in turn, generates peace, the Golden Age, divine harmony, and announces the beginning of the millennium. The printed texts of masques provide much evidence that the cognition of the created world is indeed equivalent to philological analysis, for this model of the universe is a theatrical transmutation of emblem books that "come to life" during the performance. They are self-explanatory to all who know the language of the emblems; they may with ease be decoded by the learned. For those who do not fit into the latter category, the printed texts in most cases provide full or partial explanation of the difficult passages.[95]

Moreover, cultures directed primarily towards expression have a concept of themselves as the correct text, and not as a system of rules that generates texts; each type of culture generates its own particular ideal of Book and Manual, including the organization of those texts. Consequently, according to Lotman and Uspensky, "with orientation towards rules, a manual has the appearance of a generative mechanism, while with orientation towards text, one gets the characteristic (question-answer) format of a catechism, and the anthology (a book of quotations or selected texts) comes into being."[96] A good example of this would be the book King James ordered to be written in which the basic doctrine of the divine right of kings is expounded. This is *God and the King*, published in 1615 "by his Majesties special privilege and command"; the book is written in the form of a dialogue, in which a pupil asks the questions and the tutor gives learned answers.[97] In this context, the Renaissance emblem books also come to one's mind; these may be treated as an anthology of predominantly Neoplatonic catechisms.

In this sense the masque-in-performance presents the book of the culture that made its appearance possible. The author of this book is obvious. Since in this culture the world appears as a text, immaculate precision in naming objects assumes vital importance. This explains the concern with attributes, colors, and forms in the masques-in-performance (and this does not apply to the printed texts, which often neglect such details). Jean Seznec observes that in the Renaissance, "the insistence with which theorists urge artists to read instructive texts illustrates another tendency of the period: its pedantry. . . . A painter deserves blame for taking the slightest liberty with history or Fable, and especially for representing attributes or clothing inappropriate to the figure. . . . It is thus an inexcusable fault for an artist not to give his figures the outward signs by which they may be recognized; it is no less serious . . . to make a mistake in the choice of attributes."[98] Similarly, there is no place for arbitrariness in the emblem book. Peter M. Daly is certainly correct when he writes that "the *meaning* of the emblem is *unambiguous*, it is in fact *univalent*, i.e. the context calls for only one of the several meanings associated with the natural object" (his emphasis).[99] An incorrect designation can be identified with a different context, which creates the basic opposition within this culture between "correct" and "incorrect." Thus, for example, the world of antimasque has its own expression, its own system of signs, but an "incorrect" one. This is the only source of evil and chaos in the masque world. Anything that is "incorrect" stands in opposition to the "correct" and consequently has to be treated as anticulture; it should be either destroyed or eliminated from the court world.

The Emblematic Masque

It so happens in these performances that the antimasquers are always scared or chased away before the masque proper begins.

The laws that govern the created world in masques are presented as eternal. The created model of the universe does not foresee any possibility of, or even need for, any kind of change (strictly speaking, not until the millennium, a thousand years of glory before Doomsday, which in the world of the masque is expected shortly). The recurrent motif of disorder or chaos that is troubling the court world and stemming from the antimasque or anticulture is only temporary. The laws that govern this universe, in fact the king's presence itself, as his reign in "real" life, bring back order and harmony. This model is not geared to knowledge about the future since the future is being presented as an extended "now." It is metaphorically referred to as "perpetual spring," or the Golden Age. All this is confirmed and given greater authority by infallible gods.

To conclude, I point out that the conflict between Ben Jonson and Inigo Jones, so much discussed in criticism, is really a clash of two basically different views of the masque. One, favored by Jones, saw the masque-in-performance as a "speaking emblem," where the invention of the emblematist, who is usually the artist, is of ultimate importance. The text serves the theatrical, three-dimensional emblem in the same way as mottos serve icons in emblem books. In other words, the literary element is subordinated by the dominating artistic design. The other view, advocated by Jonson, would have the poet as the chief inventor, with the scenic design serving as an illustration to the dominating poetic part of the spectacle. The first approach does not require a mechanism that would generate new texts; the text is given and the role of the inventor is to devise the wonder of theatrical equivalents of this text. The second approach is based on the concept of art and literature as generating mechanisms; only a variety of new texts can lead to aesthetic and intellectual quality.

3
The Masque of Behavior

The basic difference between courtly and everyday behavior in early Stuart England was that the former was highly ritualized and semioticized. It may therefore be treated as a set of signs encoded according to the courtly code of behavior. These signs were meaningful or signifying only to those who knew the code; to all others, courtly behavior must have seemed odd and unnatural, even nonsignifying. It could easily be caricatured, as was the character of Osric in *Hamlet*. When forced by circumstances to take part in a situation organized according to an unfamiliar behavior code, people always feel uneasy, if not ridiculous. They do not know "how to behave" and feel as if they are taking part in a performance without knowing the role and are not understanding what the other actors are doing or saying. Quite naturally, then, the semiotization of behavior leads to its acquiring the characteristics of the theater, for it includes impersonation (acting according to one's role), verbal exchanges (which sometimes reveal the features of a dramatic dialogue), and even some action similar to a "plot" in drama. Moreover, understanding the theater relies heavily on the spectators' (and the actors') knowledge of the applied conventions. The semiotization of behavior at the early Stuart court reached the point where it could have been treated as a continuous and ongoing performance.

In his influential book *Renaissance Self-Fashioning*, Stephen Greenblatt observes, "Theatricality, in the sense of both disguise and histrionic self-representation, arose from conditions common to almost all Renaissance courts: a group of men and women alienated from the customary roles and revolving uneasily around a center of power, a constant struggle for recognition and attention, and a virtually fetishistic emphasis upon manner. The manuals of court behavior which became popular in the sixteenth century are essentially handbooks for actors, practical guides for a society whose members were nearly always on stage."[1]

Consequently it is possible to assert that court life was to a

The Masque of Behavior

certain extent governed by the rules governing artistic texts and to treat it as an aesthetic form. As Heinrich F. Plett wrote, the basic features of the English Renaissance are "tropical, fictional, artificial—and thus aesthetic. The courtier appears here in the role of an artist, and the culture he fashions bears all the marks of a finished work of art."[2] This is exactly what Greenblatt means by "self-fashioning." In other words, Renaissance self-fashioning is a mechanism of control that generates required genres of behavior. Moreover, as Greenblatt observes, "literature functions within this system in three interlocking ways: as a manifestation of the concrete behavior of its particular author, as itself the expression of the codes by which behavior is shaped, and as a reflection upon those codes."[3] The same may be said about the masque: it functions as a manifestation of the concrete behavior of its particular authors and as a reflection of the codes by which behavior is shaped, and it reflects upon these codes. It is not mere coincidence that literature (including mythology, chivalric romances, pastorals, and so on) becomes a matrix on which courtiers and whole courts model their behavior and identity. Sir Walter Ralegh, in one of his attempts to win the heart of Queen Elizabeth, is said to have staged a scene of violent passion modeled on the twenty-third canto of *Orlando Furioso*.[4] Daniel Javitch also draws attention to the fact that the regular behavior of the queen's favorites was often "motivated by the conventions of chivalric romance."[5]

The masque is actually much closer to the Stuart genre of courtly behavior than is generally acknowledged. As I pointed out in the previous chapter, the boundary between the masque world and the nonmasque world of the court is not clearly marked, if at all. The true boundary is between the court world, which is signifying, and the noncourt world, which is nonsignifying. The masque therefore may be seen as part of courtly behavior, as a ritual in which the laws that govern the court are fully revealed. Revealed, too, are the most cherished values of the court. In Victor Turner's words, a ritual is any "prescribed behavior for occasions not given over to technological routine, having reference to beliefs in invisible beings or powers regarded as the first and final causes of all effects."[6] This religious or magical component of a ritual is very important, for it distinguishes the ritual from "ceremony." Rituals nearly always accompany transition from one cosmic order to another; consequently, those taking part in it experience "transformation." As Turner puts it, ceremony indicates, while ritual transforms.[7] This is exactly what happens during the masque-in-performance: the division of the court from the ordinary world is marked in the antimasque, which ends with a transformation of the court into another sphere that unites with the metaphysical order. The king becomes the sun, Neptune, a semigod; the courtiers are transformed into superhuman beings. Furthermore, the transformation of the masquers is one of the most important structural features of the masque.

In this context Victor Turner's book is worth quoting once again: "Living ritual may be better linked to artwork than neurosis. Ritual is, in its most typical cross-cultural impressions, a synchronization of many performative genres, and is often ordered by *dramatic* structure, a plot . . . which energizes and gives emotional coloring to the interdependent communicative codes which express in manifold ways the meaning inherent in the dramatic *leitmotiv*. . . ."[8] The similarity of the masque-in-performance to this definition of ritual is quite striking.

Frank Whigham points out that during the Renaissance in England, "public life at court had come under a new and rhetorical imperative of performance. *Esse sequitur operare:* identity was to be derived from behavior."[9] Belonging to the privileged upper classes had to be manifested to others, and it was done by following the strict rules of courtly behavior. It was not enough to be a courtier; one also had to act as one. When nobles frequented public theaters in London, for instance, they did it not only to see the plays, but also to be seen in the lords' room (especially designed to accommodate the courtiers) during the performance. In this way they played little performances of their own in the dual roles of actors and spectators. The lords' room functioned as a stage in its own right, or rather as a display "window" in which the courtiers enacted their roles. Even the clothes they wore were "theatrical," for the actors' apparel came from their noble patrons' wardrobes (noblemen's personal garments were customarily used as theatrical costumes). Therefore, in public theaters and during court performances of plays, both actors and courtiers wore similar clothes, a feature that linked the groups together.

Since complexity of courtly behavior was enormous, semioticians speak of a complex system of behavioral genres.[10] The court was physically divided into many "compartments" in which different genres of behavior operated. In other words, the transition from one space into another was accompanied by a change in the genre of behavior. For example, one type of genre would be present during James's favorite sport, hunting (which often included "ceremonial" elements such as smearing of the courtiers'

The Masque of Behavior

faces with the animal's blood),[11] and a different one would occur during the reception of a foreign envoy at Whitehall. Undoubtedly there was a hierarchy of the degree of semiotization of space and behavior at court. In some places one could talk and behave "more freely" than in others. To make the system more complex, the presence or absence of the monarch or members of the royal family led to the changing semiotization of a given behavioral space. In the presence of the king, for instance, one had to behave in a certain way; however, with the king absent, to behave in the same way, even in the same space, would of course have been improper. To behave within the genre one had to follow a certain decorum, so any deviation was ungentlemanlike and unladylike, and therefore "unaesthetic."

The very beginning of the Jacobean age marked a tendency to multiply the units of courtly life into more and more units of "performance." These units range from royal residences—each of which governed by a different genre of behavior (the "ritual" of hunting was not, for instance, a part of behavior at Whitehall)—through the newly created gardens with their chapels, grottos, sanctuaries for love, caves, fountains, statues, and the like, to the Banqueting Houses[12] in Whitehall, especially designed to accommodate the presentation of the masques. If one were to draw a model of the degree of semiotization at court, the Banqueting House during the masque performance would be at the very top. A sacred space of the ritual, not everyone was admitted here. The entrance to the hall marked the boundary between two cosmic orders: inside, during a sophisticated ritual involving all of the arts, the court united with the metaphysical sphere that governs this world. "Ceremony" and "theater" were transformed into a ritual.

As discussed below, even some places on the routes between the royal residences or during "progresses" could become additional units of the ongoing court performance. All of this deepened the complexity of the system of the genres of behavior and stressed its basically theatrical nature. From this point of view the masques may be seen as the peculiar genre of behavior of the courtiers taking part in them, either as actors (masquers and dancers) or as spectators. As is discussed in greater detail elsewhere in this book, the boundaries between these two roles were not very clearly marked, although both roles included costuming, acting, and dancing.

For instance, a contemporary account reveals that it was customary for the women during the masque performance to take off their masks: "They consider the mask as indispensable for their face as bread at the table, but they lay it aside willingly at these public entertainments."[13] Sir John Harington also remarked in passing that it was a custom at court for "The great Ladies [to] go well-masked, and indeed it be the only show of their modesty."[14] Thus the courtiers onstage "acted" in part by wearing masks to cover their true identity; the women offstage "acted" by taking off the masks revealing their true identity. Both reversed their usual courtly appearance. "Usual," however, applies to other spatial units of the court: the "reversal" is in fact a norm established within the new genre of behavior that operated in the Banqueting House. It is one of the distinctive features of this genre.

Other places demanded different costumes. When, for instance, in 1636 the queen and her ladies attended a masque at the Middle Temple, a contemporary source relates that "the Queene was pleased to grace the entertainment by putting of[f] majesty and putt on a citizens habit, and to sett upon the scaffold on the right hande amongst her subjects"; another source also reveals that the ladies of the court were "clad in the Attire of Citizens" as well.[15]

As observed by Peter N. Skrine, "the increasing importance given to masques and masquerade as society's favourite diversions coincided from the later sixteenth century onwards with a growing delight in going . . . "unknown" and in discovering . . . the truth about your fellow men through deliberate concealment of your own identity."[16] Men as well as women concealed their identity: a contemporary source states that the Spanish ambassador came to one of the masques in "disguise."[17] And Baldessar Castiglione, in his extremely popular and influential book *The Courtier,* advised his readers that a courtier should not dance certain dances in public "unless he were in a maske. And though it were so that all men knew him, it skilleth not, for there is no way to that, if a man will shelve himselfe in open light about such matters, whether it be in armes, or out of armes, because to be in a maske, bringeth with it a certaine libertie and license. . . ."[18]

I have noted earlier that the spectator seating order for a masque-in-performance was significant: the closer one sat to the king, the better view of the perspective stage one had and the more important one was in the court hierarchy. The seating order was of such importance that it can be considered the first signifying element of the spectacle. At the start of the masque-in-performance courtiers quickly noticed where everyone was seated. One's position could be a cause of pride, embarrassment, or even

The Masque of Behavior

humiliation. An agent of Savoy's contemporary account of a masque staged on 29 December 1613 proves the point:

> After they had set down a place was given to the Spanish ambassador immediately next to the queen, who sat on the left hand; in the middle sat the king; on the right hand beyond the baldachin and opposite the Spanish ambassador sat the prince. Lower down on a stool was the Flemish ambassador. Then a place was given to the bride [Frances Howard] at the foot of the balustrade, on a cushion.
> On the queen's side three velvet-covered chairs were brought and placed in a row next to the Spanish ambassador. The first was given to the wife of the Lord Chancellor of England, the second to the ambassadress of Spain, and the third to that of Flanders. Next there followed a bench at the head of which the Lord Chamberlain gave me a place, and on the same bench he provided places for all the Countesses and Barons of the court, the closest of whom to me was the wife of the Earl of Aubigny, brother to the Earl of Lennox. No more eminent place could have been desired for your Highness in my person—much to the confusion of the other [Lotti], who was positioned on the opposite side more than ten places down than I. . . .[19]

In spite of all its similarities to and probable origin in theater the masque may be seen as a genre of behavior since it is one part of the larger court structure. The phenomenon of the transformation of traditional theater forms into masques to a certain extent paralleled the change of artistic drama into folk plays, as described by Petr Bogatyrev.[20] The traditional theater forms become a necessary part of the structure that the particular court culture creates. That the European court culture in the first half of the seventeenth century was a relatively homogeneous phenomenon would explain the similarities between court entertainments in different countries in this period.

King James remarks in *Basilikon Doron* that "It is a trew old saying, That a King is as one set on a stage, whose smallest actions and gestures, all the people gazingly doe behold."[21] Since its source was in the living monarch, the theatricality of behavior was not restricted to royal residences. It actually followed the royal couple wherever it went, and its very presence changed the ontological status of reality from "normal" or empirical to the illusionary artistic reality of a performance. After all, King James was a "little god" himself. People all over the country felt the need to welcome and communicate various messages to their monarch in what they considered to be the language and behavior of the court. It is significant that out of a great variety of possibilities they usually selected a theatrical means of expression. Royal entries provide a good example. Along with other sorts of "entertainments," these were often written by professional playwrights.

For instance, the royal entertainment at Cawsome House was devised by Thomas Campion (who also wrote masques) and was presented for the queen on 28 April 1613. The fact that it was later printed in a quarto form with one of the masques proves the close affinity of the two texts. Both describe very similar genres of behavior. In June of that year the queen enjoyed a spectacular riverside entertainment at Bristol that included a "sea battle" between Christians and the Turks. Some of the Turks were taken prisoners and "were presented to her Majesty, who laughing said, that they were not only like the Turks by their apparell, but by their countenances."[22] The speeches and a detailed verse description of the entertainment at Bristol were later printed as a booklet (its layout similar to a printed masque).[23] Sometimes even "ordinary" people provided theatrical entertainment for the queen. As Anthony à Wood writes, on 11 June 1613 the queen passed through the parish of Bishop's Cannings, very near Devizes. The vicar of this parish, George Ferebe, having heard earlier that the queen would pass through his parish,

> composed a song of four parts, and instructed his scholars to sing it very perfectly. . . . He dressed himself in the habit of an old Bard, and caused his scholars, whom he had instructed, to be clothed in Shepherds' weeds. The Queen having received notice of these people, she with her retinue made a stand at Wensdylee; whereupon these musicians, drawing up to her, played a most admirable Lesson of four parts with double voices, the beginning of which was this:
>   Shine, O thou sacred Shepherds' Star,
>   On silly shepherd swaines, &c.
> Which being well performed also, the Bard concluded with an Epilogue, to the great liking and content of the Queen and her Company.[24]

From the very beginning of James's rule in England, theatricality was inseparable from courtly behavior. This was manifested not only by special occasions like progresses or by triumphal entries, but also by an "ordinary" visit to a nobleman's house. For instance, in May 1604 the king and queen visited Sir William Cornwallis at his house at Highgate and were entertained by a private show, *The Penates*, devised by Ben Jonson. It began as soon as the royal couple entered through the gate: they were received there by the Penates, or household gods. After the wel-

The Masque of Behavior

coming speeches the king and queen were led to the garden, where they heard a speech by Mercury himself. They were soon joined by other mythological characters, including Mercury's mother, Maia, who praised James and Anne. This was the morning part of the entertainment. After dinner, when the king and queen went into the garden again, they met with Mercury once more and were introduced to further deities. Thus the royal couple was not only addressed directly by the actors of this "show," but became actors themselves. Strictly speaking there was no real difference between these roles and those in the Banqueting House during a masque-in-performance. The appearances of mythological gods and allegorical characters before James and Anne evidently were common experiences both inside and outside their court.

In discussing the evolution of the poetics of behavior, Yuri Lotman points out the characteristic transition from stock role to plot:

> Plot is in no way a chance component of everyday behaviour. Indeed, the appearance of plot as a definite category organizing narrative texts in literature may ultimately be explained by the need to select a behavioural strategy for activity outside it. [¶] Everyday behaviour acquires a full-fledged interpretation only when each separate chain of real-life actions can be related to a meaningful, fully realized sequence of activities that has a unified meaning. On the level of coded message, such a sequence serves as a generalized sign of situation, of the chain of actions and results: in other words, plot.[25]

Assuming a mythological role was not uncommon for an individual and for a whole people. As pointed out by Jean Seznec, this tendency originated during the Middle Ages, when people claimed a mythological hero as ancestor, and persisted into the Renaissance.[26] In this way "princely pride found ample satisfaction in these claims of mythological sponsorship and heredity"[27] and was of course celebrated in various works of art. Seznec also notes that assuming mythological roles led at some courts to "acting out literally and in all seriousness the comedy of Olympus."[28] In many different ways the courts of the early Stuarts enacted the roles of the courts of "Neptune," "Jove," "Solomon," and the "Sun."

The behavior of the vicar and his scholars described above would be nonsensical if not related to a certain plot in which the queen acted the pastoral role of the "Queen of Shepherds." Similarly, ever since his first appearance in London, King James acted the role of Solomon, Jove, or "England's Caesar." Both James and Anne assumed many more stock character roles. The main sources for their behavioral plots were mythology, ancient history, and the Bible. Since these roles and sets of plots were generally known to the court group, it was possible to distinguish the signifying from the nonsignifying. (Lotman calls the mythology of everyday and social behavior the totality of the plots that encode a person's behavior.) The theatrical behavior of the vicar acquired meaning only in relation to the plot within a particular genre of behavior. As such it was accepted as an episode of that plot and was understood as a pleasant compliment to the queen.

A number of outdoor events in which courtiers and members of the royal family took part were equally theatrical in character. These ranged from "progresses" and "entries" to mock sea battles and knightly tournaments. The latter, usually called "tilts," often included actors impersonating mythological divinities who gave the reasons for the tournament and also stressed the ancient chivalrous tradition that was being carried on. As G. P. V. Akrigg observes, "Often the tilting was cast in a semi-dramatic setting, with triumphal chariots first entering, from which allegorical characters delivered speeches of compliment to the King and wove some fanciful myth of chivalry to account for the jousting and to introduce the contestants."[29] Tilting was of course a splendid occasion not only to demonstrate knightly skills but also to proudly display richness of apparel and elaborate entourage. A 1609 letter by Dudley Carleton describes a courtly tilt:

> The Duke of Lennox exceeded all in feathers; the Lord Wolden in followers; and Sir Richard Preston in a pageant, which was of an elephant with a castle on his back; and it proved a right *partus elephantis,* for it was long in coming, till the running was well entered into, and was then as long a creeping about the tilt-yard, all which time the running was intermitted.[30]

During the tilt of June 1610, a Scottish nobleman came in a raincloud, complete with thunder and lightning, that opened (like in a performance of a masque) before the king to disclose women and children in rich dresses.[31] And Lord Campton exceeded all others in his "pageant" for the tilt, as a contemporary account relates, for he

> buylded himself as it were a bowre uppon the topp of the walle which is next to St James Parke, it was made in the maner of a sheepcote and there he sate in a graye russet cloke as long as a gowne, and he had a

The Masque of Behavior

sheepe crooke in one hand and a bottell hanging thereon and a dogge in chayne in th'other hand, as thoughe he had bine a sheepharde, and thorowe the topp of the bowre there stoode up as it were the mast of a ship gilded rounde about with goulde and uppon the topp thereof there was fastned a panne with fyre burning in it, and as some thought there was a pitche in it and an iron to marke sheepe withall. . . .[32]

From there Lord Campton sent a squire to present a speech to the king; when the knight eventually made his entry into the tiltyard, all his men were wearing straw hats and had their faces "paynted as blacke as the deuill."[33]

But there was even more theatrical behavior in connection with tilting. Before the particular occasion, "real" challenges were announced by heralds and sent in writing to the possible candidates. Sometimes these heralds appeared at court, as was the case on 31 December 1609. Sir Charles Cornwallis's *Life of Prince Henry* states that on that occasion King James

not onely for his [Henry's] owne creation [as Prince of Wales], but also that the world might know what a brave Prince they were likely to enjoy, under the name of *Meliades,* Lord of the Isles[34] (an ancient title due to the first-borne of Scotland), did, in his name, by some appointed for the same purpose, strangely attired, accompanied with drummes and trumpets, in the Presence, before the King and Queene, and in the presence of the whole Court, deliver a Challenge to all Knights of Great Britaine, in two Speeches; . . . the summe was, that Miliades, their noble Master, burning with an earnest desire to trie the valour of his young yeares in foreigne countryes, and to know where vertue triumphed most, had sent them abroad to espy the same, who, after their long travailes in all countreyes, and returne; shewing, how no where in any continent, save in the fortunate Isle of Great Britaine, they had found his wishes; which ministring matter of exceeding joy to their young Meliades, who (as they said) could lineally derive his pedegree from the famous Knights of this Isle, was the cause that he had now sent to present the first fruits of his chivalrie at his Majestie's feete. Then, after returning with a short speech to her Majestie, next to the Earles, Lords, and Knights, excusing their Lord in this their so sudden and short warning; and lastly, to the Ladies; they, after humble delivery of their chartle concerning time, place, conditions, number of weapons and assailants, took their leave, departing solemnly as they entred.[35]

A curious challenge of the kind described above has been reproduced by Nichols. Four knights of the "Fortunate Island" challenge all the other knights on the basis of the following claims: "1. That in service of Ladies no Knight hath free-will. 2. That it is Beauty maintaineth the world in Valour. 3. That no fair Lady was ever false. 4. That none can be perfectly wise but Lovers. Against which, or any of which, if any of you shall dare to argue at point of launce and sword . . . we the said Four Champions shall . . . be ready. . . ."[36] Evidently it was customary to respond to challenges in writing. The above was answered by some unidentified knights:

> We confidently entertain your challenge with your circumstance proposed already, seeing the event in the cause, for old defended virtue of women is expired; and men, overcome with women, are made less than themselves, and far inferior to the valour of uneffeminate Knights. . . . Wherefore we deny your assertions . . . [and] offer your second considerations. . . . 1. That a man at the yeares of discretion hath his love in his own hand. 2. That Beauty melteth Valour, and maketh the tongue far readier than the sword. 3. That fairest Ladies are falsest, having fairest occasions. 4. That to love and to be wise, were ever two men's parts. Against you, armed with the truth of these, we shall come with sharpe arguments. . . .[37]

Cornwallis also writes that the king himself read the challenge and had a good laugh. On a number of occasions tilts were parts of cycles of events, which could include masques. In this way, tilts complement, develop, or announce certain motifs of masques. Since the tilts have text significance, one text can shed light on all the others. This mechanism of intertextuality will be discussed in the following chapters.

As pointed out above, particular genres of behavior were to a large extent determined by the space within which a given behavior was taking place. To apply other than prescribed genres of behavior would not only be inappropriate, but would also be a violation of "proper" behavior (proper within a given space, that is). This means that even the favored genre of theatrical behavior could be out of place when enacted in a "wrong" space and in a wrong time. During a formal reception a foreign ambassador could not possibly address the queen as the "Queen of Nymphs" nor label James his "Sun." However, if he took a speaking part in a court entertainment, both forms would be perfectly acceptable and correct. For an example, consider a contemporary source. The well-known Jacobean letterwriter, John Chamberlain, reports that on the night Prince Henry died

The Masque of Behavior

there fell out a very ridiculous accident. A very handsome young fellow, much about his [Prince Henry's] age and not altogether unlike him, came stark naked to St. James's, while they were at supper, saying, he was the Prince's ghost from Heaven with a message to the King; but by no manner of examination or threatening could they get more out of him, or who set him at work. Some say he is simple, others mad. He belongs to one of the Chancery. All the penance they gave him was two or three lashes, which he endured, as it seemed, without sense, and keeping him naked as he was all night and the next day in the Porter's Lodge, where thousands came to see him. The King sent to have him dismissed without more ado or inquiry.[38]

It is significant that Chamberlain calls the incident "ridiculous." He does so not because messengers from heaven cannot possibly appear at the court; it is just the opposite. Scores of them do appear in the masques, conveying various messages to the king or queen. The young man tried very hard to act according to what he thought was one of the accepted genres of behavior. He impersonated a ghost, he wore a costume (his nakedness), and he presented a speech strikingly reminiscent of the gods' messengers' speeches in the masques, all of which would make him a perfect masque character. However, his timing was wrong, as was his choice of space. Messengers from heaven appeared at James's court only during special occasions, during court entertainments, and during the masques in particular; these took place in a separate part of the royal palace, in the Banqueting Hall. This is why the sudden appearance of the young man in a space where a different genre of behavior was being observed (the court ceremony of dining) appeared ridiculous to those present. In addition, and in spite of all the similarities to actual scenes in the masques, the young man's performance failed to create meaning by relating itself to an existing plot of behavior. Simply put, a plot of that kind did not exist. To begin, messengers always came from the mythological heaven and never from the Christian one. Second, no ghost of the members of the royal family ever appeared in masques. And third, the dining ceremony did not transform the court into a metaphysical sphere, where communication with the outer world was possible: this was possible only during the masque-in-performance.

In this context one has to agree with Kevin Sharpe's point about the courtly masque:

> the court masque . . . was the court itself, that very same stage on which the monarch and his attendants performed the daily rituals of

> court ceremony and government. On the occasion of a court masque, the king's public audience chamber became a theatre, but for many in attendance the performance was doubtless not as distinguished from other presentations of ordinary court life—receptions, ceremonies and banquets. . . . The masque . . . was indeed a celebration of the monarch, but as such it should not be detached from the rituals of court life. Speeches in praise of the king in the masque were not the slavish expressions of a culture of sycophancy; they were the conventional modes of address to a sovereign, normal in the courtly discourse. Because the masque spoke to the court in the language of the court, it should not be read as propaganda or flattery. It should perhaps be regarded as a court ceremony at which, as in all ceremonies, those present both perceive and perform, and participate in, an experience in which the everyday and the mystical [?] become one, indistinguishable. The court masque then is a political event; it is kingship in action.[39]

The above is of course true only for the masque-in-performance.

To treat the masque as a genre of courtly behavior means that as such the masque should be able to enter into larger sequences of courtly events connected with the particular occasion. A theatrical performance, performed by professional actors, can also become a part of that sequence, but it will not be a manifestation of courtly behavior. In most cases it will be only loosely connected, if at all, with the current "plot" of behavior at court, and its subject matter and motifs will not be continued and developed by other genres of behavior. The only exception to this was propagandist plays, the goal of which was to stir the spectators to required behavior. But the masque-in-performance reveals this unique ability to become part of a whole sequence, or cycle, of courtly genres of behavior, and may be analyzed in relation to the remaining parts.

Part 2

4
Masque Cycles and Courtly "Festivals"

One may say that the manifestations of early Stuart courtly culture are particular mythologizing and epideictic forms of literature (for example, the pastoral and the panegyric), painting (again with heroic and mythological tendencies), along with music, theater, architecture, garden architecture, and ceremonies (such as the royal entry, the code of courtly behavior). However, these manifestations are not isolated but originate in the monarch himself and in uncountable variants announce to the world the basic constituents of Stuart ideology. In a sense, the masque-in-performance combines all of the above components and may therefore be treated as the fullest manifestation of Stuart culture. However, being a fusion of various arts, the masque itself is a component of a larger text of Stuart culture and cannot be treated in isolation from that culture. Reconstructing the cultural milieu helps to discover the complex, many-faceted layers of meaning that these—to use Francis Bacon's word—"toys" created. In other words, the masque cannot be isolated from courtly behavior, from ritual, from courtly literature, taste (aesthetics), art, music, or other courtly entertainments (again, the political context is not my concern here).

One of the curious features revealed by at least half of the Jacobean and some of the Caroline masques is their origin, which is to be sought in the sequences of spectacles designated to celebrate a given occasion. Being created as part of a cycle of signifying events, particular masques should be treated as inseparable elements of the cycle, or "festival." In other words, they create their meaning fully only within the context of other related texts. These texts may be other masques written by other authors, but they are always accompanied by spectacles of a different nature, by court ceremonies of various kinds (such as the creation of the Prince of Wales or the Knights of the Bath or Knights of the

Garter), by tilts, sea battles, fireworks, parades, and the like. A cycle of events of that kind would actually be what Roy Strong calls the Renaissance festival, which usually embraces three forms: "the state entry into a city, the exercise of arms, and forms of spectacle making use of acting, singing, music and dance that took place within a palace."[1] All of these are fused together not only by their more or less simultaneous appearance during the celebrations of the same occasion, but in a number of cases they are variants of the same motifs and deal with the same or at least similar subject matter. One element of a given cycle creates meanings in relation to the remaining elements, constituting a signifying cycle that may be treated as one complex and syncretic text. I use the term *syncretic* because particular components of the cycle may belong to different systems. For example, a "parade" through the streets of London may have been followed by a "sea battle" on the Thames and fireworks at night; the following day might have a tilt and a masque. The cycle would culminate in a splendid production of a pastoral play and yet another masque that included lots of music and dances. All of these elements constitute the "iconosphere" of the court and city cultures.

It would go beyond the goal of this book to deal with all the cycles and festivals involving masques that evidently existed in the early Stuart period. Table 2 illustrates the scope of the phenomenon. In a number of instances, however, the evidence is too meagre or unavailable to allow a detailed account and analysis of the cycle that actually took place. Of those having evidence, I select and discuss in detail only several to show certain rules by which masques-in-performance created meanings. The sources for the masque-in-performance may be traced in the extant printed or literary masques, especially in those cases where detailed descriptions of the remaining elements of the cycle have been preserved. In some instances contemporary booklets describe all or selected events connected with particular occasions. Sometimes the celebrations are reflected in other literary works, which often provide a contemporary author's interpretation of the events. Additional information may be gathered from private and diplomatic correspondence and diaries and memoirs.

One of the intriguing features of the cycles of events, of which masques were part, is that in a number of cases they seem to have been devised and planned by people other than those who actually wrote the scripts for particular elements of a given cycle. It is reasonable to assume that the overall plan of celebrations was always established in consultation with the monarch, who had

Masque Cycles and Courtly "Festivals"

Table 2
Cycles of Masques and Other Entertainments

1603/4
1 January — *The Masque of the Knights of India and China* (lost)
6 January — *The Masque of Scots* (lost)
8 January — *The Vision of Twelve Goddesses*
? January — Running at the Ring

1604/5
27 December — "Lord Willowby's Masque" (lost)
6 January — Creation of the Knights of the Bath
6 January — Creation of the Duke of York
6 January — *The Masque of Blackness*

1606
5 January — *Hymenaei*
6 January — *Barriers* (speeches by Ben Jonson)
24 July — *The Entertainment of the Two Kings at Theobalds* (by Ben Jonson)
24–28 July — *The Masque of Solomon and Queen Sheba* (lost)
29 July — Play by the Children of the Queen's Revels
30 July — *Abuses* (play)
4 August — Shows of skill in weapons and wrestling; running at the ring
5 August — Bull- and bear-baiting, a tilt, fireworks
7 August — King Christian installed as Knight of the Garter
10 August — Fireworks showing the victory of the lion over seven deadly sins

1609/10
31 December — "Challenge at Court" (with speeches by Ben Jonson?) (lost)
6 January — Prince Henry's *Barriers* (by Ben Jonson and Inigo Jones)
7 January — Parade of the prince and his knights to Saint James's

1610
31 May — Prince's welcome on the Thames
3 June — Creation of the Knights of the Bath
4 June — Creation of the Prince of Wales
5 June — *Thethys' Festival* (masque)
6 June — Tilt

1611
1 January — *Oberon* (masque)

Table 2—*Continued*

? January	*Barriers*[1]
6 January	Planned date for *Love Freed From Ignorance and Folly* (masque)
? January	Second masque planned by the queen[2]

1612

1 January	*The Masque of Twelve Months*
? January	Barriers and tilts
? January	"The Queen's Masque" (lost) planned, but canceled[3]
6 January	*Love Restored* (masque)
6 January	Running at the ring

1613

7 February	Creation of Frederick as Knight of the Garter
? February	Fireworks
13 February	Sea battle
14 February	Marriage of Elizabeth and Frederick; *The Lords' Masque* presented
15 February	*The Memorable Masque*
16 February	Planned date for Beaumont's masque, listed below
19 February	Tilt
20 February	*The Masque of the Inner Temple and Gray's Inne*

1613/14

26 December	*The Somerset Masque*
27 December	*Challenge at Tilt*
29 December	*The Irish Masque* (repeated on 3 January)
1 January	Tilt
4 January	*The Masque of Cupid* (lost)
6 January	*The Masque of Flowers*
6 January	Samuel Daniel's *Hymen's Triumph* (play)—postponed until 2 February

1614/15

1 January	*The Golden Age restor'd* (masque)
8 January	The same repeated
13 January	"The Inner Temple Masque" (lost)

1615/16

? December	*The Masque of Christmas* (lost)
6 January	*Mercury Vindicated* (masque)
6 January	The same repeated

1616

1 November	*Civitatis Amor* (show on water)

Masque Cycles and Courtly "Festivals"

Table 2—*Continued*

4 November	Creation of the Prince of Wales, followed by a dinner entertainment and barriers
6 November	Running at the ring
9 November	Banquet and a play at Drapers' Hall

1616/17
25 December	*The [Mock] Masque of Christmas*
5 January	Creation of George Villiers Earl of Buckingham
5 January	John Fletcher's *The Mad Lover* (play)
6 January	*The Vision of Delight* (masque)
17 January	"The Middle Temple Masque" (lost), presented for Buckingham
19 January	*The Vision of Delight* repeated

1617/18
1 January	*The Masque of Amazons* (lost)
5 January	*Cupid's Revenge* (presented by the Children of the Whitefriars)
6 January	*Pleasure Reconciled to Virtue* (masque)
15 February	The same repeated with the addition of *For the Honour of Wales*
19 February	*The First Antimasque of Mountebanks*

1621
3 August	*The Masque of Gypsies* (1st version)
5 August	*The Masque of Gypsies* (2d version)
9 September	*The Masque of Gypsies* (3d version)

1626
? February	Pastoral play, followed by "The Queen's Masque" (lost)

1628
? February	"The Middle Temple Masque" (lost)
? February	"The King's Masque" (lost)

1631
9 January	*Love's Triumph Through Callipolis* (king's masque)
22 February	*Chloridia* (queen's masque)

1632
8 January	*Albion's Triumph* (king's masque)
14 February	*Tempe Restored* (queen's masque)

Table 2—*Continued*

1634
3 February — *Triumph of Peace* (queen's masque)
13 February — The same repeated
18 February — *Coelum Britannicum* (king's masque)

1638
6 February — *Luminalia* (queen's masque)
7 February — *Britannia Triumphans* (king's masque)

---

1. See Chambers, *Elizabethan Stage*, 3:386.
2. See John More's 15 December letter to Sir Ralph Winwood, in *Ben Jonson*, ed. Herford and Simpson, 10:518.
3. See Herford and Simpson, 10:531.

final say in the ultimate content and schedule. No doubt even the minutest details were discussed. For instance, while planning the details of the creation of Henry Prince of Wales, his father insisted that Henry would not arrive at Parliament on horseback. In addition, one of the masques prepared for the celebrations of the marriage of Frederick and Elizabeth was called off, presumably because of its extreme political overtones. Also, Inigo Jones consulted with King Charles about scenic designs. Many more examples could be provided, which lead one to suspect that the poets and artists had much less to say in the final shape of the courtly entertainments than is generally acknowledged. The much-discussed conflict between Ben Jonson and Inigo Jones could only have had an indirect impact on the masques-in-performance. The important decisions were made above their heads and it seems likely that—adamant as these two men may have been—both of them had to follow instructions and orders from their superiors. It was only in the printed text that Jonson and others were relatively free to exercise their creativity.

From their first appearances at the Stuart court, masques enter into larger texts of court celebrations. There is of course an important difference when texts enter a cycle by mere coincidence than when they do so as an ordered part of a larger whole that reveals the features of an artistic text. The first recorded Jacobean masque, now lost, was presented in October 1603 as part of welcoming celebrations of Prince Henry. In a letter dated 17 October, Sir Thomas Edmonds informed the earl of Shrewsbury that "The Queen did the Prince the kindness at his coming hither to entertayne him with a gallant Maske."[2] The first masque "cycle," it seems, was presented at Christmastide 1603. On 23 December

Masque Cycles and Courtly "Festivals"

1603 Lord Cecil wrote to the earl of Shrewsbury from Hampton Court (where the court had moved because of the plague): "Other stuff I can send yow none from this place, wheare now we are to feast seven Embassadors; Spain, France, Poland, Florence, and Savoy, besydes Masks and much more. . . . Both the K.' and Q.' Majesties have an humor to have some Masks this Christmas time; and therefore, for that purpose, both the younge Lordes and chief Gentlemen of one pte, and the Queene and her Ladyes of the other pte, doe severallie undertake the accomplishing and furnishing thereof; and because theere is use of invention therein, speciall choice is made of Mr. Sanford to dyrect the order and course of the Ladyes. . . ."[3] The above account leaves no doubt that there were two masques in preparation, one by the lords, the other by the ladies led by the queen. Actually there were three masques staged in a sequence during Christmastide 1603/4, of which only one survives: this is Thomas Campion's *Vision of the Twelve Goddesses*. "The Masque of Lords" (sometimes referred to as *The Masque of the Knights of India and China*) was staged on 1 January 1604,[4] and the masque that was to establish a tradition of a Twelfth Night performance was *The Masque of Scots*.[5] Unfortunately, both are lost. However, one fact is certain: the masques were prepared as a sequence and may therefore be treated as parts of one text, a "macromasque" of some sort.[6]

The king of Denmark's visit in 1606 was in fact a three-week long festival filled with royal entries, pageants, fireworks, tilts, plays, and other sorts of entertainment, including a masque. The latter was preceded by an "Entertainment of the Two Kings at Theobalds," devised by Ben Jonson. The production of the masque itself (now lost) was a failure, owing to the intoxication of both the actors and spectators (see chapter 1). On the following nights, Christian IV saw three unnamed plays presented by the King's Men, one unnamed play by the Children of the Queen's Revels, and a production of *Abuses* by the Children of the Paul's. This was followed by shows of skill in weapons and wrestling, then running at the ring, in which both kings took part. There was still more: the royal guest saw bull- and bear-baiting, took part in a tilt, and towards the end of his visit was installed as a Knight of the Garter. On his departure the Danes presented a splendid show of fireworks. This is worth closer attention, for fireworks became an important part of great celebrations, and—unlike the displays known today—they always "told a story"; that is, they presented a "mime" show of some sort that included mythological or legendary characters involved in some action within an allegorical setting. From the semiotic point of view fireworks were given text-significance and may therefore be treated as having importance equal to that of other elements of a given sequence. Unfortunately the only evidence for them is in contemporary descriptions such as the kind that described the fireworks in 1606:

> The Devise of Wild fire was in Pageant-wise, betweene foure round pillars uppon a lighter framed, where the seven deadly sinnes in their lively colours, shape, and characters, sate chained fast, and for their wickednesse bound to endure eternall punishment, and over their heads in the midest of them, uppon the rop of a pinacle was a fierce lion cowchaunt, signifying sudden vengeance, holding in his teeth the loose end of the chaine, which compassed them about, and from the lyon's mouth the fire first did issue forth, and from thence, without any confusion or further ayde, by degrees and distinct proportion, descended into all parts, making sundry sorts of sounds, with loftie rocketts and fire flakes mounting in the ayre . . . and for the space of more then a quarter of an hower the foresaid images sate burning in Etnae's flame resembling hell's endles torments prepared for such, offendors, but it in the end they were consumed.[7]

In fact it was possible for the masques to continue and develop the motifs of the "plot" of fireworks. A detailed example is discussed in the following chapter.

Marriages of the nobles often provided good occasions for a great variety of celebrations, of which masques were an important and almost indispensable part. As early as in 1604, for instance, the marriage of Sir Philip Herbert and the Lady Susan Vere was celebrated at court, and Carleton writes that a masque was presented in the court hall. Characteristically it was not just any masque, but one prepared especially for the occasion; Carleton says that "for conceit and fashion [it] was suitable to the occasion."[8] A contemporary record gives further details: "On St Ions night [27 December] A maske wth Musicke presented by the Erl of Penbrok the lord Willowbie &: 6: knighte more of ye Court."[9] The Christmas festival thus started included several plays (by Shakespeare, Chapman, and Heywood) acted at court, followed by the celebrations connected with the creation of the duke of York and the Knights of the Bath (the latter usually took three days), culminating with the production of another masque. This was, in fact, Jonson's masque debut: *The Masque of Blackness* was ordered by the queen herself. Thus Jonson's first masque is actually a part of a larger text of court festivities. So were many other masques that he wrote. Jonson's *Hymenaei* (5 January 1606) was

Masque Cycles and Courtly "Festivals"

followed by *Barriers* (6 January), for which the poet wrote lengthy speeches; the two masques were printed as one text in the folio edition of 1616. Similarly Jonson's elaborate *Barriers* for Prince Henry, which took place on 7 January 1611, were preceded by a "Challenge," now lost, presented by two messengers of "Meliadus" on 31 December (Jonson probably wrote the speeches for the challenge as well); this festival of knighthood ended with a splendid parade of the prince and his defending champions, in full armor, to Saint James's. Jonson's *Oberon*, presented in January 1611, was also accompanied by barriers and was to be followed by another masque, *Love Freed From Ignorance and Folly*, postponed until 3 February. Other examples are shown in Table 2.

Another "marriage masque" was Ben Jonson's *Hue and Cry After Cupid*, presented in honor of Viscount Haddington and Lady Elizabeth Ratcliffe in February 1608. Similarly an unnamed masque was presented at the wedding of Sir John Villiers at Hampton Court on 29 December 1617. The grand wedding celebrations of the marriage of James's daughter Elizabeth with Palatine, and, a year later, the marriage of the earl of Somerset with Francis Howard are discussed in greater detail below.

Ducal investitures were another occasion for composing masques. Thus, as mentioned above, the creation of the duke of York in 1605 was preceded by the creation of the Knights of the Bath and followed by the production of Ben Jonson's *The Masque of Blackness*. In 1610 Henry was created duke of Wales and the celebrations of the event included a show on water, the creation of the Knights of the Bath, a masque by Samuel Daniel, a tilt, a sea battle, and fireworks, all of which required a week to be performed. Similarly, the creation of Charles the duke of Wales in 1616 was celebrated by a water pageant (similar to that in 1610) devised by Thomas Middleton, barriers, a tilt, and a play. The "Prince's" masque of 1612—that is, Ben Jonson's *Love Restored*— was performed in the Banqueting House on 6 January, following a running at the ring that took place on the same day and in which both the king and the prince participated.[10] Chamberlain also refers on 29 January to Prince Henry's devotion to plays and to his "martial sports of tilt, turney and barriers, which he followed so earnestly that he was every day five or six howres in armour."[11]

The masques presented on such occasions, as indicated above, were not "invented" independently of the event. Just the opposite is true: there is enough evidence to allow the claim that they were always in one way or another connected with not only the occasion itself but with other elements of a given cycle. Of course, this implies that they were always ordered to be written "on a given subject." In this context, a discussion on one of the critics' favorite topics—whether Ben Jonson (or other poets who devised masques) supported the regime or not—is pointless because it assumes that the writer had freedom he in fact did not necessarily have. Any criticism of current affairs that one occasionally encounters in the extant texts of the masques does not necessarily express the writer's beliefs, just as the sycophancy of the masques that a number of critics found distasteful is not necessarily the author's. The one who paid demanded. The sums involved were too large to dismiss: poets could be paid from twenty to thirty times more for a masque than for writing a traditional play. In addition, the prestige of "inventing" masques must have been much greater in those times than one can readily suspect.

Generally speaking, the masques entered into larger texts in two ways: first was the instance when single masques were part of a sequence of events celebrating a given occasion; the other was when two or more masques were presented in a cycle, in connection with the same courtly event. For instance, two masques were scheduled to be performed in the Hall and in the Banqueting House on Shrovetide in 1628; a contemporary source relates that "The Gentlemen of the Temple being this Shrovetide to present a masque to their majesties, over and besides the king's own great masque, to be performed in the Banqueting House by an hundred actors."[12] Both of these masques are lost, but there is no doubt that they can be treated as a cycle. Similarly, when a Venetian report states that in February 1626 "the queen and her maidens represented a pastoral, followed by a masque," one may assume that the two formed an artistic sequence and may therefore be treated as one text-in-performance.[13]

The following example, selected to demonstrate how masques were incorporated into larger texts, belongs to the first group. It is a single masque that was devised and performed as part of a sequence of events celebrating the creation of the Prince of Wales in 1610. Because the masque has received some critical attention, I discuss it briefly in this chapter, focusing only on those elements that are relevant to the analysis of masque cycles in the chapters that follow.

The creation of Henry Prince of Wales in early June 1610 was a splendid occasion for the magnificent weeklong celebrations. The ceremony itself and the accompanying spectacles form a cycle of related "theatrical" events and may therefore be treated as one text. Their order was as follows:

Masque Cycles and Courtly "Festivals"

Thursday, 31 May 1610	Citizens of London welcome the prince on the Thames
Sunday, 3 June	Creation of twenty-five Knights of Bath
Monday, 4 June	Creation of Prince of Wales
Tuesday, 5 June	Samuel Daniel's masque *Tethys Festival* staged at court
Wednesday, 6 June	A tilt takes place, followed by a sea battle and fireworks

That all of these activities were parts of one event was recognized by contemporaries. Dudley Carleton wrote to Sir Thomas Edmonds:

> The first part of the Prince's Creation *was acted* on Thursday last, when he came from Richmond by water, accompanied by many of the Nobility, and was met by the water by the Lord Mayor and all the Companies. . . . The Knights of the Bath have their College, and *perform their Ceremonies* at Durham House, from whence they are to ride in public show to Whitehall. All the rest of the Ceremony that belongs to the Prince shall be performed in as private a manner as may be . . .[14] (emphasis added).

The "festival" nature of the celebrations has been recognized also by twentieth-century critics. Roy Strong accurately observes that "from January 1610 onwards the young Prince was to become the driving force behind a sequence of festivals that were designed explicitly to present himself and his policy to both court and public."[15] But he is only partly right when he adds that if Henry "had lived, the art of festival in Stuart England would have taken a very different course from that which ended in the sterility of the self-adulatory masques of the Caroline age,"[16] for the cycles continue long after Prince Henry's death in 1612, and "England's Renaissance" does not seem to have been entirely "lost," as Strong wants us to believe.

The cycle of celebrations began on Thursday, the last day of May, 1610, when the lord mayor and his aldermen, along with the representatives of all London major companies, welcomed Prince Henry on the Thames and assured him of their "love." The event must have been considered important, for its description appeared in print in a separate quarto edition entitled *Londons Love, To the Royal Prince Henrie, Meeting Him on the River of Thames, at his returne from Richmonde, With a Worthie Fleete of Her Cittizens*. . . .[17] Presumably written by Anthony Munday,[18] the booklet is dedicated to Sir Thomas Cambell, lord mayor of London, and to "all the Aldermen his worthie Bretheren" (A3), who are referred to as the "Pollitique body." In introductory comments the author stresses the loyalty of the magistrates and notes that

> Plato termeth Magistracy, to be the *Anchor, Head,* and *Soule* of any Citty: & holdeth it for the same thing in any commonwealth, as the Heart is in the body of a liuing creature, or as Reason in the Soule: which being the chiefe and essentiall parts of either, the life and existence of the whole, is in that power, & their cheerful motion, giues courage and alacritie to all other partes of the bodie. (A4v)

This assertion is said to be confirmed by "Londons Loue to Royall Prince Henrie," who is to be created Prince of Wales, and by the earl of Chester in the "assembly of the high Court of Parliament." This last detail is extremely important, for no true prince can be created without Parliament. To prove this, the author gives a brief historical account of the lives of eleven princes that preceded Henry and concludes:

> All these fore-named Princes of Wales, were created sollemnely, by and in the Court of Parliament. . . . And those that were created out of Parliament, were Princes of hard and disaster fortune: For Richard the second was deposed: Edward the fifte murdered, and Richard the third, his Sonne dyed with in three months after, as in iust iudgement of God for his Fathers wickedness. (B2)

Moreover, Munday writes that it was the lord mayor's and aldermen's own decision to welcome the Prince on water with appropriate celebrations. Companies of the city took part in their barges and had "their Streamers and Ensignes gloriously displayed."

The author seems to have been historically inclined, for he goes on to give an account of the mythological history of Britain, which is of course strikingly similar to that described in city pageants or in the masques. According to the myth, "Neptune being called King, or God of the Seas, had by his Queene Amphitrita diuers Children . . . each one of them he made King of a seuerall Island. Britayne, which himself tearmed to be *Insula beata,* he bestowed vpon his fourth, but best affected sonne *Albion*" (B3r–v). This island enjoys Neptune's special favor, and therefore when its mortals celebrate such a magnificent occasion as the investiture of the Prince of Wales, the supreme powers above cannot sit indifferently. For exactly this reason, the author assures us, the gods in great bountie, must needs add applause vnto it, and out of their riche aboundance, enable their meaner power, by their helpe, and expresse also their owne lyking thereof, by some familiar addition or other. [¶] Whereof let vs thinke of *Neptune*, that out of his spacious watrie wildernes, he then suddenly sent a huge Whale and a Dolphin, and by the power of his commanding Trident, had seated two of his choycest Trytons on them, altring their deformed Sea-shapes, bestowing on them the borrowed bodies of two absolute Actors . . . personating in them, the seuerall *Genii* of *Corinea*, the beautiful Queene of *Cornewall*, and *Amphion*[19] the Father of harmonie or Musick. (B4)

When the fleet of citizens led by the lord mayor met the prince's barge, "Corinea," the "genius" of Cornwall, presented a speech while riding on a whale. In it she compares the citizens' and magistrates' love to Jacob's ladder, which symbolically links heaven and earth.[20] She also asks the prince to accept this love and to protect the city with "the large extended wings of *Ioues Birde* the Eagle" (C3). As the fleet proceeded towards Whitehall, the author writes that even the Thames appeared "proude of this gallant burden" and "not a wrinckle appeared in her brow" (C3). When the prince was ready to land, he was approached by "Amphion" riding on his dolphin (and representing the "Genius of Wales"), who presented another speech saluting the prince. Once again Henry was asked to accept the lord mayor's and citizens' love and is reminded that it was they who "haue brought a Royall freight to landing" (D). Thus the text constantly stresses the role and importance of the city. Prince Henry may be royal, he may even be a little god on earth, but he is nevertheless physically brought to Whitehall by those who represent the people of London, and he is going to be created Prince of Wales in a Parliament that also represents the people. Thus it is people who bring their prince to their Parliament; all other ways can only lead to disaster and calamity.

The same event is briefly described in *The Order of Solemnitie of the Creation of the High and mightie Prince Henry* . . ., whose anonymous author indicates that during the progress by the river, the hierarchy of importance was observed: "the Companies went before, the meanest in place first, the rest according to their seuerall rankes successiuely ensuing, and lastly the Lord Mayor attended with his two Sea-monsters on eyther side, going immediately before the Prince and conducting his ioyfull passage to the Citie."[21]

This description leaves no doubt that the whole encounter on the river was not improvised; it was planned as a theatrical spectacle, with action, impersonation, speeches, and music (for example, drums and trumpets). In this spectacle all elements were significant, as for instance the fact that it was the lord mayor who was accompanied by the "Sea-monsters." These were not ordinary creatures, for they represented Cornwall and Wales, and—most important—both were brought before the prince by the people of London.[22]

Saturday was the start of the ceremonies connected with the creation of the Knights of the Bath. The same booklet gives their detailed description. The young men had to go through a number of painstaking rituals, which included many scenes that may be labeled theatrical. For each "scene," for instance, they had to change costume. The description provides examples of theatrical behavior that dominated at court during the preparations. On Sunday morning, for instance,

> they were wakened with musicke, and at their vprising inuested in their Hermits habits, which was a gowne of gray cloth girded close, & a hood of the same, with a linnen coyse vnderneath, and a handkercher hanging at his girdle, cloth stockings soled with leather, but no shooes; and thus apparrelled, their Esquires gouernours, with the heralds wearing the coats of armes, and sundry sorts of winde instruments going before them, they proceeded from their lodging . . . till they cam to the chapell. . . . [After their oath] they departed to their chamber to be disrobed of their Hermits weeds, & new reuested againe in Robes of Crimson taffata. . . . [Following the afternoon service] at the Chappell doore as they came forth, they were encountered by the Kings Master Cooke, who stood there with his white Apron and Sleeues, and a Choping-knife in his hand, and challenged their spurres, which were likewise redeemed with a noble in money, thretening them neuerthelesse that if they proued not true and loyall to the King his Lord and Mast[er] it must be his office to hew them from their heeles. . . . On Monday morning they al met together again at the Court, where . . . they were cloathed in long roabes of purple sattin with hoods of the same. . . . And thus apparelled they gaue their attendance vpon the Prince at his creation. (C3–D2)

Equally theatrical in character was the ceremony of the creation of Prince of Wales. It was to be followed by a sea battle and fireworks, but for some reason these events were postponed until Wednesday. The ceremony created the official heir to the throne, who was expected to continue his father's policies in political and religious matters. This was precisely the theme of Daniel Price's sermon at Westminster on the previous day. Price called for the struggle to maintain peace and repeatedly appealed to the prince to continue the king's or Solomon's policies.[23] Much more important here, however, is the Tuesday night court performance of Samuel Daniel's *Tethys Festival*.

The masque is a direct continuation of the "welcoming show on water" and celebrates the investiture. The similarities to the former event, as described in *Londons Loue*, are striking. As mentioned above, Munday states why the mythological gods are interested in the creation of Prince of Wales: England is Neptune's elect island (as Albion was his favorite son) and he cannot therefore remain "indifferent" to what is going on there. He sends two Tritons to present speeches before the prince. In the masque, the general scheme is exactly the same, but here it is Tethys (the queen of the ocean, and wife to Neptune) who sends two Tritons to James's court. They deliver Tethys's message and presents for James and Henry. In their speeches, "inuestiture," "Rites," and the "new Prince" are mentioned, which leaves no doubt that the masque is directly linked with the "present occasion." The solemnities are the reason why Tethys decided "t'adorne the day" and to appear in person at James's court with her choice nymphs. The Tritons address the king directly, calling him the "great Monarch of Oceanus," and refer to Henry as "the hope and delight / Of all the Northerne Nations." They also advise the prince not to unsheathe the sword "but on iust ground" (an echo of the Sunday sermon) and not to expand his "Emperie" beyond reasonable boundaries, "For Nereus will by industry unfold / A Chimicke secret, and turn fish to gold" (sig. F).

Further similarities between the two spectacles abound. *Londons Loue* takes place on water, on the Thames, with the participation of many ships and barges; *Tethys Festival* begins with a perspective view of the harbor.[24] The former ends with the prince entering Whitehall; the latter begins with the messengers from the gods doing the same. The whale and the dolphin on which Tritons arrive in *Londons Loue* reappear in *Tethys Festival* as part of the design for the second scene, in which the action is moved from the "harbor" to the court. As for the allegory, Neptune and Tethys are the mythological equivalents of King James and Queen Anne. In the spectacle on the Thames, it is the messengers from Neptune, or James, that welcome the prince and, accompanied by the lord mayor, take him to Whitehall to be created Prince of Wales. The royal and civic powers join their trust and legal powers to enable the creation.

John Pitcher suspects that Samuel Daniel was responsible for the total design of the masque, pageant, and symbolic journey down the river (Anthony Munday being the author of the Tritons' speeches only).[25] It is true that, as Munday says, both of the Tritons that welcomed the prince on the river were ordered by "Neptune's prophet, or poet." But one must not forget that events of such great political importance as the investiture of the Prince of Wales could not have been devised by just anyone, not even the court's most trusted poet, without the king's consent. It is an established fact that James did take part in planning the details of the celebrations. As the Venetian ambassador informed the Doge and the Senate in a report of 16 June (n.s.), "the King would not allow him [Prince Henry] on this occasion, nor yet on his going to Parliament, to be seen on horseback. The reason is the question of expense or, as some say, because they did not desire to exalt him too high."[26]

By Tuesday night James's role had already been played. Now it was the queen's turn. She appeared in her masque as Tethys, the wife of Neptune, accompanied by her nymphs, all of whom turn out to be English rivers. In the final transformation she changed back into her human shape. In the ritual of the masque the queen's "return" to human nature marks the end of the ritual and the beginning of the revels. Thus, it is James and Anne who celebrate the occasion.

On Wednesday there were more attractions: tilting was followed by a sea battle on the Thames and fireworks. A contemporary account relates that

> Uppon Wednesday afternoone, in the Tilt-yard, there were divers Earles, Barons, and others, being in rich and glorious armoure, and having costly caparisons, wondrous curiously imbroydered with pearls, gould, and silver. . . . They presented their severall ingenious devices and trophies before the King and Prince, and then ran at Tilt, where there was a world of people to behoulde them. And that night there were other naval triumphes and pastimes upon the water, over against the Court, with shippes of warre and gallies fighting one against another, and against a great castle builded upon the water. After these batels then for an houre's space, there were many strange and variable fier-workes in the castle and in all the shippes and gallies. . . .[27]

As is apparent from Table 2, the masque cycles and "festivals" were the feature of the Jacobean period rather than of the Caroline. The death of King James ended a clearly distinct phase in masque history. To begin, there is a surprising several-year period

Masque Cycles and Courtly "Festivals"

immediately following Charles's accession when no masques were staged at all. The reason seems to have been the inseparable link of the masque-in-performance with King James, whose divine wisdom the masques celebrated in ritualistic spectacles. When James died, it was contradictory to masque "ideology" to present the spectacles before a substitute, even though he was the royal heir. After all, it was King James's (and nobody else's) book of wisdom that was transmuted into a theatrical system of signs. As mentioned earlier, the masque may be seen as an attempt to create three-dimensional "speaking" and "singing" emblems based on *Basilikon Doron* and on James's general worldview. Inigo Jones described the masques as pictures with light and motions. Moreover, King James was the deity at court; he was the sun and Neptune. His death was not taken into account in the fictive world of the masque. The two "texts," that of King James and that of the masque, were united: the death of the first meant the death of the second as well.

Consequently, new masques staged at court had to be different from the Jacobean ones. And indeed they were. One of their curious features is that they tend not to enter into cycles with other types of texts; they do not even cross the confinements of the court. In other words, they become almost completely separated from the world outside the court. Caroline masques tend to be more varied in their structure, having many more antimasques with elements of opera, drama, and even folk entertainments. This means that the masque-in-performance, instead of reaching out to the text of the noncourt culture, became almost completely isolated from the outside world. Of course, this was also the characteristic feature of Charles's autocratic rule without Parliament. The self-adulation of the court did not require corroboration and support from the common people; in the same way the masque became fully satisfied with itself and did not need to flirt with mundane forms of entertainment. When the two worlds met again, the only "masque" they could stage was King Charles's execution, which ironically took place in front of the Banqueting House.

One of the distinctive features of Caroline masques, however, is their tendency to form minicycles of two masques each, one prepared by the king, the other by the queen. There seems to have developed some sort of competition between Charles and Henrietta, and in fact most Caroline masques may be grouped in pairs. In 1631, for instance, Jonson and Jones wrote *Love's Triumph Through Callipolis* for the king, and *Chloridia* for the queen. In 1632,

Albions Triumph was the king's masque, whereas *Tempe Restord* was the queen's. Two years later, the queen presented *The Triumph of Peace*, and the king entertained the court with *Coelum Britannicum*. The last of the documented "pairs" was *Luminalia* (the queen's) and *Britannia Triumphs* (the king's), presented on 6 and 7 February 1638.

The "competitive" character of these masques implies their relatedness. They ought to be treated together, if not as one text, then at least in relation to one another—as they must have been received in their own time.

Table 2 includes over twenty early Stuart court "festivals" and masque cycles. As mentioned above, the scope of this book does not allow discussion of all of them. The table, however, suggests a number of possibilities for further research. For instance, it is tempting to assume that the plays selected to become parts of a festival functioned as such and, moreover, created meanings in relation to other elements of a given sequence of court entertainments. This function would be unique for the occasion, and therefore short-lived, but is certainly worth considering in literary studies. A play of that kind did not have to be written for the particular occasion, or festival, and authorial "intentions" did not really count; but through becoming a part of signifying celebrations, the play acquired the function of a part of a larger text and consequently acquired new meanings that the text could not create outside the given sequence. For instance, can the court performance of Ben Jonson's *Alchemist*, which took place on 1 January 1623, be related to the planned peformance of his masque *Time Vindicated to Himself and His Honors*, scheduled for the Twelfth Night? Moreover, it would be particularly interesting to investigate this pehonomenon in plays by Shakespeare, and would perhaps end the endless disputes over—to give just one example—whether or not Shakespeare wrote *The Tempest* for the wedding celebrations in 1613. This is actually not relevant, for what is really important is the new function the play acquired when staged as part of the whole sequence.

5
Masque Cycle I

Although particular masques staged during the celebrations following the marriage of Elizabeth and Frederick have gained considerable critical attention, so far they have not been analyzed in detail as a whole. Yet all evidence seems to indicate that one ought to treat the extant masques not only as parts of a masque cycle, but also as parts of a larger whole that would incorporate all other types of festivities, like fireworks, a tilt, and a sea battle. All these elements may be treated as components of one surprisingly consistent text that is logical and creates meanings on several levels. When treated independently, the particular elements of the ten-day wedding celebrations are deprived of their original richness. One could further argue that the individual elements make sense only when treated as parts of one text. It does not really matter that we do not know the authors—who may have been Francis Bacon or a group of people—since their overall plan for the celebrations may have been supervised by King James. Establishing authorship is not essential at this point;[1] instead, I attempt to scrutinize the significant elements of the wedding festivities (each devised by an individual author) as one text-in-performance. In so doing I follow a contemporary opinion of John Finett, who stated that "the solemnity of the marriage" was *"one continuous Act though performed divers daies"* (emphasis added).[2]

For the sake of clarity, the order of the major events of the celebrations are:

Sunday, 7 February 1613	Frederick installed as Knight of the Garter at Windsor
Tuesday, 9 February	The court returns to Whitehall
Thursday, 11 February	Display of fireworks
Saturday, 13 February	Sea battle on the Thames
Sunday, 14 February	The marriage ceremony: *The Lords Masque* presented at court

Monday, 15 February	The running at the ring; *The Memorable Masque* presented at court
Tuesday, 16 February	Planned date for the presentation of *The Inner Temple and Gray's Inn Masque*
Saturday, 20 February	Performance at court of the above masque

Let us begin with events that occurred a week before the actual marriage ceremony. On Sunday, 7 February, Frederick V, the duke of the Rhenish Palatinate, was installed at Windsor as Knight of the Garter, thus becoming one of the chosen nobles of Europe whose knightly patron was Saint George. This patronage was significant, even though the historical existence of the saint was largely doubted in the seventeenth century. Saint George's patronage signified all the virtues and honor of knighthood. Equally significant was the fact that this knightly order was part of the English tradition, Saint George was also the patron of England, and only English monarchs could elect new Knights of the Garter. Since the beginning of Queen Elizabeth's reign, the Knights Companions were summoned to Whitehall to hold a special "Chapter" for the election of new knights.[3] The king was the sovereign of the order, and, in theory at least, represented the epitome of the order's values. In this way England, and Whitehall in particular, were considered the center of knighthood, with James's court often described as the Temple of Knighthood. As A. Nixon, author of *Great Brittaines Generall Ioyes: Londons Glorious Triumphs*, wrote in his verses commemorating "Prince Frederick [being] created Knight of the Garter":

> . . . The order of Saint George
> That at this day is honoured through the world
> The order of the Garter now is cal'd. (antiquity
> Famous through all the world for honour and
> Grace'd by a King, and fauoured of his peeres.[4]

Earlier in the poem the poet has a vision—significant to this discussion—in which

> . . . me thought I saw
> A royall glimmering light, streaming aloft,
> A Titan mounted on the Lions backe,
> Had cloath'd himself in fier pointed beames
> To chase the night and entertaine the Moone.[5]

As Frances A. Yates put it,

Masque Cycle I

the very special significance attached to the Order of the Garter was again an Elizabethan tradition. There had been a great revival of the Order, its ceremonies, processions, and ethos, during the reign of Elizabeth, who had used it as a means to drawing the noblemen together in common service to the Crown. When the Palsgrave became a Garter Knight he enlisted under the banner of the Red Cross of St. George in defense of the causes for which the Order stood, the fighting of the Dragon of Wrong and the defense of the Monarch.

The story of St George and the Dragon and of his romantic adventures in attacking wrongs and defending the oppressed was blazoned in fire in firework display given by the King's gunners shortly before the wedding, on the night of 11 February.[6]

Shows of this kind were relatively new in England. Alan St. H. Brock, in *History of Fireworks,* notes that James was introduced to the new and superior type of fireworks by his brother-in-law, King Christian IV (of Denmark), in 1606.[7] During the Dane's visit to London, discussed briefly in the previous chapter, his gunners staged magnificent fireworks. These were in the form of a cube with a pillar at each corner, surmounted by "a lion holding the eight capital vices in chains." The show lasted for forty-five minutes and impressed James so much that he persuaded his brother-in-law to leave one of the artificers behind. When a few months later James ordered fireworks for Christmas, they were, according to a contemporary source, "contrived by a Dane, two Dutchmen and Sir Thomas Challoner."[8]

In February 1613 fireworks were also prepared, at high cost, by the gunners to the king: their fullest description is in John Taylor's *Heaven's Blessing and Earth's Joy.*[9] Taylor distinguishes five displays of fireworks and names the devisers. First was the show in which Lady Lucida, the queen of the Amazonians, rejects the love of the "hell-commanding" magician "Mango." In his fury, Mango magically raises "a strong impregnable pavilion" in which he "immures and encloses this beautiful Amazonian Queene and her attendant Ladies." To secure the guard, Mango erects "another strong tower as a watch-house, wherein he placed a fiery dragon and an invincible giant." To this pavilion comes Saint George, who is allowed to enter and is told the story of the queen's imprisonment. He vows to free the queen and is entertained with fireworks. Afterwards Saint George mounts his horse and rides towards the enchanted tower. The second part of the show begins with a fierce combat in which the dragon is slain, a sight that must have impressed the spectators gathered on the banks of the Thames. As soon as the dragon is dead, the giant enters and, as Taylor describes it, "at their first encounter the blowes on both sides fell like thunderclappes, enforcing lightning and fiery exhalations to sparkle from whence their powerful stroakes lighted." At last the giant falls and begs for mercy, which is granted if he shows how to besiege the castle. The giant tells Saint George that "there is an enchanted fountaine, and whosoever can attaine to drinke of it shall be he whome the Fates have ordained to the conclusion of the Castle's glory." In the meantime Mango mounts an invisible flying devil and "in a moment alights within the castle," which "hath at the top . . . a fiery Fountaine, which burnes and sends up rackets into the ayre." Eventually the magician is taken by Saint George, bound to a pillar, and "burned with fire and lights." Fireworks from the castle continue until "the maine Castle is fyered," and in the next "episode" the whole edifice explodes.

This is not the end of the show, however. The ruins of the castle are now called the Castle of Envie, situated on the Rock of Ruine, encompassed by the Sea of Disquiet. An allegorical spectacle follows. The captain of the castle is called Discord, his lieutenants are Lawless, Ancient Hatred, and the like. The castle is besieged by three ships called "Good-will," "True-love," and "Assurance." These attack the castle, which is, to use Taylor's words, "utterly razed, demolished, and subverted, with rackets, breakers, blowes." The last episode is in turn emblematic in character. It was composed of a pyramid or an obelisk with a "triangled spire, with a globe fixed on top," from "whence proceeded many rackets, fires, blowes" and such.

The connection of the fireworks, and especially of Saint George, with the recent investment of Frederick as Knight of the Garter has been noticed by others, as is apparent from the above-quoted passage by Frances Yates.[10] However, the meaning of the fireworks, especially when considered part of a larger text (the whole program of the marriage celebrations), seems to go beyond mere variations on the theme of Saint George. The fireworks "tell a story," so to say, in five acts, of which the first three are directly connected with the saint; the fourth is allegorical, and the last emblematic. The story of Saint George represents the eternal struggle of good against evil (shown by the dragon and the magician). So is the allegorical siege of the Castle of Envie. In both cases the forces of evil are utterly destroyed, and the victory is celebrated in the last, emblematic "act." Because of the political context of the marriage of Elizabeth and Frederick, the fireworks seem to have more specific meanings, which I attempt to elucidate.

A poetic description of most of the events connected with the marriage celebrations is given by M. Joannes Maria de Franchis in his lengthy work entitled *Of the Most Auspicatious Marriage: Betwixt, the High and Mightie Prince Frederick . . . and the most Illustrious Princesse . . . in III Bookes.*[11] The poet claims to have been eyewitness to all the events he describes (the poem was entered in the Stationers' Register in June, several months after the marriage). Many similarities between this poem and the masques staged during the wedding festivities suggest that de Franchis may actually have been influenced by the court spectacles. Whether or not this is true, the poet clearly follows the recurrent imagery of the masques and quite consciously develops and expounds their religious and propagandist motifs. The poem is basically an amalgam of a fictitious, mythological plot and historical facts, the function of which was to praise the marriage and show its great significance and ramifications that will influence the future of the world. By including a narrative description of real events, seen by thousands of people in London, the poet joins the fictitious plane of his work with the historical one, thus making the first of these planes "more true" and his entire interpretation of the events more trustworthy. The poem begins with conventional dedications, followed by "The Argument, or Epitome," which is surprisingly similar to "arguments" found in masques. For this reason it is worth quoting at some length:

> Ivpiter, by meanes of Mercury his messenger, summons a Convocation of the Gods to conferre and dispose of things here below; at this Synod, Religion made her appearance, being ful of afflictions, & depriued of [the] accustomed coelestiall pompe . . . [Religion explains] with teares, and sobbes, that this happened to her, because she was so torne and persecuted in the world, by wickednesse and superstition . . . [Jove ordains that the remedy is] the linking together of two royal families in a most profitable marriage, long since preordained by Fate, for the reformation of these corrupted times: And then he repeated the aunceient oracle of the goddesse Themis, now upon the point to be performed, in the person of the most illustrious Lady, the Princesse of great Brittany, and of the most noble Prince Palatine. . . . (A3)

Also Juno, the goddess of marriage, sends down her ambassador, Iris, accompanied by Cupid, Venus's son. They arrive at Heidelberg, where with his golden dart, Cupid struck Frederick's heart. The young prince, "not yet knowing the obiect of his desire," was walking in his gallery when suddenly "his eye lighted on the picture of the L. Elizabeth" (A4). As preordained by Fate, Frederick fell in love with Elizabeth. This achieved, other gods appeared in James's dream to inform him that "the coming of the Prince Elector into his kingdome, was by the ordinance of heauen." The espousals are proclaimed, the bridal day comes, and all the festivities are meticulously described by the poet. He does not leave out the fireworks, which according to him were devised by Vulcan himself. (A number of characters from the poem also appear in the masques written for the occasion, as, for instance, Jove, Ivno, Muses, Iris, Mercury, Nymphs, Vulcan, Thames, and Rhine).

In the poem Frederick is presented not only as a great prince but also as a savior of mankind in general and religion in particular. His greatest enemy is the dragon. As the poet at one point declares,

> 56. The miracle of ancient yeares reuiues,
>   The boy that lying in cradle crush'd the Snakes:
> And tam'd the monster in our *Frederick liues*,
>   The Palatine with Brittaine ioynd shall bring
>   Earths golden dayes againe, times blessed spring.

The above refrain is reiterated throughout part 2. The significance of the dragon is fully and clearly revealed in the poem: he represents the "infernal" forces of evil that oppress Religion;[12] he also represents false religion, "the Dragon conquering by dissentions" (stanza 71). However, the end of his power has come, for the ancient decree of Fate is now materialized through the marriage of Elizabeth and Frederick:

> That which the Fates foretold vs for our good,
> What Heauen and Earth, and Seas so long desird
>   Now comes to passe, the Palatine of *Rhein*,
>   Is linckt with *Brittains* blest, most royall line.
>
> (2.72)

This union will lead to all sorts of changes: wars will cease, envy shall be bound, and all evil chased away. Among other things,

> Vaine Superstition vailes to Pietie,
> Deceit to Truth, Doubt vnto Demonstration,
> Darkness to Light, *Pluto* to *Ioues* deity,
> Hell to bright Heauen, Damnation to Saluation.
>
> (2.80)

Masque Cycle I

And, what is most important:

> The *Serpent Elaps* shall no poyson keepe,
> The *Dragon Amphisbaena* dwine away.
>
> (2.76)

The dragon's fall is predicted early in the poem, in part 1, when Jove assures Religion that her power will be restored through the marriage of Elizabeth and Frederick:

> . . . Yet shall my Loue augment thy precious name
> . . . .
> Behold thy primitiue pureness, free from blame
> Return'd restores true ioy: See *Babel* cries,
> Because the ruling Dragon thence fast flies.
>
> (1.84)

> His Crest is laid, fire quenched and sting rebated
> Dear loue, sweet peace, sound faith, and vertue springs;
> The furies and their terrors are abated:
> Now time his daughter Truth from darknes brings.
>
> (1.85)

Since the "infernall Dragon and his lernian" shakes with terror at the sight of Frederick (2.56), there is good reason to identify Saint George of the fireworks with Prince Palatine. Of course, it is not a matter of chance that Frederick comes to Britain, for King James's court is called

> great *Arthurs* court,
> Where pious *Iames* raignes and maintaines our lawes
> Of holy truth and right.
>
> (2.12)

Most interesting here is de Franchis's description of fireworks that comes almost at the very end of his poem. The king, accompanied by his peers, Queen Anne, Prince Charles, Elizabeth, and Frederick "ascended" to a "lofty stately Turret made for view," which looked so rich and grave that it reminded the poet of Jove ascending to the throne (3.113). A description of fireworks soon follows:

> Scarce this was done, when by *Vulcanian* arts,
> A fell, fierce, fiery Dragon gins to mount:
> Who with his taile the ayre so swiftly parts,

> As makes a thunder, Teeth withouten Count.
>   Whet, gnash, and crash, his Irish Dart tongue there,
> Threatens to kill and poyson who comes neere.
> Saint *George* on horseback with his speare and sheild,
> Confronts the Serpent, and with martiall looks
> Makes towards the *Dragon* in the airy field,
> And with vndaunted spirit his speare he shook,
>   The Dragon, in whose scales laid hart and might,
> Prouokes this worthy warriour to the fight.
>
> (117–18)

A detailed description of the combat continues until stanza 122, where at last Saint George kills the dragon. Because they share a number of common features, the dragon of the poem and the dragon of the fireworks may with ease be identified as one. This naturally leads to the parallel of Frederick and Saint George. Thus, the fireworks—as seen by the poet—present a vision of Britain's anticipated victory, now strengthened by the new union, over the dragon and all that he can possibly represent.

As indicated above, the three "acts" of Saint George's fight against evil forces are followed by two allegorical scenes, the first of which is a sea battle. This actually is a siege from the sea of the "Castle of Envie," undertaken by three ships, "Good-will", "True-love," and "Assurance." This allegory, of course, is reminiscent of morality plays, and again de Franchis's description elucidates the allegory. According to the poet, the battle signifies the victory of the British over Turkish infidels. This is yet another victory of Saint George, and his flag is displayed to "honor the day" (3. 132).

The fireworks sea battle was repeated on the Thames with real warships on Saturday, 13 February. Again, a Christian fleet fights against the Turks. As John Taylor relates in the quoted work, this struggle immediately evoked memories of the battle of Lepanto (of which King James had apparently written a poem) and the defeat of the Spanish Armada.[13] Thus, past days of military glory are brought to mind in order to suggest and strengthen the possibility of future victories. In this particular case, however, Taylor insists that the battle ends with a draw: "the victorie inclyning to the nether side, all being opposed foes and combined friends; all victors, all triumphers, none to be vanquished and therefore no conqueror."[14] This conclusion is contradicted by de Franchis, who has no doubts on who won and who lost, and also by the anonymous author of *The Magnificent Marriage of the Two Great Princes* (1613).[15] The latter source reveals that the Turks yielded both the Castle and gallies, and submitted to the conquest of the English Admirall, who fired many of the said gallies, sacked the Castle, and tooke prisoner of the Turke's Admirall, with divers Bashawes and other great Turkes. . . . After the performance . . . the English Admirall, in almost triumphant manner, carried as prisoner the Admirall of the gallies . . . with the Bashawes and the other Turkes, guarded, to his Highness' Privie-stairs at White-hall, where his Grace, Prince Palsgrave, and his Lady remained, which prisoners of war were led by Sir Robert Mansfield [Mansel] to the Lord Admiral's, and by him they were conveyed to the King's Majestie as a representation of pleasure, which to his Highness moved delight, and highly pleased all the present.[16]

What is striking in this description is the theatricality of the details: not only does the sea battle take place between the Christians and the Turks, but this distinction between the two sides (played by Englishmen, of course) is further continued after the naval battle. A theatrical convention is extended to include the court. The captured "Turks" do not cease to impersonate infidels after they had been defeated. They are taken by the guard to the court as if they were real prisoners of war. The court officials, including the Lord Admiral and King James himself, "pretend" (therefore act) to treat them as such. It may be said that a specifically theatrical form of behavior is accepted by some of the spectators, who thus become actors in a spectacle entitled "The British Victory over Infidels." The allegory presented in the fireworks is materialized in a "real" defeat of the enemy's navy, a "real" triumph of the victorious forces. The sea battle was prepared on the order of the Lord Admiral and his message is quite clear: the strength of Britain lies in its naval force. It is also obvious that the Turks were not the only enemies of the true Christians (or Protestants).

This prophecy of the Protestant victory, which parallels de Franchis's poem, was followed by the marriage ceremony on Sunday, 14 February 1613. A many-faceted event, this union of two virtuous individuals would lead to the strengthening of the Protestant union and other benefits. The masques that celebrated the marriage quite naturally were variations on the many levels of the union: as such they may be treated as one text, as I will attempt to prove.

The procession of the young couple to the chapel at Whitehall started from the Banqueting House. The author of *The Magnificent Marriage* writes that the Banqueting House was "new" and "erected of the purpose to solemnize this Feast."[18] This cannot be identified with the second of the Whitehall Banqueting Houses, erected in 1606/7 in place of the old "rotten sleight builded banquetting house" designed by David Cunningham.[19] Inigo Jones was paid three hundred pounds for his part "in preparing and fitting the Banquetting house against *three* Maskes to be performed there"[20] (emphasis added). This clearly implies that three masques were to be staged in the Banqueting House. This by no means is a revelation: scholars have known this for decades, and since exactly three masques are extant, everything makes sense and seems to be obvious. However, other pieces of evidence have been neglected that indicate, for instance, that simultaneously preparations were made for another masque to be performed in the court hall. Payments were made for "the Maske in the Hall" and "alsoe for diverse woorkes and raparacions in making ready the hall with degrees and galleries for a Maske to be performed before the king by the gentlemen of the Temple."[21] The same source reveals that the "old" Banqueting House (the one erected in 1606/7) was being prepared for another masque.[22] This means that the masque to be performed in the hall was the fourth one. Moreover, John Chamberlain's account leaves no doubt that the masques were in fact performed in two different places: "On Monday night was the Middle Temple and Lincolns Ynne maske presented in the hall at court, whereas the Lords was in the bancketting roome."[23] A payment was also made for "making ready tholde banquetting house for a nother Maske at the Marriage of the Lady Elizabeth"; Orgel and Strong think that this must refer to "one of the two other masques for the wedding,"[24] but the entry implies that there were possibly two masques to be staged on the day of the marriage, on Sunday night.

Another puzzling entry is a payment for "building a newe banquettinghouse upon the Tarras for the feastes to be keapte at the marriage of the Palsgrave and the Ladie Elizabeth," quoted by Orgel and Strong as a reference to the Banqueting House in which the masques were actually performed.[25] However, this "newe banquettinghouse" seems to have been a separate structure. In fact there are two banqueting houses: the old one, now newly "furnished" for the performances, and the new one, a temporary, wooden structure, erected *ad hoc* for the feasts. In other words, the new Banqueting House is a separate wooden structure erected for the wedding in the empty space of the terrace adjoining the stone Banqueting House of 1606/7. It had nothing to do with the actual performances, for it was used as a large dining hall.[26] On 21

February, for instance, "a great supper was held there, in a large roome built of purpose for the time over the North Terras."[27]

A quarter of a century later, when the famous Rubens ceiling was in danger of damage from the smoky torches used during masque performances, Charles I instructed a new masquing place to be built. A contemporary source writes of "a new house being erected in the first Court at Whitehall, which costs the King 2500£, only of Deal Boards, because the King will not have his Pictures in the Banqueting-house hurt with Lights";[28] the same source also reveals that "A great Room is now [November 1635] in building only for this Use [for the masques] betwixt the Guard-Chamber and Banquetting-house, of Fir, only weather-boarded and slightly covered. At the Marriage of the Queen of Bohemia I saw one set up there, but not of that Vastness that this is."[29]

Thus the procession to the chapel begins in this new wooden Banqueting House, and after the marriage ceremony, the newlyweds returned "to dine in state in the new Banqueting-house with the Prince, the Ambassadors . . . and all the Lords and Ladies who had been attendant on the Marriage."[30] The interior of the new building was apparently decorated for the occasion. As a report of the Venetian ambassador states, immediately following the marriage ceremony the newlyweds and their guests "passed into a great chamber, especially made for this wedding, accompanied by the Master of the Ceremonies. Here was presented a great table and the hangings of the Hall represented the defeat of the Spanish in '88, which may be was a miracle as is expressed in the legend that surrounds it. . . ."[31] Thus the wedding was considered an appropriate time to recall the great glory of England's military victory over the Spaniards (in fact Catholics). In this way the motifs and ideological significance of the preceding sea battle find their continuation at court.

The masque that followed, Thomas Campion's *The Lords Masque*, was not staged there, but was held in the "old" Banqueting House. On the following night, George Chapman's *The Memorable Masque of the Two Honorable Houses or Innes of Court, the Middle Temple, and Lyncolns Inne* was presented in the court hall. On Tuesday, the sixteenth, Francis Beaumont's *The Masque of the Inner Temple and Gray's Inne* was to be staged in the same place, but the performance was canceled. The masquers, Chamberlain writes,

> were feign to return as they went without doing any thing; the Reason whereof some say, was because the Hall was so full that it could not be

avoided nor room made for them, and most of the principall Ladyes that were in the Galleries to see them land, excluded: but the most probable is, that the King was satiated and overwearied with Watching, that he could hold out no longer, and so was driven to put it off till *Saturday;* when it was very well performed in the new Banquetting-House, which for a kind of Amends was granted to them, though with much Repining and Contradiction of their Emulators. The next Day the King made them all a solemn Supper in the new Marriage Roome. . . .[32]

Since the unforseen cancelation of the masque no doubt meant additional cost and labor for its "producers," for all scenery and machinery had to be moved from the hall to the Banqueting House, this explains why Chamberlain mentions much "repining and contradiction."

All of these somewhat confusing pieces of evidence give the following schedule of masques presented during the wedding festivities:

Sunday, 14 February	Thomas Campion's masque
Monday, 15 February	George Chapman's masque
Tuesday, 16 February [postponed until Saturday, 20 February]	Francis Beaumont's masque

However, as indicated above, some sources mention four masques. Where, then, is the missing one? One point is certain: the fourth masque, if there was one, had to be the last in the cycle. In the British Library MS (Addit. 10, 444) a contemporary source refers to the masque of Sir Francis Bacon as having two parts. Could this possibly mean that the *Inner Temple and Gray's Inne's Masque,* of which Bacon was chief contriver, was considered part 1, to be staged on Tuesday? And was it to be followed by Bacon's part 2 on Wednesday? Until further evidence is found, no positive answer can be given to these questions. It does seem certain that a fourth masque was planned (and for some reason not performed); perhaps the evidence for this may be found in the remaining three masques.

Thomas Campion's *The Lords Masque* was presented on Sunday, after the marriage, as the first masque in the cycle. The text survives in a quarto edition of 1613 (STC 4545), where it appears as an "annex" to another work of Campion, *A Relation of the Late Royal Entertainment Given by the Right Honorable the Lord Knowles at Cawsome-House neere Redding . . . Whereunto is annexed the Descrip-*

Masque Cycle I

tion, Speeches, and Songs of the Lords Maske, presented in the Banquetting-house on the Mariage night of the High and Mightie, COVNT PALATINE, *and the Royally descended the Ladie Elizabeth.* Contemporaries praised this masque for the splendor of the production and for its dances, although Chamberlain complained that it was too long and therefore tedious.[33] Twentieth-century critics, on the other hand, have paid hardly any attention to this piece, and I. A. Shapiro noted in the introduction to his edition that the "unity of action, with logical and explicit connexion between episodes, is not, however, among the merits of *The Lords' Masque*."[34] The general impression is that for many critics this particular piece does not make much sense.

Campion begins with a description of scenery: "The Scene was diuided in two parts from the roofe to the floore, the lower part being first discouered . . . there appeared a Wood in perspective, the innermost part being of releaue, or whole round, the rest painted. On the left hand from the seate was a Caue, and on the right a thicket, out of which came Orpheus . . ." (sig. C). The choice of Orpheus as the leading character in the masque has puzzled its critics. Shapiro commented that this was

> an interesting reflexion of Campion's personal preoccupations. Apparently it did not occur to him that his audience might wonder why Orpheus, rather than Mercury or another of Jove's usual messengers, should be employed to release Entheus (Poetic Inspiration) from Mania's caue, though it is possible that he meant us to infer that Entheus could be released only by that Orphean music which could tame wild beasts and move trees, rocks, and rivers as Elizabethan writers frequently remind us.[35]

In Campion's text, following Orpheus's opening speech, "Mania the Goddess of madness" appears "wildly out of her caue." Orpheus informs her that he is Jove's messenger, and that Jove demands Entheus to be set free (he is held captive by Mania). Mania agrees, although reluctantly, for she worries that once the doors are open, all the lunatics will escape. Orpheus assures her that

> Ioue into our musick will inspire
> The power of passion, that their thoughts shall bent
> To any forme or motion we intend.
>
> (Cv–C2)

And to "the sound of strange musicke twelue Franticks enter, six men, and six women, all presented in sundry habits and humours: there was the Louer, the selfe-Louer . . . Vsurer . . . in the middest of whom Entheus (or Poeticke furie) was hurried forth, and tost up and downe, till by vertue of a new change in the musicke, the Lunatickes fell into a madde measure, fitted to a loud phantasticke tune . . ." (C2). According to Renaissance beliefs, madness was caused by an incorrect mixture of the elements fire, water, air, and earth, of which man's body consists, and only harmony of the elements could effect sanity. The "Franticks" cannot make proper use of poetic inspiration: they can only toss him "up and downe." Orpheus brings along harmony, and Mania and her "Franticks" depart, leaving behind Entheus in an emblematic costume. He wears on his head a wreath of laurel, "out of which grew a paire of wings, in the one hand he held a booke, and in the other a pen" (C2). The divinely inspired music contrasts, of course, with the "strange" music to which Mania's captives enter the stage. And it is analogous to the proper use of poetry.

Francis Bacon's *The Wisdom of the Ancients* has interesting attributes of some of the characters that appear in Campion's masque. According to Bacon, Orpheus represents the image of philosophy: "for the person of Orpheus, a man admirable and divine, and so excellently skilled in *all kind of harmony,* that with his sweet ravishing musicke did, as it were, charm and allure all things to follow him" (emphasis added). By the strength of his harmonious music, he is also said to "draw all manner of wild beasts unto him" that forget completely about "their savage fierceness."[36] It is worth noting that in the masque Orpheus appears at one point with "severall wild beasts . . . about him tamely placed."

In a later dialogue Orpheus tells Entheus that Jove set him free

> . . . to create
> Inuentions rare, this night to celebrate,
> Such as become a nuptiall by his will
> Begun and ended . . .
>
> (C2v)

At this point one might recall de Franchis's poem in which the princely marriage is presented throughout as divinely inspired. In addition, in the masque Jove releases poetic inspiration from captivity and orders Entheus to create a spectacle celebrating the nuptials. Thus Jove stands behind the masque, and the text (or spectacle) unfolds as an *ad hoc* improvisation. In this way the masque itself is an example of the proper use of poetry, conspicuously contrasted with the "franticks," who can only toss the poetic inspiration in a futile way.

Inspired by Jove, Entheus calls forth Prometheus in a song, asking him to bring all the lights taken from heaven and to show them to "human sights." The magical box of the stage begins to work. "In the end of the first part of this Song," Campion writes, "the upper part of the Scene was discovered by the sodaine fall of a curtaine, then in clowdes of seuerall colours . . . appeared eight Starres of extraordinarie bignesse, which so were placed, as that they seemed to be fixed betweene the Firmament and the Earth; in the front of the scene stood Prometheus, attyred as one of the ancient Heroes" (C3). Entheus asks him

> In Hymens place aide vs to solemnize
> These royall Nuptials, fill the lookers eyes
> With admiration of thy fire and light.
>
> (C3)

Thus, no one is pretending that this is not a spectacle; the theatrical illusion of a different location is destroyed at the very beginning of the text. Everything takes place here and now, and both sides (those on stage and those in the auditorium) recognize this fact.

A song follows, to which the stars dance. The song celebrates the union of the Rhine and the Thames and predicts both Beaumont's masque—in which the two rivers are actually married—and in this masque the transformation of the stars into masquers. "Vpon their new transformation," Campion says, "the whole Scaene being Cloudes dispersed, and there appeared an Element of artificiall fires, with seuerall circles of lights, in continuall motion, representing the house of Prometheus, who then thus applies his speech to the Maskers" (C4). Francis Bacon acknowledges that the ancients claimed that Prometheus made a man of clay and then stole fire from heaven and "communicated it with men."[37] What is important in Campion's version is the fact that Prometheus stole fire from heaven in order to put life into the clay figure he had embossed. Fire is the source of life. Similarly, the "fierie spirits" accompany the masquers as they descend. The appearance of Prometheus has a miraculous effect on the statues of women, as mentioned in the description above. Entheus addresses Prometheus, indirectly explaining the whole scene to spectators or readers:

> See, see, Prometheus, four of these first dames
> Which thou long since out of thy purchas'd flames
> Didst forge with heav'nly fire, as they were then
> By Jove transform'd to statues, so again
> They suddenly appear by his command
> At your arrival.
>
> (D)

The time has come to bring the ancient statues to life, which also implies that Jove's anger is gone; the time is ripe for reconciliation and forgiveness. Following Prometheus's invocation to Jove, in which he pleads to have these statues "made . . . women fit for love," a transformation takes place (which parallels the appearance of the masquers) and the statues "come to life." Since there are eight masquers, Jove is asked to provide four more women, which he does. Dances and songs follow, praising the bride and the bridegroom, thus fusing, as in de Franchis's poem, the mythological past with the historical present. Both men and women are labeled "new-born" (Dv).

The marriage of Elizabeth and Frederick marks an important moment in human history, as preordained by Jove. What was treated as a criminal act in the past (the theft of fire) is now given an "official" sanction with a divine seal. Prometheus's fire brings new life and marks the beginning of a new phase in history. What this will bring is prophesied by Sybilla, who appears within new scenery:

> The whole scaene was now againe changed, and became a prospective with Porticoes on each side, which seemed to go in [?] great way, in the middle was erected an Obeliske, all of siluer . . . on the side of this Obeliske, standing on Pedestals, were the statues of Bridegroom and Bride, all of gold in gratious postures. This Obelisk was of that height that the toppe thereof touched the highest cloudes, and yet Sybilla did draw it forthwith a threed of gold. . . . (D2v).

Here is a typical emblematic scene, so characteristic of the masques. The obelisk that Sybilla pulls by a golden thread finds analogy in one of Henry Peacham's emblems (21), where a crowned Lady, the "Glorie of Princes," stands with her hand around a brick obelisk (called "Pyramis" by Peacham);[38] the last lines of the accompanying poem read:

> The Pyramis the worldes great wonderment,
> Is of their fame, some lasting Moniment.

Masque Cycle I

This in turn derives from Ripa, who presents a "beautiful Lady, with a golden Circle around her Forehead, interwoven with many precious Jewels. Her Golden Locks signifie the *magnanimous Thoughts* that possess the Minds of Princes. She holds a Piramid, signifying their *Glory,* in causing magnificent Fabricks to be erected, signilising them to all Posterity."[39]

Sybilla is asked to prophesy, which she does in Latin verse:

> . . . Patrem vultu exprimit,
> Parens futura masculde prolis, Parens
> Regum, Imperatorum; additur Germaniae
> Robur Britannicum; ecquid esse par potest?
>
> (D3)

Her prophesy is significant for further discussion of the remaining masques, for Sybilla not only tells that the great race of kings and emperors will spring from this union, but also that all the peoples of the world will unite in one true religion and in love. Once again, it is stated that this "cultus unus" is the only way to the redemption of mankind, which in turn is possible only through the union that will initiate it—the marriage of Elizabeth and Frederick (who as Saint George is also Christ's foremost knight). The harmony of the dances pays the young couple appropriate honor:

> Turn, turn, and honour now the life these figures bear
> Lo, how heav'nly natures far above all art appear!
> Let their aspects revive in you the fire that shin'd so late
> Still mount and still retain your heavenly state.
> . . . .
> This pair, by Hymen join'd, grace you with measures then,
> Since they are both divine and you are more then men.
>
> (D3v)

This is followed by the blessing of Elizabeth and Frederick by Sybilla, Prometheus, and Entheus, and by a concluding dance of the masquers.

The text of the masque creates meaning by alluding to classical mythology, contemporary emblem books, and to the "present occasion." The marriage, it appears from the text, is a direct continuation of the Promethean myth; this time, however, it is decreed by Jove himself. Entheus, who literally creates the spectacle through his poetic vision, represents "Poetic Fury," or *Furor Divinus.* His vision, hence the whole masque, is inspired by Jove, who now himself sends to humanity the fire of redemption that will bring new life. He does this (ironically using Prometheus as his messenger) only for the marriage of Elizabeth and Frederick, who by analogy will begin a new era in history, allegorically represented by the obelisk of their everlasting fame. This new period is to be characterized by harmony, which is revealed by music, poetic speeches, and dances. This time Promethean fire brings life and harmony to people: the union of these two people has changed the world.

The Stuart masques are usually known by the abbreviated titles created by later editors. For example, the full title of George Chapman's masque, staged on Monday, 15 February 1613, is:

The Memorable Maske of the two Honorable Houses or Inns of Court; the Middle Temple, and Lyncolns Inne. / As it was performed before the King, at White-Hall on Shroue Munday at night; being the 15. of February. 1613. / At the Princely celebration of the most Royall Nuptialls of the Palsgraue, and his thrice gratious Princesse Elizabeth.&. / With a description of their whole show; in the manner of their march on horsebacke to the Court from the Maister of the Rolls his house: with all their right Noble consorts, and most showfull attendants. / Inuented, and fashioned, with the ground, and speciall structure of the whole worke, By our Kingdomes most Artfull and Ingenious Architect Innigo Iones. / Supplied, Aplied, Digested, and written, / By Geo: Chapman.

The fact that Chapman included the description of the "march" through London of the masquers and accompanying persons is significant. The printed text is defined by Chapman himself, on the title page, as "a description of their *whole* show" (emphasis added), and therefore has to be treated as one text, of which only one part is a performance at court. This distinction is supported by the text—which I intend to show—since the performance part of the printed text has to be treated as a part of a larger whole. Otherwise a significant portion of its meaning is lost. Similarly, the actual performance of this masque cannot be analyzed in isolation, for it created meaning by relying on the spectators' knowledge of the preceding progress through the city.

In his twelve-page description of the "march" (which in itself is proof of the importance Chapman attached to it), Chapman listed the order of this "performance" as follows:

1. Fifty gentlemen of the two Inns of Court, on horseback, attended by footmen

Masque Cycle I

2. A "mock-Masque of Baboons" (which appears in the performance at court)
3. Two "Carts Triumphall," made especially for this purpose and not appearing in the masque. The carts were "adornd with great Maske heads, Festones, scroules, and antick leaues, euery part inricht with siluer and golde." In them twelve musicians were seated, attired as "Virginean Priests, by whom the Sun is there adorn'd" (Av).
4. "Chiefe Maskers" on horseback, with faces covered with "vizards of oliue collour" (A2v) and two Moors attending each horse
5. Torch-bearers, also attended by Moors
6. A final chariot, the most adorned of all. It had the "whole frame fill'd with moulded worke; mixt all with paintings, and glittering scarffings of siluer; ouer which was cast a Canopie of golde, boarne vp with anticke figures" (A3). Inside this chariot sat Capriccio, and "on a seate of the came Chariot, a little more eleuate, sate *Eunomia*, the Virgine Priest of the Goddesse *Honour*; and the earthy Deity, *Plutus*; or Riches . . ." (A4).
7. ". . . a full guard of two hundred Habardiers & two Marshals" (A4) attending the entire entourage.

That the progress was part of the whole show is additionally proven by the fact that it was watched by those who would be the most distinguished spectators during the performance at court. Chapman writes that "all these so marching to the Court at White Hall, the King, Bride & Bridegroom, and all the Lords of the most honord priuy Councel, and our chief Nobility, stood in the Gallery before the Tilt-yard, to behold their arriuall . . . being then honorably attended through the Gallery to a Chamber appointed, where they were to make ready for their performance in the Hall . . ." (A4v).

The account of the latter event begins with a description of the scenery, basically a landscape. It is worth quoting extensively.

an Artificiall Rock, whose top was as neere as high as the hall itselfe. This Rock, was in the vndermost part craggy, and full of hollow places, in whose concaues were contriv'd, two winding paire of staires, by whose greeces the Persons aboue might make their descents, and all the way be seene: all this Rocke grew by degrees vp into a gold-colour; and was run quite through, with veines of golde: On the one side whereof eminently raised on a faire hill, was erected a siluer Temple of an octangle figure, whose Pillars were of a compos'd order . . . ouer which stood a continued Plinthe; whereon were aduanc't Statues of siluer: Aboue this, was placed a bastarde Order of Architecture, wherein were keru'd Compartements: In one of which was written in great golde Capitoles, HONORIS FANVM. Aboue all, was a Coupolo, or Type, which seem'd to be scal'd with siluer Plates. . . . For finishing, of all, vpon a Pedistall, was fixt a round stone of siluer, from which grew a paire of golden wings; both faign'd to bee Fortunes: the round stone (when her feet trod it) euer affirm'd to be rouling; figuring her inconstancy: the golden wings, denoting those nimble Powers, that pompously beare her about the world; On that Temple (erected to her daughter, *Honor;* and figuring this kingdome) put off by her, and fixt, for assured signe she would neuer forsake it. . . . On the other side of the Rocke, grewe a Groue, in whose vtmost part appear'd a vast, wither'd, and hollow Tree, being the bare receptacle of the Baboonerie. . . . (Sig. a–av)

Thus the set was composed of three adjoining elements: the huge rock in the center, the Temple of Honor on a hill on one side, and the Grove with a fallen, hollow tree on the other. In the description the Temple is said to be "figuring this kingdome," i.e. Great Britain, which suggests that the other elements of the set do not do that. Since the "action" takes place directly in front of the temple (as is apparent from the dialogues and songs that follow), all the "heres" on the stage refer to England (as opposed to the "there" of the remaining two elements of the set). Moreover, the rock is said to have "arrived" here with the aid of some miraculous force. Capriccio claims that this was the motion of the earth that "hath brought one of the most remote parts of the world, to touch at this all-exceeding Iland" (B2v–B3). This is possible because Britain does not move with the rest of the world—it is the world that moves around Britain: "this Ile is (for the excellency of it) diuided from the world . . . and that though the whole world moues; yet this Ile stands fixt on her feete, and defies the Worldes mutability, which this rare accident of the arriuall of Riches [Plutus] . . . most demonstratiuely proues" (B3). The rock is also an island, and—like Britain—is inhabited. "With this dull Deity Riches," Capriccio says, "a rich Iland lying in the South-sea, called Poeana . . . is by earths round motion mou'd neere this Britan Shore. In which Island (beeing yet in command of the Virginian continent) A troupe of the noblest Virginians inhabiting; attended hether the God of Riches. . . . For hearing of the most royal solemnity, of these sacred Nuptialls; they crost the Ocean in their honor, and are here arriu'd" (B3r–v).

Thus Chapman presents a detailed "geography" of the stage

set: the hill and the temple are located on the British soil, whereas the rock is in fact another island, Poeana, off the coast of Virginia, and is still governed by the Virginians. Poeana crossed the ocean and "touched" with the British shore. This implies that what the audience sees on stage is Poeana "anchored" somewhere along the British coastline. It is also the island of riches and gold, being one of the dominions of Plutus, the god of riches. Even if Capriccio's words are not entirely trustworthy, they are confirmed on several occasions by Plutus himself, as when he says about Capriccio: "This is a man of wit indeede, and knows of all our arriuals" (B3). The Virginians go to the trouble to make the distant journey in order to take part in the celebrations of the royal wedding. This is predominantly the matter of honor. As the goddess herself later claims, she was responsible for bringing the Virginians to this "most famed Ile" (D2).

The grove with a fallen tree, in turn, is not a part of Poeana, for it is inhabited by Capriccio's companions, the baboons, whom he has brought along to present an antimasque. Plutus does not know them at all, for he asks Capriccio where they "abide," which means that they cannot possibly be inhabitants of any of his dominions. Thus the grove and the tree may be a part of Britain as well, although they are symbolically located opposite the Temple of Honor. What is, however, most relevant to this discussion is the fact that if one takes into account only the description of the performance at court, the Temple of Honor to a certain degree will appear as located "somewhere in Britain," presumably on the British shore (since it adjoins the anchored island of the Virginians). The extant text devoted to the performance at court is not specific about the temple's location. It may be argued, of course, that the temple is directly linked with the court (direct access is possible both ways), but this feature does not distinguish the temple from the rock: the masquers also descend from the latter and dance on the court floor. Similarly, the baboons enter the court directly from the grove. In this sense, the temple, the grove, and the rock are in exactly the same physical and functional relation to the court. Moreover, unobstructed communication is possible between the four locations—the temple, the grove, the rock, and the court hall—as if distances disappeared owing to the miraculous power of the magical box of the stage. However, from the description of the performance at court, taken in isolation, it appears that the existence of the court sphere is not essential for anyone to enter the Temple of Honor, nor to make direct communication with Honor, Eunomia, and Fama. If the "court" part of the printed masque is considered an independent text, the Temple of Honor would appear to be located somewhere outside the court, most likely somewhere along the British shore. In other words, the stage set does not have to be treated allegorically: it may just as well represent a mimetic landscape ("somewhere along the British shore").

This conclusion changes entirely if one treats the printed text as an inseparable whole. To begin, this second approach explains the puzzling comment made by Plutus early in the masque: when Plutus tells Capriccio about his love for Honor, he mentions that "the sweetnesse of whose voice, when I first heard her perswasions, both to my self, and the *Virginian* Princes arriu'd here, to doe honor and homage, to these heauenly Nuptialls, so most powerfully enamour'd mee, that the fire of my loue flew vp to the sight of mine eyes: that haue lighted within mee a whole firmament of bounty . . ." (C3v–C4). It seems, then, that both Plutus and the Virginian princes had met and conversed with the goddess of Honor before the court performance began, implying some preperformance action that is not further explained or alluded to and makes the reader or spectator think that he or she missed something. However, taking the "description of their whole show" into account reveals that Honor, Plutus, and the Virginian princes rode together in a chariot from Sir Edward Phelips's house in Chancery Lane to the Whitehall.[40] The description, quoted at length above, proves that this was a lavish show in which hundreds of people took part. It seems symbolical that both Sir Edward's house and the Inns of Court were located between the city and Whitehall, for this particular masque was sponsored, prepared, and staged by two Inns of Court and Chapman dedicated his printed text to Sir Edward Phelips, the Master of the Rolls, and to the Inns of Court.

In the masque, Plutus, the god of riches, is allowed to enter the court/Temple of Honor only because he has undergone a transformation: owing to the miraculous power of his love for Honor, he has regained sight and wisdom. As Chapman himself put it in "The aplicable argument of *the Maske*," "*Plutus,* (or Riches) being by *Aristophanes, Lucian &c.* presented naturally blind, deformed, and dull witted; is here by his loue of Honor, made see, made sightly, made ingenious; made liberall" (A4). When approached by Plutus, Eunomia (or Law) decides that he can join in a union with Honor. Similar, by analogy, is the function of James's legal institutions (represented here by the Inns of Court) that guard the court from intruders like Capriccio and his baboons; these are fit for the antimasque only.

A parallel union of riches and honor is that of London and James's court. This insight, again, is apparent only when one takes the whole text into account. In his dedication to Sir Edward Phelips, Chapman says that the masque "renewed" the ancient spirit and honor of the Inns of Court. He praises Sir Edward for his "most laborious and honored endeuors (for his Maiesties seruice; and honour of the all-grace-deseruing Nuptialls . . .)," and states directly that in the Master of the Rolls "Honor, hauing neuer her faire hand more freely and nobly giuen to Riches (being a fit particle of this Inuention) then by yours [hand], at this Nuptiall solemnity. . . ." It is therefore significant that the procession passes through both London and the court in order to reach the Temple of Honor.

Equally important here is the fact that the progress to the court, as described by Chapman, is reminiscent of welcoming celebrations of foreign envoys or ambassadors. The Virginian princes and Plutus are given a ceremonious welcome as if they were real princes, as if they had actually arrived from abroad. They are met by the "representative" of Britain, Honor, in the house of the guardian of the law, the Master of the Rolls, and taken to the court by the gentlemen of the Inns of Court. Not only were all of the gentlemen dressed up for the occasion, but some of them wore "costumes," which stresses the theatrical character of the progress. The two marshals, for instance, leaders of the guard of two hundred halberdiers, were said to have been "Commaunder-like attir'd." The costumes of the Virginians and the deities, of course, deepened the sense of theatricality of this show.[41]

So this was the time when the princes and Plutus had a chance to converse with Honor and when Plutus fell in love with her and regained his sight, wisdom, and bounty. Overwhelmed by his passion, Plutus decides—as is apparent from the remainder of the text—to join in a union with Honor, a state that is apparently possible to achieve only in her temple. Thus, passing through London is not only the way to the nuptials that the princes came to honor, but it is also a road to the Temple of Honor. The latter is located, quite appropriately, at James's court, a feature that is obvious only when the progress is treated as an inseparable part of the whole show. The text, in fact, identifies the court with the temple. Whitehall is the Temple of Honor and one cannot enter a communal union with Honor outside the court (as is the case with the Knights of the Garter, who cannot be created outside the court[42]). Thus the journey to the court is a significant element of the text's meaning, and there is no reason to neglect it as irrelevant to a literary analysis.

Moreover, the Temple of Honor may be associated with the traditional concept of the Temple of Knighthood. This identification was common in the Renaissance in general and very frequent in England in particular (being the seat of the Order of the Garter), as was acknowledged by many writers. For instance, Elias Ashmole, author of *The Institutions, Laws & Ceremonies of the Most Noble Order of the Garter*,[43] in his introductory chapter on the nature of knighthood discusses the traditional value of Virtue and Honour:

> The *Romans* had so great an esteem of *Honor* and *Vertue*, that they deified them, and dedicated *Temples* to their Worship. . . . In [its] structure, the Temple of *Vertue* was contiguous to that of *Honor*, and so situated that there was no other passage thereunto, but through the Temple of *Vertue*; thereby mystically shewing and admonishing, That *Honor* was not to be attained by any other ways thou by *Vertue*; That *Vertue* was as the Guardian of *Honor*; and those that undertook any notable Action, unless they carried themselves valiantly, and squared their actions by the Rúle of *Vertue*, could make no entrance into future Honor.[44]

This is exactly what Plutus says in the masque, when he asks Eunomia to admit him inside the Temple of Honor, so that he could "ioine with Honor":

> And since to Honor none should dare accesse,
> But helpt by vertues hand (thy selfe, chaste *Loue*
> Being *Vertues* Rule, and her directfull light)
> Help me to th'honor of her speech and sight

Thus it is only through Virtue that entrance to the court/temple is possible. The inner structure of the masque world parallels that belonging to the Roman tradition. In this way James's court continues ancient tradition, and in Chapman's "aplicable argument of *the Maske*" we read that "Honour, is so much respected . . . that shee hath a Temple erected to her, like a Goddesse; a Virgine Priest consecrated to her (which is Eunomia, or Lawe; since none should dare accesse to Honor, but by Vertue; of which Lawe being the rule, must needes be a chiefe) and a Herrald (call'd Phemis, or Fame . . ." (A4). It is also important that Eunomia is introduced in the masque as a "Daughter of Ioue" (Dv), which stresses Law's divine origin.[45] Access to the Temple of Honor is possible only through another temple, that of Knighthood, since it is James's court. In this way the world of the masque becomes a model of the Jacobean world: not as it was, but as it was created in the Stuart ideology.

The text, then, makes the following parallel: access to the Temple of Honor is possible only through Eunomia's or Law's rule as to whether a given person is virtuous enough; similarly, James's court, being the Temple of Virtue or Knighthood in its own right, is guarded by legal institutions that prevent the unvirtuous from entering the court. Capriccio and his baboons cannot possibly have access to honor; neither would have Plutus, had he not fallen in love with the goddess. But who is this Capriccio, anyway? He is an emblematic character who also appears in Henry Peacham's *Minerva Britanna:*

> A Youth arraid, in sundry cullors light
> And painted plumes that overspred his crest
> . . . .
> His right hand holdes, the bellowes to his eare,
> His left, the quick, and speedie spurre doth beare.
>
> Such is Capriccio, or th'vnstaied mind,
> Whome thousand fancies howerly do possesse,
> For riding post, with every blast of wind,
> Is nought hee's steddie, save vnstablenes.
>
> (P. 149)

In Chapman, the appearance of Capriccio is described as "a Rock, Mooving and breaking with a cracke about Capriccio, he enters with a paire of Bellows on his head, a spur in one hand, and a piece of golde Ore in the other . . ." (B2). D. J. Gordon wrote that Capriccio "stands for unprincipled wit . . . working at the service of the highest bidder: the bellows . . . here show that Capriccio can puff up with glory all who affect him. . . . To pay for the services of such a creature is to buy—the wrong use of wealth—false honour. . . ."[46] This description is confirmed by Capriccio himself, who explains to Plutus that he wears "these Bellowes on [his] head, to shew I can puff vp with glory all those that affect mee: and besides, beare this spurre, to shew I can spur-gall, euen the best that contemne me" (C2).

As pointed out by Gordon, the evil correlative of honor is ambition, or the "desire to move beyond one's proper place, to threaten the subversion of that order which is the fabric of society and the universe."[47] The function of honor is precisely to maintain this order. Consequently, argues Gordon, "the expression of this fundamental order is law. Honour therefore must come within the rule of Law."[48] Plutus can enter the union with Honor only after his transformation, only after among other things he gains bounty. To again quote D. J. Gordon: "[Chapman] also shows the reconciliation of Plutus or Wealth with Virtue or Honour. Behind this, I suspect, lie traces of the old dispute about true nobility, and a part played in it by wealth . . . [for] the true use of wealth was . . . an element of nobility: this was the virtue of liberality. . . . Liberality was an important kingly virtue—as James himself had emphasized in his *Basilikon Doron*."[49]

The union of Riches with Honor, however, is only one of many unions in the masque.[50] Marriage is a union of two people, but it is only a pretext to talk about other unions that constitute the nature of this universe. Examples are the union of humanity and true religion, through which the union of heaven and earth is achieved; the union of kingship and loyalty, of knighthood and virtue; the union of the elements that leads to individual, social, and political harmony; and so on. All of these unions have to be taken into account when discussing this immensely complex text. Through a seemingly trivial "plot" the poet presents a vision of the nature of the universe. It should not surprise us, then, that Ben Jonson claimed that apart from himself, only Chapman could write masques.

The importance of the location of the masque has already been discussed above. One should realize, however, that the Great Britain of the masque is equipped with peculiar qualities that make this country distinct from all others. First, some of the physical laws that govern the created (and the empirical, as a matter of fact) world do not apply to Britain. They simply do not operate there. Characteristic is the way in which Britain is presented as immune to the rotation of the earth (also indicated above). Another curious feature of the world of Britain is that it is equipped with its own sun.

Actually there are at least two suns appearing in the masque. Early in the text the Virginian priests are mentioned "by whom the Sun is there ador'd" (Av). They accompany the princes, and—as Honor says—have crossed the ocean (significantly called the "Britan Ocean")

> To this most famed Ile, of all the world,
> To do due homage to the sacred Nuptials

Masque Cycle I

> Of Law, and Vertue, celebrated here,
> By this Howre of the holy Eeuen I know,
> Are ready to perform the rites they owe.
>
> (D2)

There is no doubt that the Virginians are devout worshippers of the sun. Phoebades is their chief priest of the sun, and he comes out and sings "(shewing the custome of the Indians to adore the Sunne setting)." In the song the following wish is expressed:

> Kisse Heauen and Earth, and so combine
> In all mixt ioy our Nuptiall Twine.
>
> (D2v)

After the song the "mount opened, and spred like a Skie" and masquers are discovered in a mine of gold. However, when Honor hears the Virginians' song, she (and her opinions are for obvious reasons authoritative) speaks against them:

> This *superstitious* Hymne, sung to the Sunne,
> Let vs encounter with fit duties done
> To our cleere Phoebus; whose true piety,
> Enioyes from heaven an earthly deity.
>
> (Emphasis added)

Thus Phoebus is the mythological sun that shines over Britain. He, and not any other sun, should be worshipped in accordance with true religion. As noted by Gordon, "the image of the king (and James in particular) as sun is too common to require further illustration, but James is also, here, explicitly, sun-as-God."[51] This "earthly deity," mentioned by Honor, is a direct allusion to James's *Basilikon Doron*, where his theory of the divine right of kings is expounded and where he literally calls kings "little gods" on earth.

In response to Honor's words, songs in praise of Phoebus follow. These are preceded by the following "stage-direction," which leaves no doubt that Phoebus is in fact equaled with James: "Other Musique, and voyces; and this second Stance was sung, directing their obseruance to the King" (D3v). Later songs develop the theme.

> *Rise, rise O Phoebus, euer rise,*
> *descend not to th'inconstant streame,*
> *But grace with endles light, our skyes,*
> *to thee that Sun is but a beame.*
>
> (D3v)

The Chorus adds,

> *O may our Sun not set before,*
> *he sees his endles seed arise:*
> *And deck his triple crowned shore,*
> *with springs of humane Deities.*

(D3v)

The message of these direct appeals to the monarch is clear: King James/British sun should not die/set before he sees his "endles seed arise" (heirs),—that is, not before Great Britain ("triple crowned shore") sees the royal line secured with "humane deities." In poetic terms, the setting (hence temporary) sun of the Virginians is contrasted with the everlasting rise of the sun of Britain. The priests of the first sun pray for the sunset:

> *Set, set (great Sun) our rising loue*
> *shall euer celebrate thy grace:*
> *Whom entring the high court of loue,*
> *each God greetes rising from his place.*

(D4)

The followers of the other sun (of James) sing a song that in its form is similar to a religious prayer:

> *Rise stil (cleare Sun) and neuer set,*
> *but be to Earth her only light:*
> *All other Kings in thy beames met*
> *are cloudes and darke effects of night.*

(D4)

The brightness of the British sun is contrasted with the lesser brightness of the astronomical sun (see also the passage, quoted above, in which the sun is said to be "but a beame" when compared with the British Phoebus), and a parallel contrast is that between James and other kings. In this "prayer" a wish is expressed that Phoebus/James would be the only light for the whole earth.

In the next stanza James is praised, as was the Jacobean habit, for his wisdom, and is called the "learned king."[52] He is to play a vital role in the future of the world.

> [Chorus] *Blest was thy Mother, bearing Thee,*
> *Thee only Relick of her race,*

> *Made by thy vertues beames a Tree,*
> *Whose armes shall all the Earth embrace.*
>
> (D4v)

These words leave no doubt about the ramifications of James's reign: he is to be earth's "only light," superior to all other kings. The tree of James's virtue is expected to embrace all of the earth.[53] At this point the masquers are identified with the Virginian princes and are asked to renounce

> Your superstitious worship of these sunnes,
> Subiect to cloudy darknings and descents,
> And of your sweet deuotions, turne the euents
> To this our Britan *Phoebus,* whose bright skie
> (Enlightned with a Christian Piety)
> Is neuer subiect to black Errors night,
> And hath already offer'd heauens true light,
> To your dark Region, which acknowledge now;
> Descend, and to him all your homage vow.
>
> (D4v)

The religious tone of the demand is unambiguous, and what the Virginians are asked to do may be expressed in religious terms: they are to renounce the worship of their "false" sun and worship the British Phoebus, the Christian god, offering to all willing "heauens true light." Note that Chapman surprisingly uses the plural form "Sunnes" in the quoted passage, but since there is a clear identification of the true sun with King James, the "sunnes" may stand for other monarchs who do not equal James in his virtue and wisdom. What is more important, they do not have the "true light" of heaven to offer, as James does. Naturally, the "sunnes" also stand for false religions, which contrast with James's true "Christian Piety." Recall at this point that in de Franchis's poem, discussed above, the marriage of Elizabeth and Frederick was said to bring all sorts of changes to humanity; among other things "Vaine Superstition" turns to "Piety," "darkness" to "light," and "Pluto" is transformed to "Ioues deity" (2.80). As indicated above, this will also bring peace to all people, the golden age.

All this evokes a strong biblical echo of Isaiah 60:

18. [When the days of glory come] Violence shall no more be heard in thy land, wasting nor destruction within thy borders. . . .

19. The Sunne shall be no more thy light by day, neither for brightnesse shall the moone guie light vnto thee: but the LORD shall be vnto thee an euerlasting light, & thy God thy glory.
20. Thy Sunne shall no more goe downe, neither shall thy moone withdraw itself: for the LORD shall bee thine euerlasting light, and the dayes of thy mourning shall be ended. [Authorized Version of 1611]

The masquers descend obediently and pay homage through their dances. Thus they are an example for other nations, ruled by minor kings and worshipping false suns, to follow. In the masque Honor is presented as the daughter of Fortune, and she is adored in a temple erected for her. This temple stands for Great Britain, which by analogy makes King James the high priest of the temple (quite appropriately for the head of the Church of England). Another feature that makes Britain unique among nations is the fact that she does not physically move with the rest of the world: it is other countries that orbit around her, like planets around the sun. Thus the function of Britain is similar to that of the astronomical sun: she spreads light, being—symbolically—the source of sight, wisdom, true religion, life, and salvation. Of course, it is not only Britain that is presented as the sun among other countries. King James is the sun among other monarchs. It is only through the true love of virtues that Britain/James represents that those goals can be achieved. Plutus is not the only example of a positive transformation (conversion) in the masque: he is followed by the Virginian princes. The implication is that Britain can transform this world and bring it closer to heaven. The goal is the ideal union of heaven and earth: Elizabeth's and Frederick's marriage is an example of this happening. The latter event is also, of course, an element of the recurrent motif of the union of riches and honor, an analogy that is made early in the text:

> Ope, Earth, thy womb of gold,
> Show, Heaven, thy cope of stars.
> All grand aspects unfold,
> Shine out and clear our cares;
> Kiss, Heaven and Earth, and so combine
> In all mix'd joy our nuptial twine.
>
> (D2v)

The fact that the Inns of Court represent the legal order of the realm, guarding the court in the same way that Eunomia guards

Masque Cycle I

the Temple of Honor, has already been discussed above. Equally important, however, is the fact that the Houses and the Gentlemen (not to mention their "assistants") represent London. The Virginians are welcomed in London and pass through it in their progress. One enters the court through London, and no other access is available (at least not in the world of the masque). On yet another level, as critics of the masque have noticed, the appearance of the Virginians in Britain suggests both the wealth of the newfound lands (to be exploited by the British) and the union of the Old World and the New under James I.[54] In this "marriage," as Jack E. Reese put it, "Plutus who is depicted as the guardian of the Virginian gold mines, represents the riches of the New World, and Honour the dignity of the Old, that is, the English court under James."[55] This is also a variant of the motif of the marriage of heaven (the world of values of James's court) and earth and its riches (Virginia).

The next and the most obvious union referred to in the masque is the marriage of Elizabeth and Frederick, who are mentioned directly in sig. D3v. King James is described as the "only Relick" of yet another union—that of his parents. Particular importance, it seems, is attached here to James's mother (his father is not mentioned at all), who is twice described as "Blest" in giving birth to James. The king in turn is compared to the Tree of Virtue, and through the image of the tree's branches embracing the world, he is united with the whole earth: "Made by thy vertues beames a Tree, / Whose armes shall all the earth embrace" (D4v). Once again earth joins with divinity. The nuptials are then compared to the union of Love and Beauty, who are presented as twins. In a song in their praise, the origin of love and beauty is given:

> Bright Panthaea [?], daughter to Pan[56]
> Of the Noblest Race of Man,
> Her white to Eros giuing
> With a kiss joined Heauen to Earth
>
> (Ev)

To the union of Love and Beauty, other elements were added: Virtue, Bounty, and Innocence, and so "the golden world was made" (E2). The latter is directly identified with the time of the nuptials:

> Now may the blessings of the golden age,
> Swimme in these Nuptials.
>
> (E2)

And last, "our Nuptiall paire" is ordered not to be disturbed, and

> Now close the world-round sphere of blisse,
> And fill it with a heauenly kisse.

Thus this union is also a joining of the "world" and heaven. By becoming a mother Elizabeth will undoubtedly be "blessed," like her grandmother. Their union marks the beginning of the golden age. Frederick and Elizabeth are further identified with Love and Beauty in the final speech of Plutus:

> Come Virgine Knights, the homage ye haue done,
> To Loue and Beauty, and our Britan Sun,
> Kind Honor, will requite with holy feasts
> In her faire Temple.
>
> (E2v)

And the union of Honor and Riches (Plutus) is said to be eternal. They enter the temple, leaving the young ones to their "ioys," so that

> . . . may Heaven & Earth as highly please
> As those two nights that got great *Hercules.*
>
> (E3)

To conclude, Chapman's *Memorable Masque* conspicuously focuses on a single element—earth. Plutus, the god of riches, lives underground. The golden mines, representing of course the riches of the earth, are both presented and talked about on stage. Earth is also one of the elements, along with water, fire, and air. It is an important constructive element of this world, and general harmony depends on the union of the four elements. This applies to the microcosm of man and macrocosm of the universe. Earth and its riches play an important function in the created world of the masque, for Plutus gains sight and wisdom and enters into a union with Honor. As he himself proclaims, this moves him to "humanity, and bounty" (C3v). The inhabitants of the planet Earth, if they join with virtue and honor, may also reach a union with heaven. As an element, earth is an important factor and a constructive element that constitutes man's humors, influences his life, and eventually determines his salvation; as a planet, in her geocosm earth contributes to the macrocosmic union with heaven. As seen from this point of view, it is perhaps significant

Masque Cycle I

that the masquers arrive at court by land, thus marking yet another echo of that union.

The third masque in the cycle was by Francis Beaumont and entitled *The Maske of the Gentlemen of Grayes-Inne, and the Inner Temple, Performed before the King in the Banqueting-house at Whitehall, at the marriage of the Illustrious Frederick and Elizabeth, Prince and Princesse Palatine of the Rhene.*[57] Like Chapman's, this masque is also composed of two major parts: the progress by water and the performance at court. The first part did in fact take place on Tuesday night, but the second one was postponed and eventually presented on the following Saturday. Only in print do both parts appear together.

Also, since the first part of Beaumont's masque is a description of the progress from London to court, constituting an important and significant element of the whole text, it cannot be omitted from critical scrutiny.

Beaumont's description says that

> . . . the Maskers with their attendants and diuers other gallant young Gentlemen of both houses [the Inns of Court], as their conuoy, set forth from Winchester house which was the *Rende vous* towards the Court, about seuen of the clock at night.
>
> This voyage by water was performed in great Triumph. The Gentlemen Maskers being placed by themselues in the Kings royall barge with the rich furniture of state, and adorned with a great number of lights placed in such order as might make best show.
>
> They were attended with a multitude of barges and gallies, with all variety of lowde Musicke. . . . (A3r–v)

As was the case with the previous occasion, the king, his family, and the highest nobles watched the progress. This time, however, this was done by water. The latter fact is not a mere coincidence, for water is the element that the masque focuses on. "Of this show," Beaumont writes, "his Maiesty was gratiously pleased to take view, with the Prince, the Count *Palatine,* and the Lady *Elizabeth,*—their highnesses at the windowes of his priuy gallerie vpon the water, till their landing, which was at the priuy staires: where they were most honorablie receiued by the Lord Chamberlain, and so conducted to the Vestry . . ." (A3v). Again, the theatricality of the procession is quite obvious, with Francis Bacon (to whom the printed text is dedicated) "officially" greeting the masquers as if they were "real" guests of honor.

158   THE MASQUE OF STUART CULTURE

The description of the first part is followed by an "Epistle" to Bacon and to the two Inns of Court. In this, Sir Francis is made responsible for the invention. John Chamberlain confirms this fact:

> On Tewsday yt came to Grayes Ynne and the Inner Temples turne to come with theyre maske, whereof Sir Fra: Bacon was the cheife contriver, and because the former came on horse backe, and open chariots, they made choise to come by water from Winchester Place in Southwark: which suted well enough with theyre devise, which was the mariage of the river Thames to the Rhine.[58]

Next comes the "Devise of Argument," which is worth quoting extensively:

> Ivpiter and Juno willing to doe honour to the Mariage of the two famous Riuers *Thamesis* and *Rhene,* imploy their messengers seuerally, *Mercurie* and *Iris* for that purpose. They meete and contend: then *Mercurie* for his part brings forth an Anti-masque of all Spirits or diuine Natures. . . . He raiseth foure of the *Naiades* out of the Fountaines, and bringeth downe fiue of the *Hyades* out of the Cloudes to daunce;[59] hereupon *Iris* scoffes at *Mercurie* for that he had deuised a daunce but of one Sexe, which would haue no life: but *Mercurie* . . . in token that the Match should be blessed both with Loue and Riches[60] calleth forth out of the Groues four *Cupids,* and brings downe from *Jupiters* Altar four *Statuaes* of gold and siluer to daunce with the Nymphs and Starres: in which daunce the *Cupids* being blinde, and the *Statueaes* hauing but halfe life put into them . . . giueth fit occasion to new and strange varieties both in the Musicke and paces. This was the first Anti-masque.
>   Then *Iris* for her part in scorne of this high flying deuise, and in token that the Match shall likewise be blessed with the loue of the Common People, calls to *Flora* her confederate . . . to bring in a May-daunce or Rurall daunce consisting . . . of a confusion, or commixture of all such persons as are naturall and proper for Countrey sports. This is the second Anti-masque.
>   Then *Mercurie* and *Iris* after this vying one vpon the other, seeme to leaue their contention: and *Mercurie* by the consent of *Iris* brings downe the *Olympian* Knights, intimating the *Iupiter* hauing after a long continuance reuiued the *Olympian* games, and summoned thereunto from all parts the liueliest, & actiuest persons that were. . . . The *Olympian* games portend to the Match, Celebritie, Victorie, and Felicitie. This was the main Masque. (B2–3)

As early as in the title of the masque, quoted in full above, Beaumont identifies Prince Frederick with the Rhine. He is, after all, the duke of the Rhenish Palatinate. It is not difficult to associate the English princess with the Thames. Quite appropriately, the marriage of the young is presented as an allegorical marriage of the two rivers. Moreover, the masquers and the accompanying persons arrive at Whitehall by the Thames, for water is the element on which the masque focuses, just as *The Lords Masque* focused on fire, and *The Memorable Masque* focused on earth. Having this in mind, the opening stage design appears significant: it is, indeed, "full of water":

> The Fabrick was a Mountaine with two descents, and seuered with two Trauerses. At the entrance of the King the first Trauers was drawne, and the lower descent of the Mountaine discouered; which was the Pendant of a hill to life, with diuers boscages and Grouets vpon the Steepe or hanging grounds thereof, and at the foote of the Hill, foure delicate Fountaines running with water and bordered with sedges and water flowers." (B3r–v)

Iris tells Mercury, who was sent by Juno

> To celebrate the long wisht Nuptials,
> Heere in *Olympia*, which are now perform'd
> Betwixt two goodly Riuers, which haue mixt
> Their gentle rising waues, and are to grow
> Into a thousand streames . . .
>   and I am sent from her
> The Queene of Mariage, that was present heere,
> And smil'd to see them ioyne.
>
> (B4)

Thus, the "long wisht" marriage of the two rivers and the nuptials that follow take place in Olympia (a mythological location). This is the "here" of the masque world. As usual in masques, the entrance of the king signals the show to begin, and since the king's presence is a significant part of the text (and the performance text, of course) the "here" of the masque is identified with the "here" of the Banqueting House, or the court. In a way the court is transformed into an allegorical Olympia that includes all current events, the marriage, and the wedding celebrations. So, when Iris tells Mercury that the Queen of Marriage was present "here" during the marriage ceremony, she incorporates the latter into the masque world. It also enables us to set the masque in time: it takes place after the marriage ceremony.

Iris asks Mercury about Jove's interest in this particular marriage, which has led him to interfere with Juno's own domain. Mercury explains

> That when enamor'd *Ioue* first gaue her [Juno] power
> To link soft hearts . . .
> He then forsaw, and to himself reseru'd
> The honor of this Marriage.
>
> (B4v)

What makes this union exceptional, then, is the fact that it is the only one reserved by Jove for himself to "sponsor." The poetic concept, of course, is highly reminiscent of de Franchis's poem, discussed above, which is also strengthened by the appearance of a number of the same characters in both works.

To "bless" this feast Mercury summons "the Nymphs of the fountains," who dance and are soon joined by five "Hyads," who "descend softly in a cloud from the firmament" (Cv). Because Iris does not like this "liuelesse dance," Mercury summons four cupids and also four gold and silver "Statuaes" directly from Jupiter's altar. They all dance together in the first antimasque. The nymphs (called also "Naiades") and the Hyades represent springs and rain clouds, the source of water for rivers. (How appropriate it is that the Hyads descend on a cloud!) They dance with cupids (or love) and the statues from Jove's altar, and the dance itself becomes an allegory of the princely marriage.

As part of the competition, Iris calls Flora to rush in a "Rurall company," and the May Dance follows, as indicated in the "Argument of the Masque," quoted above. The dancers are rustic types like a servingman, country clown, chambermaid, country wench, and so on, all familiar characters to an early seventeenth-century audience. Note that in de Franchis's poem, as part of celebrations following the fall of the infernal dragon, the poet foresees

> Crafts-men leaue work, May-games in euery towne
> Let Courtiers act some amorous Comedie,
> With Iigs at end on't, to the Plow-iaggs by.
>
> (3.84)

The May Dance constitutes the second antimasque. The main one follows, and Mercury brings Jove's message:

> . . . the Olympian games
> Which long haue slept, at these wish'd Nuptials,
> He pleas'd to haue renew'd, and all his Knights

Masque Cycle I

> Are gathered hither, who within their tents
> Rest on this hill, vpon whose rising head
> Behold *Ioues* Altar, and his blessed Priests
> Mouing about it . . .
>
> (C4r–v)

Thus the theme of knighthood is again evoked and continues the motif of Frederick—Saint George/Whitehall, the Temple of Knighthood, and the like. The marriage becomes an important moment for chivalry, for it is honored by Jove with the renewal of an ancient knightly tradition, the Olympian games. The link of the games with the actual tilt on Monday following the marriage is deepened by de Franchis's description of it in which he calls it an "Olympian game." The poem reads:

> Now *Mars* withall to please his *Cyprian* Dame,
> Next day prepares a chiefe *Olympian* game.
> A stately place within the Court is built,
> Smooth as a die, round, emptie, spatious,
> Prepar'd for Martiall Knights to run at tilt,
> And try in arms who was most valorous:
> > In gathering armour euery Gallant's bent,
> > To try his warlike force at Tournament.
>
> (3.133–34)

The main masque begins with a change of scene:

> The second Trauers is drawne, and the higher ascent of the Mountaine is discouered, wherein vpon a leuell after a great rise of the Hill, were placed two Pauilions[61] . . . and behind the Tents there were represented in prospectiue, the tops of diuers other Tents, as if it had been a Campe. In these Pauilions were placed fifteen *Olympian* Knights . . . and the Knights appeared first, as consecrated persons all in vailes . . . in the midst betweene both the Tents vpon the very top of the hill, being higher leuell then that of the Tents, was placed *Jupiters* Altar gilt, with three great Tapers vpon golden Candlesticks burning vpon it: and the foure *Statuaes,* two of gold, and two of siluer, as supporters, and *Jupiters* Priests in white robes about it. (D)

Again the king's presence is stressed, for "Vpon the sight of the King, the vailes of the Knights did fall easilie from them, and they appeared in their owne habit" (D). Although one would expect to see Jupiter (or at least his statue) on stage, he is not there. The king's powers, however, are equally divine. It is his very presence that makes the veils drop off the knights. Small wonder, for he is the Jupiter of the masque (where the statue of the god seems to be "missing"), and it is his altar presented on stage, with the three burning tapers standing for the three parts of Great Britain. Jupiter's priests descend and sing a song addressed to the knights, who follow and lay aside their weapons.

These are no ordinary dances, for

> . . . at the wedding such a paire,
> Each dance is taken for a praier,
> Each song is sacrifice.
>
> (D2)

In the third song the knights are asked to dance with the "Nymphs," which they do. After the dances they "leade them to their places. Then loude Musicke sounds, supposed to call them to their *Olympian* games" (D2v).

It is impossible, however, to stop time—as the penultimate song says and

> The Knights daunce their parting Measure and ascend, put on their Swords and Belts, during which time the Priests sing the fifth and last Song
>
> > Peace and silence be the guide
> > To the Man, and to the Bride
> > . . . .
> > If we should stay, we should doe worse,
> > And turne our blessing to a curse,
> > By keeping you asunder.
> >
> > (D3)

With these words the masque ends and the masquers leave for their games. What is missing is the actual tilt at court that would in a way have been an "extension" of the masque world. This event, however, had taken place on the previous day, which makes the parallel between the masque world and the court even more obvious. A contemporary description reveals that on Monday

> the King's Majestie in his owne person, accompanied with his brave-spirited Sonne, Prince Charles of Great Brittaine, the Royall Bride-groom Count Pallatine, the Duke of Lineux, with divers other of the Earles and Barrons of Scotland, together with the praise-worthy Peeers of the Netherland Provinces, performed many famous races at the Ring, an exercise of much renowne and honour and the Knightly

sports and the Royall delights onely befitting the dignity of Kings and Princes, and of the chiefest Nobility.[62]

Witnessed by a multitude of spectators, one may assume that all those who were present at the performance of the masque had actually seen the tilt. The same description says that "The Queen's Majestie, with her daughter the Princess Elizabeth, attended on by many of the greatest Ladies of the land, being placed in the galleries and windowes of the Banquetting-house, in the presence of many thousand of his [James's] subjects, the King mounted upon a steed of much swiftnes, was the first who began the honourable pastimes."[63] This sporting event, however, is not the end of the direct fusion of the two worlds of the masque and James's court, for the king enjoyed the masque so much that he invited the masquers and their attendants (some forty people) to a banquet. "The masque of the Gray's Inn and Inner Templars came off very well," Chamberlain writes, "and the masquers were entertained by the King, but at the cost of the Prince and his followers, who laid wager for the charges of the feast, and lost it in running at the tilt."[64] In a different letter he refers to the same event: "The next night the King invited the maskers . . . to a solemne supper in the new mariage roome. . . . The King husbanded the matter so well that this feast was not at his owne cost, but he and his companie wan yt upon a wager of running at the ring of the Prince and his nine followers, who payed thirty pound a man. . . ."[65] Clearly part of the attraction of the renewed Olympian Games was gambling. The Olympian knights leave the stage to run at their tilt, in which it seems two parties competed. Naturally the Jupiter party won and the money was used to celebrate the event with the remaining actors. The boundaries between the fictitious world on stage and empirical reality are lost completely. James's court is the Mount Olympus of knighthood.[66]

In considering the three masques as one text, a cycle of a formal and thematic integrity, one notes that a common feature is that each focuses on a single element: the first one focuses on fire, the second on earth, and the third on water.

Of the numerous references to fire in Thomas Campion's *The Lords Masque*, let me recall only several that reveal the function of fire in the created world of the masque. Entheus, who is freed from Mania, is described by Orpheus as being equipped with a "celestial" talent (poetic talent), a spirit, as it is called, of "fiery" scope. When he feels inspiration he says, "I feel the fires / Are reddy in my braine which Jove inspires" (C2v). Entheus envisions Prometheus standing before the "lights" that he attempted to steal, so that the earth would be "enflamed" with "the affects of Love and honour'd Fame." Thus it was not merely the physical fire that Prometheus tried to bring to humanity, but a spiritual one as well. In this way the word *fire* and all related words acquire both a specific and a much broader meaning in the masque. Entheus then asks Prometheus to

>   bring thy golden theft,
> Bring, bright Prometheus, all thy lights,
>   Thy fires from Heav'n bereft
>   Shew now to human sights.
>
>   (C3)

Poetic inspiration is of divine origin, and it is the "heavenly" fire that initiates it. In this way the entire masque and the marriage itself is inspired by divinity. Prometheus is called the "patron of mankind,"

>   powerfull and bounteous,
>   Rich in thy flames, reverend Prometheus
>   . . . .
>   fill the lookers' eyes
>   With admiration of thy fire and light.

And when Prometheus's "dancing lights" approach, a song says,

>   This night concludes the Nuptiall vow,
>   Make this the best of nights,
>   So brauely crowne it with your beames,
>   That it may live in fame,
>   As long as Rhenus or the Thames
>   Are knowne by either name.

Thus it is the heavenly light that "crowns" the marriage and guarantees eternal fame. The source of this light is James himself.

This celestial "fire" plays another important function in the world of the masque; it is, literally, the source of life. One of the scenes displays statues with "a history" above them depicting a pictorial "story." The conceit was to show a new version of the mythological story. Prometheus first molds a clay figure of a woman, then steals the fire and puts life into the figure. An enraged Jupiter turns it into a statue. This heavenly fire/light has the power to put life into inanimate matter. Before it is done on a larger scale, earth is said to be (in the quotation above) "dull," or dead. So is humanity spiritually dead. But now, during this special night Jove shows exceptional bounty: he has not only forgiven Prometheus his sin, but asks him to bring the statues back to life, as expressed in the song:

> Divine Prometheus, Hymen's friend,
> Leade downe the new-transformed Fires,
> And fill their breasts with love's desires;
> That they may revell with delight,
> And celebrate this Nuptiall night!

Jove's wrath "relents" and life returns to the statues and "then for more." The marriage of Elizabeth and Frederick not only fulfills the ancient prophecy, but brings about Jove's mercy and a new life to all people who will be transformed by divine fire and light. In this way the marriage becomes a spiritual redemption for the world.

Even the masquers in Campion's text are made of fire, for they are metamorphosed stars. Their costumes are significant: "The ground of their attires was massie cloth of siluer, embossed with flames of embroidery; on their heads they had crownes, flames made of gold plate enameled, and on the top a feather of silke, representing a cloud of smoake" (C4).

George Chapman's *The Memorable Masque* focuses on the element earth, as has been shown in detail above. Let me briefly recall that Plutus, representing the riches of earth, enters into a union with Honor, and the masque produces a number of related unions. An honorable use of riches (bounty) is an important noble attribute of man and woman. A union with honor brings one closer to heaven, which is an act impossible to achieve without generosity and bounty. The masque plays on the meanings of the word *earth*; not only does it denote an element that brings harmony to the microcosm of humanity, but it also signifies the planet earth inhabited by people. The conversion of earth's nations to true religion (following the example of the Virginians) under Britain's and James's lead will bring universal harmony—a union of earth and heaven.

As indicated above, Francis Beaumont's *The Masque of the Inner Temple and Gray's Inn*, scheduled for the third night of the wedding and celebrating an allegorical marriage of the Thames and the

Rhine, focuses on yet another element—water. The scene opens with a view of running water fountains; the nymphs, who are celebrating the union of two rivers, are described as

> The Nymphes of Fountaines, from whose watry locks
> Hung with the dew of blessing and encrease,
> The greedy riuers take their nourishment.
>
> (B4v)

The fountains, of course, are located at the foot of the Mount Olympus, the mountain of the gods, and their water flows from this mountain. The allegorical marriage of the two rivers is analogous to the marriage of Elizabeth and Frederick and to other unions such as that involving knightly virtues. The latter is presented as a revival of the ancient tradition of the Olympian Games. It actually parallels the function of fire in the previous text; it is the marriage of Elizabeth and Frederick that makes the revival possible. The event marks a new era for humanity, for it gives an example of renewed knightly virtues. This again brings people closer to the most important of all unions—that with heaven.

The three masques are in fact about the union of elements. They could even be labeled

The Masque of Fire   (*The Lords Masque*)
The Masque of Earth   (*The Memorable Masque*)
The Masque of Water   (*The Masque of the Inner Temple and Gray's Inn*)

This common ground strongly suggests an overall integrated plan contrived by whoever commissioned the masques. However, one obvious text is missing: The Masque of Air. This omission would have impaired the validity of this interpretation had it not been for David Norbrook, who in a recent essay has provided what seems to have been "the missing link."[67] As noted by Norbrook, one of the many surviving pamphlets describing the festivities contains a strange anomaly; its fairly accurate account of the events provides a summary of a masque that was never presented. This pamphlet was published by D. Jocquet in French in Heidelberg in 1613 under the title *Les triomphes, entrees, cartels, tournois, ceremonies, et aultres Magnificences, faitesen Angleterre, & au Palatinat, pour le Mariage & Reception, de Monseigneur le Prince Frideric V. Comte Palatin du Rhin . . . Et de Madame Elisabeth.* The text gives a

Masque Cycle I

completely false account of events that took place on Tuesday. As we know, this was the night when Beaumont's masque was canceled. The Heidelberg summary, however, states that the masque was staged on that very night. Moreover, as Norbrook indicates, this violation of facts seems to have been done intentionally.[68]

To quote Norbrook's summary of the masque:

> The masque begins with a song by the Nine Muses, who sing the praises of King James. They are joined by Atlas who is weary with trying to hold up the world and has been guided by the muses to England, where their mistress Truth has chosen to live. He has given up his burden to Aletheia (Truth), who is represented on stage by a huge reclining statue reading a Bible and holding a globe in her left hand. The first three Muses, Urania, Clio and Terpsichore, call on the nations of Europe to pay tribute to King James for his patronage of the Truth. Part of the huge globe opens to reveal Europe and her five daughters, France, Spain, Germany, Italy and Greece, each of whom has three pages dressed in national costume; they are followed by the Ocean and his wife the Mediterranean with their vassals the chief rivers of Europe. After bowing to Aletheia they make their offerings to the royal couple. After an anti-masque of pages the princes of Europe appear and dance with the princesses. Atlas now calls on the next three Muses to summon Asia and her daughters, and again there are three main dances, first of the princesses, then of the pages, and then of the princes and princesses together. Finally, Africa and the princes and princesses of this least Christian continent pay tribute. Each dancer wears a national costume and dances in a national style. After the dances the nine Muses come together again and call on the princes and princesses of the world to abandon their old quarrels and imitate James in his zeal for the true religion. In a witty reference to the "device" of the masque Atlas thanks the nations for leaving the world: the weight of their sins was an intolerable burden to him. The masque ends with one more spectacular effect: the globe splits in two and disappears, leaving behind it a paradise guarded by an angel bearing a flaming sword, with a skull at his feet. Truth invites the queens and their followers to overcome their fear of death with repentance and faith and enter Paradise. Atlas and the Muses lead the nations into Paradise and the sword and skull vanish; then the gates of Paradise close behind them.[69]

This summary forms a perfect conclusion of my points about the three masques and entertainments occasioned by the marriage. Practically all the motifs developed in individual performances meet in this ostentatiously ideological piece. Led by the divine guidance of King James and England, all the world unites in conversion to true religion. As David Norbrook put it, "The wedding of Frederick and Elizabeth is viewed [in the last masque he calls *The Masque of Truth*] primarily not in dynastic terms, as the union of two royal houses, but in ideological terms as a confessional alliance. The Palatinate was the most militantly Calvinist of all European states, and the masque text regards this as the chief attraction of the marriage: James, guardian of the Calvinist church in England, will unite with the leaders of the Palatinate and all other states will follow their religious example."[70]

Bounty, honor, virtue, and love combined in a harmonious union mirror a perfect balance of the four elements that govern both man's micro- and his macrocosms. James's court is an example for others to follow, for it is there that the Temple of Honor is erected; it is there that mundane characters like Plutus can gain wisdom, sight, and bounty; it is there that true religion finds faithful worshippers; it is there that the love of the newlyweds appears in its purest and divine form; and it is there that the ancient tradition of chivalry is revived. To follow these examples means to enter into a broader harmony with nature, with the universe, and with God. The latter, of course, is the union with the fourth element—air. In its elaborate use of apocalyptic imagery, this last masque, as David Norbrook observed, reflects the growing belief in the coming of the Golden Age and of the Millennium.[71] Thus I suggest that *The Masque of Truth*, being the missing element in the cycle, is basically about the religious union of all nations and continents under the leadership of James and England. This union is essential for the apocalyptic union with God. In a theological sense this might be called the "masque of air," for the union with Christ is to take place "in the air," as prophesied in Paul's first epistle to the Thessalonians, chapter 4: "16. For the Lord himself shall descend from heauen with a shour, with the voyce of the Archangel, and with the trumpe of God: and the dead in Christ shall rise first. 17. Then we which are aliue, and remaine, shalbe caught up together with them in the clouds, to meet the Lord in the aire: and so shall wee euer bee with the Lord" (the Authorized Version, 1611).

Had this piece been performed, it would indeed have been one of the most elaborate masques ever presented with its spectacular changes of scenery and numerous actors in colorful costumes. The extant description leaves no doubt that a number of scenes were emblematic in character. For instance, Aletheia (Truth) is represented in the masque by a huge reclining statue reading the Bible and holding a globe in her left hand; a variant of this emblem is in Peacham's *Minerva Britanna* (134), where Truth has an open book in her hand, a palm (as a sign of victory) in the other, and with her right foot on the globe, looks up at the sun.[72]

It is interesting to note that all the masques of the cycle refer to one another. *The Lords Masque* refers to the union of the Thames and the Rhine, which is the subject of *The Masque of the Inner Temple and Gray's Inn*. That masque deals with the union of religion ("cultus unus"), which is finally realized in *The Masque of Truth*. Chapman's *Memorable Masque* mentions Atlas holding the globe and he also appears as a major character in *The Masque of Truth*.

The features of the celebrations discussed above allow them to be treated as a consciously contrived sequence of spectacles. This sequence, governed by an overall structure and characterized by inner logic and consistence, may therefore be treated as a macrotext created by whoever planned the whole program, possibly Sir Francis Bacon, who was one of the people involved in the planning. The three extant masques are central to this sequence. Since each of the masques concentrates its imagery on one element, earth, water, or fire, it is very likely that originally there was a fourth masque that concentrated on the fourth element, air. Fortunately, a contemporary description of this missing masque has been found. "The Masque of Air" concludes the major motifs developed by the other three masques and presents a vision of the world united under James's rule in one religion, which in the closing scene leads the human race to paradise. The most important fact is that the masques create meanings in relation to each other, which means that only by taking the masques and other events as a whole is it possible to understand their full significance.

6
Masque Cycle II

The "occasion" for the second masque cycle that I discuss in detail was the marriage of Frances Howard and Robert Carr, the earl of Somerset, which took place late in December 1613. Again the particular masques have been analyzed by critics but have been treated in isolation, as independent of each other. However, all the masques staged during the wedding celebrations form one cycle and may therefore be treated as one text. When treated as such, the masques create meanings that are otherwise lost to critical scrutiny. This is why critics have often dismissed the individual masques as not significant to the study of the form.

Once again there were four masques staged for the occasion, in addition to a knightly tilt. Their order was:

26 December 1613 (Sunday)	Thomas Campion, *The Somerset Masque*
27 December 1613 (Monday) and 1 January (Saturday)	Ben Jonson, *Challenge at Tilt*
29 December 1613 (Wednesday)	Ben Jonson, *The Irish Masque*
4 January 1614 (Tuesday)	Thomas Middleton, *The Masque of Cupid* (lost)
6 January 1614 (Thursday)	anon., *The Masque of Flowers*

The original title of Thomas Campion's masque was totally different from the one introduced by later editors and critics: it was *The Description of a Maske: Presented in the Banqueting roome at Whitehall, on Saint Stephens night last, At the Mariage of the Right Honourable the Earle of Somerset: And the right noble the Lady Frances Howard* (London, 1614). In his description of the "scene," Campion writes that

> On the vpper part there was formed a Skye with Clowdes very arteficially shadowed. On either side of the Sceane belowe was set a high Promontory, and on either of them stood three large pillars of

Masque Cycle II

golde: the one Promontory was bounded with a Rocke standing in the Sea, the other with a Wood; In the midst betweene them apeared a Sea in perspective with ships, some cunningly painted, some artificially sayling. On the front of the Sceane, on either side was a beautiful garden, with six seates a peece to receaue the Maskers: behind them the mayne Land, and in the middest a paire of stayres made exceedingly curiously in the forme of a Schallop shell. . . . (A2v)

As is apparent from the above description, the center of the stage was occupied by a perspective view of sailing ships. The latter, of course, is a recurrent motif in sundry emblem books. For instance, in Whitney's collection of emblems a sailing ship is presented in emblem 137; the accompanying epigram reads that just as a ship keeps its course and reaches its destination, in spite of all perils, winds, and waves, so man will attain heaven if he keeps his course in this world:

> And if he keepe his course directe, he winnes
> That wished porte, where lastinge ioye beginnes.

On the other side of the scene, Campion says, there is a rock in the sea, which again is an emblematic representation, with the sea standing for the world and the rock for human constancy.[1] Similarly, the wood on the other side of the stage could also be linked with emblematic tradition.[2] Equally emblematic in character are the other elements of the design—the garden, the "mayne Land," and the stairs "in the forme of a Schallop shell." Thus the whole design may be treated as an emblem, and therefore as a meaningful unit of the spectacle (and of the printed text, of course). As the author concludes in his description of the scenery, "in this manner was the eye first of all entertayned."

The masque begins with the entrance of four Squires, who approach the king and address him directly, asking for help. The first Squire informs the spectators/readers that Fame, "Great Honor's herrald," has herself proclaimed these nuptials, which is an obvious echo of the Chapman masque staged earlier in February. Fame has also decreed that from every "quarter" of the earth three knights would come to honor the solemnity, which again echoes the similar journey undertaken by the Virginians in the previous cycle. However, the Knights' voyage to Britain was not without obstacles, and they even faced mortal danger caused by the four "enchanters," Error, Rumor, Curiosity, and Credulity. Maliciously, they caused a storm at sea and the lives of the noble voyagers were additionally endangered by the sea monsters. The enchanters are enemies not only of the Knights but of humanity in general, for they cause confusion and chaos. In an extant description of the actual performance, they are literally called the "infernal furies," and in another one the "devils."[3] The Squires ask the king for protection from the "curst Enchanters" who "turne all the worlde into confusion." Thus the king is asked to protect the world. In a compliment to James, the first Squire wishes that the "fruite of *Peace*" would become "Perpetual spring." Note that in the last masque, the one closing the cycle (*The Masque of Flowers*), Spring actually comes to James's court in January, replacing Winter for good, and the image of a spring garden, which can refer to the Garden of Eden, visually dominates the conclusion of the cycle.

Owing to divine intervention, the brave Knights miraculously were saved from the raging sea, but while standing on a cliff "to view their storm-tost friends," they suddenly vanished, transformed—again by the forces of evil—into six pillars of gold. From the very beginning, the entire world is therefore presented as suffering from the chaos caused by the evil forces that have some power over nature and over the laws that govern the universe. However, this universe is also governed by the superior power of God, who is capable of returning order. This struggle is literally described as the encounter of "Heauen and hell," by which equivalence the four enchanters are made the representatives of Hell. This agrees with the contemporary description of the actual performance of the masque, referred to above, where the enchanters are repeatedly called "infernal powers." It is apparent from the Squires' description of the perilous storm that God's power is superior to any other. It is his lightning that makes the evil "serpents" disappear, "and all was husht, as storme had neuer beene" (A3v). In the description is the following: ". . . in order to save themselves from the monsters, the men had been forced to climb the rigging to the top of the masts, from which a bolt of thunder and a flash of lightning lifted them into the air, and so they came to land on some cliffs."[4]

The confusion of the world is presented emblematically on stage as well. As soon as the Squires made their complaints and asked the king and queen for protection, Error, Rumor, Curiosity, and Credulity enter. At first, they whisper "as if they rejoyced at the wrongs which they had done to the Knights." They begin to dance and are joined by the four Winds, which enter "confusedly." The Four Elements then enter—also "in confusion"; these, in turn, are followed by the "Foure Parts of the Earth in a confused measure." As if there was not enough confusion on stage, "All these having danced together in a strange kinde of confusion, part away by foure and foure" (B).

The costumes of these strange characters were essentially emblematic in character. For instance, Error appeared "in a skin coat scaled like a Serpent, a haire of curled Snakes, and a deformed visard." Undoubtedly the costume stresses the "beastly" character of Error. Rumor, in turn, had "a skin coate full of winged Tongues, and ouer it an anticke robe, on his head a Cap like a tongue, with a large paire of wings to it." Curiosity was in "a skin coate full of eyes, and an anticke habit ouer it, a fantasticke cap full of Eyes." And Credulity was in "the like habit painted with eares, and an antick Cap full of eares" (A4). The sources for these costumes are to be found in emblem books. Serpents, for instance, appear in many emblems, and they always represent evil, or even more directly, the forces of hell.[5] Similarly, there are emblems in which eyes, ears, and tongues appear. As mentioned above, in the masque Rumor appears in a "skin coate full of winged Tongues" and in a "Cap like a tongue, with a large paire of wings to it." A winged tongue appears in the icon of an emblem in P. S.'s *The Heroical Devices*;[6] the epigram reveals that the tongue is dangerous and should be controlled by reason. A winged tongue appears also in George Wither's *A Collection of Emblemes, Ancient and by Modern*.[7]

Winds are also frequent metaphors in emblem books. Whitney, for instance, presents an emblem in which a rock is shown as being "attacked" by four blowing winds; the accompanying epigram states that one should "houlde vertue by the hand, / And in rage of wyndes, and Seas, the Rock doth firmely stand."[8] Let me recall that a rock surrounded by the sea is presented in the masque under discussion. As was the case in the Four Winds, the Four Elements are also equipped with emblematic apparel and attributes. With one possible exception, their costumes are traditional. Earth has a coat full of flowers and trees and an oak tree growing on his head; Water's coat is decorated with fishes and a dolphin adorns his head; Air's costume sports fowl and an eagle, respectively. These are natural attributes of the three elements. The costume of the fourth one, however, Fire, is puzzling, for it (quite naturally) has a mantle painted with flames, but surprisingly fire carries a salamander in the middle of his "cap of flames." This is a good example of the emblematic detail with which all the masques are filled. In this particular case, a reader or spectator may be baffled by the combination of fire with the salamander. What do they have in common? Contemporaries believed that the salamander was so cold that it could extinguish fire by simply lying on it. An icon in P. S.'s book of "devices" represents just that: a salamander lies in flames. The epigram says that the animal "is of such a cold nature that she quenches the fire like ise." Quite appropriately for the context of the masque, the emblem is also said to represent the king's desire to nourish the virtuous and destroy the wicked.[9]

All of these emblematic characters are presented in a state of confusion and chaos. During their "confused" dance, however, Eternity appears, followed by the three Destinies bringing the Tree of Gold, followed by Harmony, who is accompanied by nine musicians. Chorus speaks: "Vanish, vanish hence, Confusion" (Bv). Thus, the confusion of the elements or the chaos of the world turns out to be temporary in nature and is replaced by eternal harmony. In this context, however, the appearance of Eternity is rather unusual. Since she is followed by the three Destinies and by Harmony, it seems that Eternity literally brings in Harmony, as preordained by the Destinies. In this way a visual message is conveyed: temporary chaos is replaced by eternal harmony. One must not forget that the enchanted knights came from the Four Continents and therefore represent the whole world. They (and the world) are enchanted by the forces of evil and are responsible for the "confusion" and for the "false illusion"; and the text also states that the Knights (and the world) can be saved only by the king and queen of England and by the "Sacred Tree of Grace and Bounty." The latter is placed "heere," or at James's and Anne's court, by the Destinies "who neuer erre." The royal couple, one has to remember, are not ordinary human beings, and the masque makes it clear that even a touch of the queen's hand is divine; she is asked to pull a branch off the tree, creating thus "a diuine touch't bough" (B2). Moreover, only the queen can "all knotted spels untye." The tree has the power to disenchant the Knights (and the world), and the branch is presented to a Squire, who will use it for that purpose. In a song the Knights—now freed from the evil charm—are asked to appear at court.

In this particular masque it is the queen's superhuman power that frees the Knights from the spell. In this context, the words of one of the Squires are significant:

> Since Knights by valour Rescue Dames distrest,
> Let them be by the Queene of Dames releast:

Masque Cycle II

> So sing the Destinyes, who neuer erre,
> Fixing this Tree of Grace and Bounty heere.
>
> (B2)

Since the Knights are not only English but represent all the knights of the world, it is important to note that the Destinies, or Fate, have chosen Anne and her court as the source of power that can free the world from the forces of evil. As James is the king of all honor and chivalry, so is Anne the queen of all the "Dames" of this world, of virtue and grace. Therefore it is quite possible that this masque was in fact sponsored by the queen herself.

The masque persistently focuses on numbers and on the number four in particular. There are four Squires, four Vices-Beasts, four Winds, four Elements, and the four Continents. Since there are numerous biblical echoes accompanied by occasional prophetic statements in the text, one may suspect that the masque creates additional meanings by suggesting its source in the Bible. It cannot be a matter of mere coincidence that the fourth prophetic book of the Old Testament is the Book of Daniel. In it the number four also plays an important role. Chapter 7 contains the following:

> 2 Daniel spake, and said, I saw in my vision by night, & beheld, the foure windes of the heauen stoue upon the great Sea.
> 3 And the foure great beasts came vp from the sea, diuers one from another.

The masque has four winds that cause the great storm at sea, and the direct counterparts of the beasts are the Vices, whose costumes stress their "beastly" character. Let me recall that Error, for instance, is dressed in a coat "scaled like a serpent" and in an "antick habit painted with Snakes" (A4). It is worth noting that in the eschatological sense the serpent that appears in the Old Testament (as in Isaiah 27:1) stands for the Lord's enemies, who "in that day" (Christ's coming) will be overthrown:

> In that day the Lord with his sore and great and strong sworde shall punish Leuiathan the piercing serpent, euen Leuiathan that crooked serpent, and he shall slay the dragon that is in the Sea.

In the masque the Squires say that during the storm, serpents appeared near the ships carrying the Knights, and that it was only the lightning from heaven that saved the knights from the evil serpents. As in Daniel, the Vices-Beasts emerge from the sea to appear in their dance of confusion. As in Isaiah, it is God who destroys the "crooked Serpent," the dragon of the sea. According to the medieval and Renaissance commentaries, the four beasts of the Book of Daniel stand for the four world empires, normally interpreted as Babylon, Assyria, Greece, and Rome. The destruction of the last beast was believed to lead to the establishment of the everlasting kingdom of the saints, the "Fifth Monarchy." Since the Reformation the Protestants believed that the Fourth Monarchy and the fourth beast represented the papacy, being the head of the Holy Roman Empire. This belief led to a widespread faith in Christ's second coming and in the approaching millennium that would precede the Last Judgment. As B. S. Capp put it, "The theory of four world-empires had also a much wider appeal: it provided a means by which the whole, anarchic course of history could be reduced to a simple and satisfying pattern, and by which a divine . . . purpose was given to all events. . . . The division of Europe by the Reformation and the ensuing wars seemed to presage the impending dissolution of all things. A typical English writer early in the seventeenth century saw decay in the four elements of fire, water, air and earth; all plants were feebler. . . ."[10]

In this context, the confusion of the four elements in the masque, replaced by eternal harmony, gains a millenarian dimension. One cannot forget that these ideas were close to those of both James and Bacon. The future James I had himself declared in 1588 that the Pope was Antichrist, and that the last age (the Fifth Monarchy) was at hand.[11] One has to remember that in the Renaissance references to apocalyptic imagery were widely understood and may be found both in poetry and in drama (as, for instance, in Ben Jonson's *Alchemist*).

The parallel to Daniel continues in the masque during the scene of the Knight's descent on a cloud. This occurs after the confusion of the world had been chased away and order was restored by Harmony and Eternity: "Then out of the ayre a cloude descends, discouering six of the Knights alike, in strange and sumptuous atires . . ." (B2v). The Book of Daniel says:

> 13. I saw in the night visions, and behold, one like the sonne of man, came with the clouds of heauen, and came to the Ancient of daies,[12] and they brought him neere before him.
> 14. And there are giuen him dominion and glory, and a kingdome, that all people, nations, and languages should serue him: his dominion is an euerlasting dominion, which shall not passe away; and his kingdome that, which shall not be destroyed.

Masque Cycle II

As the masquers descend, the scene was changed: ". . . for whereas before all seemed to be done at the sea and sea coast, now the Promontories were suddainly remooved, and London with the Thames is very arteficially presented in their place" (B2v). This leaves no doubt as to the location of everything that takes place on stage. So far nothing has been said about the occasion of the masque—the marriage of Frances Howard and the earl of Somerset. The text does not seem to be concerned with that event at all, making only occasional references to the celebration. The marriage, it seems, is only a pretext for a presentation of a broader view of the way of the world, of the roads leading to eternal harmony. The masquers—relieved from their imprisonment—dance, and a song is sung that concludes with the following:

> Like lookes, like hearts, like loues are linck't together
> So much the Fates be pleas'd, so come they hether,
> To make this Ioy perseuer euer.
> Loue decks the spring, her buds to th' ayre exposing,
> Such fire here in these bridall Breasts reposing
> We leaue with charmes enclosing, closing.
>
> (B3)

Thus the Fates are said to make this joy eternal and love is said to generate spring.[13] Let me note in passing that Spring appears as a character in the last masque of the cycle, *The Masque of Flowers*. In the farewell speech of the second Squire, the Fates are mentioned again as having prophetically sung the blessings of these nuptials (B4). As was the case with the marriage of Frederick and Elizabeth, this union also turns out to have been predestined by fate. The pure love of two hearts brings harmony, and by analogy similar love in humanity will bring about universal harmony, as described in the apocalyptic prophecy of Daniel. This "divine" love is contrasted with other types of love.

An unusual passage called the "Dialogue of three with a Chorus," which follows the masquers' second dance, discusses the advantages of true marriage over "friendship between man and man." These relationships are presented as being in opposition.

> [2] Some friendship between man and man prefer,
> But I th'affection between man and wife.
> [3] What good can be in life,
> Whereof no fruites appear?
> [1] Set is that Tree in ill houre
> That yeilds neither fruite nor flowre.

[2] How can man Perpetuall be,
But in his owne Posteritie?

The Chorus sums up:

That pleasure is of all most bountiful and kinde,
That fades not straight, but leaues a liuing Ioy behinde.

(B3r–v)

One may well ask whether the dialogue was addressed to the newlywed couple or to King James, whose homosexuality was notorious and must have been embarrassing to his wife.

After the dialogue the masquers danced with the ladies, followed by four barges with "skippers" appearing on the Thames. From the Spanish description of the performance referred to above, it appears that these are the sailors of the enchanted ship who have come to ask the gentlemen to reembark because the winds and tide were right. The "merry mates" are asked to come ashore and they dance a "brave and lively" dance. This is followed by the masquers' final dance and by the squires' speeches addressed directly to the king's "Triple Majesty." The first squire wishes James "all that was euer ask't, by vow of *Ioue*, To blesse a state with . . ." (B4); in other words, with "Plentie, Loue, Power, Triumph, priuate pleasure, publique peace," and so on. This blessed state has earlier been associated with the spring, and the prophesied coming of the new harmonious age metaphorically replaces the winter of the confused age.

The celebrations of the Somerset wedding provide good material for the discussion of the theatricality of the court life in Jacobean London. Not only were the four masques planned for the period between 26 December (the day of the marriage ceremony) and 6 January (which was the traditional masquing night), but a play was to be staged (Samuel Daniel's *Hymen's Triumph*, scheduled first for 6 January but postponed to 2 February) and a tilt was to take place. The latter was announced during a special "show," which cannot really be called a masque, for in fact it is more reminiscent of medieval disputes. It was written by Ben Jonson and is usually known by the title *Challenge at Tilt*. In this brief text, two cupids appear and quarrel over the identity of the real son of Venus and therefore the one responsible for the wedding or the "feast of love." Written in prose dialogue, the "challenge" was presented at court on Monday, 27 December 1613 (the cupids talk about "yester-night's nuptials"). The dispute ends with a challenge of one cupid against the other, which is expected to reveal the truth. This is to take place on New Year's Day, and on each side ten knights are to meet at tilt. The one feature that the dialogue shares with the masques is that it breaks the theatrical illusion by insisting that it takes place here and now. The cupids do not pretend to be anywhere else but at James's court, and they refer directly to the audience. They are as "real" as the individual spectators are. The other common feature with the other texts of the cycle is that the *Challenge* continues one of the themes signaled in the previous masque. The major issue is that of the relative values of the man's and the woman's love. In this way the text identifies itself as a part of the cycle.

Several days later, on 1 January 1614, the cupids met again as leaders of the two chivalrous sides. They quarrel again (presumably to remind the spectators of the cause behind the tournament) and the tilt begins (marked briefly in the text as "the tilting"). In this way a knightly tilt becomes a part of the theatrical text and the participants become actors in a way similar to masquers in a masque. The text does not provide further details of the knights' struggle and only Chamberlain writes that

> On the New-year's day was the Tiltings of ten against ten. The bases, trappings, and all other furniture of the one party was murrey and white, which were the Bride's colours; the other green and yellow for the Bridegroom. There were two handsome chariots or pageants that brought in two Cupids, whose contention was, whether were the truer, his or hers, each maintained by their champions. But the current and praise, you must think, ran on her side. The whole show, they say, was very fair and well set out. . . .[14]

The contention between the two cupids therefore seems to suggest two different approaches to love, represented in the extratextual reality by the bride and the bridegroom, respectively. One must not forget in this context that Somerset was James's beloved favorite, with Buckingham not yet in sight. As seen from this point of view, the tilt could in fact conclude the odd discussion in the previous masque about the superiority of a male/female relationship over a homosexual one. After the tilt another actor appears, Hymen, who tells the cupids that they are both the true sons of Mars and Venus, being Eros and Anteros. In this way peace and harmony is achieved. Note, too, that Hymen reappears in person in the play by Daniel, mentioned above. Since the play is dedicated to the queen, this fact supports the possibility of

Anne's direct sponsorship of at least some of the spectacles prepared for the occasion.

A final point is that the inclusion of a tilt into a masque cycle lies within an established tradition. Knightly tilts took place when Henry was created Prince of Wales in 1610 and during the wedding celebrations of Elizabeth and Frederick. But even much earlier, in 1588, James included a tilt into the masque he wrote on the occasion of the marriage of George Gordon, sixth earl of Huntly, and Lady Henrietta Stuart, daughter of the first duke of Lennox.

The next masque in the sequence, Ben Jonson's *Irish Masque*, was staged on 29 December 1613 and was first published in the *Workes* of 1616. Continuing certain motifs of Thomas Campion's text, it is also epideictic and prophetic in character. It begins with the almost conventional antimasque motif of "simple people looking for their monarch." When at last the Irishmen notice the king, they address him directly. They have come from Ireland because they had heard about the marriage:

> *Dennise.* Tere vash a great newesh in Ireland of a great Brideall of one o'ty Lords here ant be.
> *Patrick.* Ty man Robyne, tey shay.
> *Donnell.* Mary ty man, Toumaish, hish daughter, tey shay.
> *Dermock.* I, ty good man, Toumaish, o'shuffolke. (P. 1001)

Speaking with a harsh Irish accent, they assure the king that they—or the Irish in general—are James's faithful subjects and that they "loue ty mayesty heartily" and would even fight for him and for his daughter "that is in Tuchland." Constantly referring to the king as King Yamish, they tell him that the marriage brings over to England "a doshen of our besht Mayshters" to dance at the wedding. However, there is a serious problem: they have lost all their clothes during a storm at sea. Dennise explains that "tey vere leeke to daunsh naked, ant pleash ty mayesty; for te villanous vild Irish sheas haue casht away all ter fine cloysh, as many ash casht a towsand cowes . . ."; Dermock adds that in spite of that "tey musht eene come and daunch i'teyr mantels now" (1002). Having explained the lack of nice garments, they then dance to some "rude" music, accompanied by several more "footmen." Their "rude" dance is contrasted with the one that follows, danced by the Irish gentlemen, who are the true masquers. These, as Jonson writes, danced indeed in their "Irish mantles," the only cover of their nakedness. By contrast they dance "to a solemne musique of harpes" (1003). Harps of course were considered Irish instruments; a type of harp is called to this day the Irish harp. Barnaby Rich, in his *New Description of Ireland* (1610), mentions that "Euery great man in the Countrey hath his Rymer, [and] his *Harper*."[15] He also, as part of the civilizing process, strongly advocates teaching English to the Irish and concludes that "those of the irish that haue reduced themselues to ciuility, (were it not for their Religion) are otherwise, of very good conuersation; and as well in their manners, as in the decencie of their apparell, they are very modest and comly."[16]

Jonson first contrasts the simple men's language, behavior, dances, and music with the solemn elegance of the masquers' dance and then with the "civility" of an Irish gentleman, who appears on stage and chases his "rude" compatriots away: "Hold your tongues. / And let your courser manners seeke some place, / Fit for their wildenesse. This is none, be gone" (1003). The gentleman asks the "immortall Bard" to enter:

> Aduance, immortall Bard, come vp and view
> The gladding face of that great king, in whom
> So many prophecies of thine are knit.
> This is that IAMES of which long since thou sung'st,
> Should end our countreys [Ireland's] most vnnaturall broyles;
> And if her eare, then deafned with the drum,
> Would stoupe but to the musique of his peace,
> Shee need not with the spheares change harmony.
> This is the man thou promis'd should redeeme,
> If she would loue his counsels as his lawes,
> Her head from seruitude, her feete from fall,
> Her fame from barbarism, her state from want
> And in her all the fruits of blessing plant.
>
> (F1, 1003)

It is worth noting that Francis Bacon, in one of his parliamentary speeches, praised King James for making Ireland "civil": ". . . the plantation and reduction to civility of Ireland, the second island of the ocean Atlantic, did by God's providence wait for his majesty's times, being a work resembling indeed the workes of the ancient heroes: no new piece of that kind in modern times."[17] Again, in another speech: "Ireland is the last 'ex filiis Europae,' which hath been reclaimed from desolation, and desert, in many parts, to population and plantation; and from savage and barbarous customs to humanity and civility. This is the King's work in chief: it is his garland of heroical virtue and felicity. . . ."[18]

In this context, the *Irish Masque* presents the king's power to transform the "savage" and "uncivil" men into "civilised" human beings, which is additionally expressed by the gentleman's courtly speech (presented in an impeccable English, with not a trace of an Irish accent), by the substitution of prose by poetry, and by the harmonious dance of the masquers. King James is also praised for his bringing peace to Ireland, and for "civilizing" the country in general, in John Davies's *A Discovery of the State of Ireland* (1613). For over 250 pages Davis describes the history of Ireland and the appalling mistakes of England's policy toward that country. But the reign of James changes everything: "And now I come to the happy raigne of my most Gracious Lord & Maister King *Iames;* in whose time . . . all the Defects in Gouernment of *Ireland* spoken of before, haue beene fully supplied in the first nine yeeres of his raigne."[19]

One of the major changes for the better, Davies relates, was the fact that the Irish people "were receiued into his Maiesties *imediate protection*. This bred such comfort and security in the hearts of all men, as thereupon ensued, the calmest, and most vniyersall peace, that euer was seen in *Ireland*."[20] Furthermore, King James established true public justice and "the Common people were taught . . . that they were free subiects to the Kings of England, and not slaues & vassals to their pretended Lords." In words strikingly similar to those used in the masque, Davies continues praising the changes introduced by James, which "haue reclaymed the Irish from their wildernesse, caused them to cut off their Glibs and long Haire; to conuert their Mantles into Cloaks; to conform themselues to the maner of *England* in al their behauior and outward formes. And because they find a great inconuenience in mouing their suites by an Interpreter; they do for the most part send their Children to Schools, especially to learne the English language."[21] Moreover, James is metaphorically presented by Davies as a great gardener under whose care the plantation of his three kingdoms flourishes: "the Irish were in some places transplanted from the Woods & Mountains, into Plaines and open Countries, that being remoued (like wild fruit trees) they might grow the milder, and beare the better & sweeter fruit. . . . For when this Plantation hath taken root, and bin fixt and setled but a few yeares . . . it will secure the peace of *Ireland*, assure it to the Crowne of England for euer; and finally, make it Ciuill, and Rich, a Mighty, and a Flourishing Kingdome."[22] Let me mention at this point that the last masque in the cycle, dis-

Masque Cycle II

cussed below, ends with an image of an ideal garden that allegorically represents the fruits of James's reign.

Since the king has the power to transform the Irish, there is no reason why other nations should not follow a similar transformation to "civility." Thus the function of the appearance of the Irish in the masque is to show the power of the king.

The Bard is asked to "sing some charme" that would reconfirm his former prophesies. In his song he addresses the married couple directly:

> Bow both your heads at once, and hearts:
> Obedience doth not well in parts.
> It is but standing in his [James's] eye,
> You'll feele your selues chang'd by and by,
> Few liue, that know, how quick a *spring*
> Workes in the presence of a king.
> (1003–4; emphasis added)

The very presence of the king acts as a catalyst for the laws that govern nature. The coming of spring is expected. The text says further that during this song, the masquers let their mantles fall and discovered their masquing costumes. Miraculously, their nakedness is gone and the presence of the king transforms them into "new-borne creatures" (1004). They are now just like English masquers. The "civilizing" process has been completed. It was represented in the masque by a series of transformations: "rude" behavior became courtly manners; "rude" music and dances changed to the solemn elegance of the masquers' dance; a ridiculous accent that often led to semantic confusion (as, for instance, the mispronunciation of "sit" by "shit") metamorphosed to the impeccable English of the Irish gentleman; Irish mantles became English masquing costumes; and prose changed to poetry. After their dance, the Bard sings again:

> So breakes the sunne earths rugged chaines,
> Wherein rude winter bound her vaines;
> So growes both streame and source of price,
> That lately fetterd were with ice.
> So naked trees get crisped heads,
> And cullord coates the roughest meads.
> And all get vigour, youth, and spright,
> That are but look'd on by his light.
> (1004)

Thus, it is the king's mere sight, his eyes, that have the miraculous power to cause various transformations of people, nature, and the seasons. The king is also presented as the source of light, for he is in fact the sun. An allegorical spring of the new age is about to replace the "rude" winter. One ought to remember that the Irish, before their transformation, were also described as "rude." James, the sun, will break earth's "rugged chaines." As Chamberlain writes, this meaning was highly appreciated at court, although he admits that some did not like the Irish made "ridiculous."[23] The magical powers of the king, Britain's (and the world's) prime "gardener," are further clarified and corroborated by the last extant masque in the cycle.

One of the curious features of *The Irish Masque* is the lack of any indication of the scenery. None seems to have existed. One of the possible reasons is that the masquers were not gods nor ancient heroes, descending from the mythological heavens; on the contrary, they were presented as living people who have come from Ireland to take part in the wedding celebrations. They were not allegorical characters (with the exception of the transformation of their costumes) and took part in a performance that could be entirely (and probably was) staged on the hall floor. As I have pointed out earlier, real people do not inhabit the allegorical and mythological world of the perspective stage. In fact they are excluded from that world. Thus, the *Irish Masque* lies more within the tradition of folk theater, where there is generally little significance attached to scenery, and where—as Petr Bogatyrev has pointed out—the role of scenery is taken over by props.[24]

Finally, there is yet another level from which the Irish motif may be considered. The reasons usually given by contemporaries for the colonization of Ireland were not only political (to strengthen the kingdom) or economic (to profit from farming and husbandry), but also religious. As Barnaby Rich put it:

> *This enterprize . . . thus undertaken, for the planting of the Northerne part of* Ireland, *with the* English, *cannot be but acceptable in the presence of God, when it shall draw so much to the aduancement of his glory, making way fro the* Gospell of Iesus Christ *to be truely preached in a place where there was nothing but Idolatry and superstition formerly practised; giuing light and understanding to a blind and ignorant people, to discern the way of saluation, that do rather hope to saued by the means of* Saint Patricke, *then by the mercy of God.*[25]

Thus this is also a religious mission, undertaken for the good of the local people, with their salvation the ultimate aim. The source of all evil in Ireland, of the constant uprisings and mutinies, of the cruelty of the people and their "barbarism," is not difficult to detect. It is, of course, popery, which gives the colonization ideology yet another dimension. To again quote Barnaby Rich:

> for Popery in *Ireland* is the original of a number of imperfections, that otherwise would bee reformed, and it is Popery alone that hath secluded the *English* and the *Irish* from that perfect loue and amity, which else would be imbraced on both partes as well to the glory of God, as to the great benefit of this Countrey.
>
> God bring it once to passe, that wee might all ioyne together as well *English* as *Irish*, in the true acknowledgement of one God, of one Religion, of one King, of one Law, and of one loue. . . .[26]

The colonizing process therefore was to introduce the true religion to Ireland, and the political union would lead to the religious union. All of this was possible only because of James's wisdom and his superhuman qualities, which made him the natural king to lead the world into the kingdom of the saints.

On Tuesday, 4 January 1614, the bride and bridegroom, accompanied by the duke of Lennox, the Lord Privy Seal, the Lord Chamberlain, and other nobles, went to Merchant Taylors' Hall, where—as a contemporary source writes—the "Lord Maior and Aldermenne of London, in their scarlet robes, entertayned them with hearty welcome. . . . At their first entrance into the Hall they were received with ingenious speeches and pleasant melody. . . . After supper, and being risen from the table, these noble guests were entertayned with a wassaile, two several pleasant Maskes, and a Play, and with other pleasant dances. All which being ended, then the Bride and Bridegroome, with all the rest, were invited to a princely banquet, and about three o'clock in the morning they returned to Whitehall."[27] Hardly anything else is known about the entertainment and the masques; in fact, we only know that on 18 January payment was made to Thomas Middleton in respect of the "late solemnities at Merchant Tailors' Hall" for "the last Mask of Cupid and other shows lately made" by him.[28] Writing to Carleton on 5 January, Chamberlain mentioned that after the supper with the Lord Mayor "they had a Play and a Masque, and after that a Banquet"; in the same letter he also noted that "Mr. Attorney's Masque is for tomorrow, and for a conclusion of Christmas and their shews together."[29] The latter piece has to be identified with the anonymous (unless one accepts Bacon's authorship) masque entitled *The Maske of Flowers: Presented*

By the Gentlemen of Graies-Inne, at the Court of White-hall, in the Banquetting House, vpon Twelfe night, 1613.[30] It is dedicated to Sir Francis Bacon and the implication is that Sir Francis at least sponsored the whole show:

> The dedication of it [the masque] could not be doubtful, you hauing beene the principall, and in effect the onely person, that did both incourage and warrant the Gentlemen [of the Gray's Inn], to shew their good affection towards so noble a Coniunction, in a time of such Magnificence. Wherein we conceiue without giuing you false attributes, which little neede where so many are true. . . . [A complaint is made that the gentlemen had only three weeks to prepare the masque.] which could not haue beene done, but that euery mans exceeding loue and respect to you, gaue him wings to ouertake Time, which is the swiftest of things." (A3v)

"The Deuice of the Maske" gives an outline of the plot that is useful to further discussion:

> The *Sunne* [James] willing to doe honour to a Marriage, between two noble persons of the greatest Island [England] of his vniversall *Empire*, writeth a Letter of Commission to the two Seasons of the yeare, the *Winter* and the *Spring*, to visit and present them on his part, directing the *Winter* to present them with sports, such as are commonly called by the name of *Christmas* sportes, or *Carnaual* sportes, and the *Spring*, with other sportes of more Magnificence. . . . (A4)

Winter is also to "take knowledge" of a certain challenge "which had beene lately sent and accepted betweene *Silenus* and *Kauasha* vpon this point; *That Wine was more woorthy then Tobacco, and did more cheere and relieue the spirits of man.* This to be tried at two weapons, at *Song* and at *Dance*, and requiring the *Winter* to giue order that the same *Challenge* be performed in the dayes of Solemnitie of the same Marriage. . ." (A4). Spring, in turn, is to take care of certain "youths" who had been transformed into flowers and to transform them back into men so that they could "present themselues at the same Marriage" (A4).

First to appear in the masque is Winter, presented as an old man, who "marcheth vp to the middle of the Hall, and looks round him" (B). Noticing unusual signs of spring, he expresses surprise:

> *Why thus it should be; such a night as this*
> *Puts downe a thousand weary longsome dayes*
> *Of* Somer, *when a* Sunne, *and* Moone, *and* Stars

> *Are mette within the Pallace of a King,*
> *In seuerall glory shining each on other.*
>
> (B)

But how can the sun shine at the same time with the moon and the stars? Later the text says that the firmament on stage was "like the Skies on a cleare night." On the other hand, references to the sun are constant. This seeming contradiction is readily explained by the fact that it is James himself who is the sun in the world of the masque. He is the source of light that has the power to transform people, nature, and the whole world. I will discuss this shortly.

Suddenly, Spring enters, "like a Nymph" [one must not forget that Queen Anne was the Queen of Nymphs], and "overtakes" Winter. Winter is offended: how dare you, he says, come here in January, "to giue the lie / To all Almanackes that are come forth?" The conflict is solved by Gallus, the sun's messenger, who brings a dispatch from his lord that contains orders summarized in the "Deuice," quoted above. The first "Antickmaske of the Song" begins, with Silenus and Kawasha with their followers competing in a challenge. Since the antimasque world is a topsy-turvy one, the challenge is an echo of the challenge at tilt, which had already taken place. The songs that follow, sung by the adversarial parties, bring up the motif of the dispute over the superiority of wine over tobacco. Silenus's singers express their desire to get Kawasha drunk and then to return him to his "Munkeis," where he belongs (B3v). Kawasha's singers, in turn, want to make Silenus "fall downe" after seeing Kawasha's "men of Ire"

> All snuffing, puffing smoke and fire,
> Like fell Dragon.
>
> (B3v)

As is well known, James strongly opposed the use of tobacco, even writing a pamphlet against it; he also, in theory at least, opposed the abuse of wine. In *Basilikon Doron*, he warned his son: "beware of drunkenness, which is a beastly vice, namely in a King." The challenge continues through the second antimasque of dance, in which a number of new characters appear such as Courtesan, Usurer, Midwife, Mountebank, Chimney Sweeper, and the like. All of these had the reputation of using wine or tobacco or both, in large quantities.

The seemingly trivial "plot" of the antimasques also has a serious dimension. It basically presents, as is always the case in the masques, an "antiworld" inhabited by creatures that constantly violate the harmonious order of the main masque world. They are always associated with chaos and vice. James treated his anti-tobacco campaign very seriously; he loathed people who smoked. As a contemporary account reveals, the king believed that

> Tobacco was the lively image and pattern of hell; for that by allusion, it had in it all the parts and vices of the world, whereby hell may be gained; to wit, first it was a smoak, so are the vanities of the world a smoak and vapour. Secondly, it delighteth them who take it, so do the pleasures of the world. Thirdly, it maketh men drunken and light in the head, and so do vanities of the world men are drunk therewith. Fourthly, he that taketh Tobacco, saith, he cannot leave it, it doth bewitch him; even so the pleasures of the world make men loath to leave them, so they are for the most part so inchanted with them. Besides the former allusion, it is like hell in the very substance of it, for it is a stinking loathsome thing, so is hell; it goeth in at the mouth and out at the nose, so doth the smoke of hell through the body and head.[31]

The challenge on stage therefore is in fact between two major evils, drinking and smoking. Both of these, "by allusion," are the common ways to reach hell. The latter is located outside the court and is clearly juxtaposed with the heavenly world of the main masque.

As the contestants exit, the masque proper begins with a change of scenery. This again, is an emblematic design, and its description is worth quoting extensively:

> *The Trauers* being drawne, was seene a Garden of glorious and strange beauty. . . . In the middle of the crosse walk, stood a goodly Fountaine raised on foure columns of Siluer. On the toppes whereof stoode foure statues of siluer, which supported a bole . . . in the middle whereof vppon scrowles of siluer and gold was placed a Globe garnished with foure golden Maske-heads, out of the which issued water into the bole, aboue stood a golden Neptune . . . holding in his hand a Trident, and riding on a Dolphin. . . . The Garden walls were of brick artificially painted in *Perspectiue*. The Garden within the wall was rayled about with rayles of three foote high, adorned with Ballesters of Siluer, betweene which were placed pedestalls, beautified with transparent Lights of variable colours, vpon the Pedestalls stood siluer columnes, vpon the toppes whereof were personages of golde, Lions of gold, and Vnicorns of siluer. . . .
> Euery quarter of the Garden was finely hedged about with a lowe hedge of Cipresse and Iuniper: The knottes within set with artificiall

greene hearbs, embelished with all sortes of artificiall Flowers. In the first two quarters were two *Piramides* garnished with golde and siluer, and glistering with transparent lights, resembling *Carbuncles, Saphires,* and *Rubies.* In euery corner of each Quarter were great pottes of lilli flowers, which shadowed certain lights placed behind them. . . .

The two further quarters were beautified with *Tulipaes* of diuers colours, and in the Middle, and in the corners of the said quarters were set great tufts of seuerall kindes of Flowers. . . .

At the farther end of the Garden was a Mount raised by degrees, resembling banks of earth, couered with grasse: on the top of the Mount stood a goodly Arbour . . . couered with artificiall trees, and with arbour of flowers, as *Englantine, Honnysuckles,* and the like.

The Arbour was in length three and thirtie foote, in height one and twenty, supported with termes of gold and siluer, it was diuided into sixe double arches, and three doores answerable to the three walks of the Garden. In the middle part of the Arbor rose a goodly large Turret, and at either end a smaller.

Vpon the toppe of the Mount, on the front thereof was a banke of Flowers . . . behind which within the Arches the *Maskers* sate vnseene.

Behind the Garden ouer the toppe of the Arbour were set artificiall trees appearing like an Orchard ioyning to the Garden, and ouer all was drawne in perspectiue, a firmament like the Skies in a cleare night.

Vpon a grassy seate vnder the Arbor sate the Garden-Gods, in number twelue, apparrelled in long roabes of greene rich taffata, cappes on their heads, and chaplets of flowers.

In the midst of them sate *Primauera*, at whose intreaty they descended to the Stage, and marching vp to the King, sung to Lutes and Theorboes. (C–C2)

The quoted passage proves the concern with which the author regarded the "garden," for this scene not only marks the end of this particular masque, but it also concludes the whole cycle. The prophesied coming of spring takes place at James's court. The description is detailed and technical, as if a real garden were described, and reveals the author's deep interest in and knowledge of gardening. As a matter of fact, the design is strikingly similar to the description of the ideal garden in Bacon's *Essays,* where he included a separate chapter *Of Gardens,* being one of the earliest theoretical treatises on gardens in English. Among other things, in this work we read that

> The garden is best to be square, encompassed on all the four sides with a stately arched hedge. The arches to be upon pillars of carpenter's work, of some ten foot high, and six foot broad. . . . Over the

arches let there be an entire hedge of some four foot high, framed also upon carpenter's work; and upon the upper hedge, over every arch, a little turret . . . and over every space between the arches some other little figure, with broad plates of round coloured glass gilt, for the sun to play upon.[32] But this hedge I intend to be raised upon a bank, not steep . . . set all with flowers. . . . Little low hedges, round, like welts, with some pretty pyramids, I like well; and in some places, fair columns upon frames of carpenter's work. . . . I wish also, in the very middle, a fair mount, with three ascents, and alleys . . . and the whole mount to be thirty foot high. . . .

For fountains, they are a great beuty and refreshment. . . . Fountains I intend to be of two natures: the one that spinkleth or spouteth water; the other a fair receipt of water. . . . For the first, the ornaments of images gilt, or of marble, which are in use, do well: but the main matter is so to convey the water . . . either in the bowls or in the cictern. . . . As for the other kind of fountain . . . [it may be] withal embellished with coloured glass . . . encompassed also with fine rails of low Statua's.[33]

Bacon also recommends fruit trees of all sorts in the alleys and makes a list of plants and flowers most suitable for each season of the year. For instance, tulips and honeysuckles, both mentioned in the masque, are—Bacon says—appropriate for April. Cypress and juniper, also mentioned in the masque, are among his list of plants that are green all winter.[34] The concern with the garden in the masque is a curious reflection of the new vogue in Jacobean England. Art historians have noticed the unprecedented creation of new gardens in accordance with imported designs. Roy Strong, for instance, observed in his *Renaissance Garden in England* that "this craze for the elaboration and extension in the size of the garden is vividly reflected in the anonymous *Masque of Flowers*."[35] Strong also points out the actual similarity between some of the elements of the masque garden and the actual gardens in Jacobean England. The obelisk, he claims, was in the manner of the Kenilworth garden, and the garden of New College, Oxford, was in fact the garden of the *Masque of Flowers*, even though the former was completed in the 1640s.[36] Note that the masque fountain is very similar to the one reproduced by Salomon de Caus in the second book of his *Les Raison des Forces Movvantes*.[37] As is well known, de Caus was active in England between 1607/8 and 1613, when he created elaborate gardens and waterworks on the grounds of Richmond Palace. In the mentioned design, the fountain is composed of three levels, with Neptune holding a trident and a dolphin on top—the exact arrangement as in the masque (see the description above). Furthermore, Neptune appears in a similar milieu, with pyramids, in one of Wither's emblems: the angry god causes a storm at sea, but a pyramid, here associated with virtue, is immune to the rages of the storm:

> So, howsoever *Fortune,* turnes or winds,
> Those men, which are indow'd with virtuous minds,
> It is impossible, to drive them from
> Those *Formes,* or *Stations,* which those minds become.[38]

But the exact sources of the design are not of major importance here. More important is the fact that the masque garden belongs to a certain tradition, both architectural and iconographical, and that the design creates certain meanings by referring to that tradition.

This garden, however, is not ordinary. It is inhabited by gods (at one point they are also called the "Priests"). When they come down to the hall floor and approach the king, they sing a song in which an appeal is made to "ancient powers" to "giue place," for never in history has the world witnessed "Flowers return'd to Men." The present times, however, are very special, and the Chorus sings:

> *But miracles of new euent,*
> *Follow the great Sun of our firmament.*

(C2v)

Since the song is sung by the garden gods, "their" firmament is the firmament of the garden, and the "Sun" referred to is the sun of the same garden. Since direct communication is possible between the latter and the royal hall, the garden appears to be the court's extension. The sun of the court shines on the adjoining garden, no doubt implying James. There is no astronomical sun in the firmament on stage, we are told. Thus the only sun present has to be the king, and his very appearance can cause the miracle of the transformation of flowers into men. Rather, it is a series of transformations, for nature is first transformed by James's miraculous light: winter becomes spring. In this way the garden is the visible effect of the king's rule, it reflects beauty, peace, and harmony, replacing the confusion of the world apparent in the opening of the cycle. This is further confirmed by "The Charme":

> *Hearken ye fresh and springing Flowers,*
> *The Sunne shines full vpon your earth*

> . . . .
> *Descend you from your hill,*
> *Take spirit at his will* [the Sun's],
> *No Flowers, but flourish still.*

(C2v)

The miracle presently takes place: "The bankes of flowers softly discending and vanishing, the Maskers, in number thirteen appeared, seated in their arches" (C2v). A meticulous description of the masquers' costumes follows, in which the dominating ornamental motif is of sundry flowers: "The lowd Musicke ceasing, the Maskers descend in a galland March through three seuerall doores of the Arbor to the three seueral Allies of the Garden, marching till they all met in the middle Allie vnder the Fountaine, and from thence to the Stage, where they fel into their first measure" (C3). The garden gods descend again and sing songs, each of which is said to have "reference" to somebody. The fourth song, as the text literally states, has "reference to the King":

> *All things returne with Time,*
> *But seldom do they higher clime*
> *Yet vertue soueraigne*
> *Mends al things, as they come again;*
> *This ile was* Brittaine *in times past,*
> *But then was* Britain *rude & waste,*
> <u>*But now is* Brittaine *fit to be,*</u>
> <u>*A seate for fift Monarchie.*</u>
>   *Offer we to his high deserts,*
> Cho. *Praises of truth, incense of hearts,*
> *By whom ech thing with gaine reuerts.*

(C3v–C4)

Here the past is contrasted with the present. The Britain of former times was "rude & waste" (as Ireland in recent years), whereas at present she is like a garden, full of harmony, beauty, and rich in fruits of the earth. All this makes Britain under James's rule "fit to be / A seate for fift Monarchie." What was alluded to in the earlier parts of the cycle is stated directly at its conclusion. In the emblematic tradition a walled garden often represented paradise, as in Henry Hawkins's *Parthenia Sacra, or, the Mysterious and delicious Garden of the Sacred Parthenes*.[39] Additionally, as Bacon pointed out at the very beginning of his essay on gardens, "God Almighty first planted a Garden. And indeed it is the purest of human pleasures."[40] Since "all things returne with Time," so does the garden, the Garden of Eden. Thomas Brightman's *A Revelation*

Masque Cycle II

of the revelation, first published in Latin in 1609 (with several later editions in English), contains a passage where the destiny of the Church of England, headed by James, is literally compared to "the first church of all, the Garden of Eden."[41] And Walter Ralegh, in his *History of the World,* expressed the belief that James I was the David of Ezekiel's prophecy who was to lead all the nations to the kingdom of God.[42]

The concept of England being God's elect country and the paragon of all nations was not an isolated one. Millenarian ideas were also quite common in the early seventeenth century. For instance, in D. Maxey's *Five Sermons Preached before the King,* published in the same year as *The Masque of Flowers,* King James is praised for the blessed state of England and of the true Church under his rule: "This Church of England in times past, hath seemed to be forsaken of her louer. . . . *But now as a Bride-groome reioyceth ouer the Bride, so hath God reioyced ouer this Land, and decked his Loue with ornaments, in a most excellent manner, shee is become glorious and of perfect beautie, her name is spread through the world, and other Nations doe taste and are satisfied with the breast of her consolation.*"[43]

Similarly, the celebration of the marriage in the masque is an equally good occasion to discuss broader issues. And at another point, where James is made responsible for bringing the entire country to a blessed state, Maxey speaks in definitely millenarian terms: "For I am vndoubtedly perswaded (next after the knowledge of Christ, and the true profession of the Gospel) *this day, this day* I say, is now, and hereafter shall be the most memorable and happy *Day* that in this Land was euer commended vnto posteritie these 1000 yeeres."[44]

The beginning of the millennium, it was believed, would be marked by the final fall of Antichrist. A particular role in this victory of the true church was to be played by England and the English, and—of course—by their king. This was to take place shortly. Sampson Price, for instance, in his *Heavenly Proclamation to Fly Romish Babylon,* also published in 1614, claimed that "Never was *Antichrist* and his army of *Priests* . . . more enraged to oppugne the true Church then in these *daies,* conceauing in likelyhood that he hath but a *short time,* and that the time is *at hand,* which the Lord *hath promised,* shal bring vpon *Babel* the vengeance of *the Lord* and the vengeance of *his temple.*"[45] The author further admits that he cannot predict the precise date of Rome's fall, but it is to be expected soon. And who is to lead the victorious forces of the true church? The answer is obvious: "Wee haue a good *King (and long may we haue him)* who in the lists of *controversie,* may grapple with *Antichrist* for his triple crown."[46]

Such a conviction is even more openly expressed in *The Triumphs of King Iames the First* (1610), whose author—with the help of his peculiar "scientific" methods based on numerology—proves beyond doubt that James was predestined to overthrow Antichrist:

> That which wanteth of forty two months, of a thousand two hundred and sixty dayes Propheticall, of three great dayes and an halfe; of a time, of times, and of half a time, mentioned in *Daniel,* and in the *Apocalipse:* al do signify the same tearme or space of time, and each, one thousand, two hundred and sixty *Iulian* years, which since the diminishing and fall of the kingdome of Antechrist, and which shall bee wholly ouerthrowne by *Our Prince,* accomplished by his Numbers.[47]

The transformation of flowers into men in *The Masque of Flowers* seems to create additional meanings by relying on the readers'/spectators' knowledge of the emblematic tradition. Of particular importance in this case is the image of a fully grown spring garden, opening the main masque (and concluding the cycle), in which—under the influence of the sun—some flowers turn into men. This miracle is in fact a theatrical echo of emblems paralleling the relationship that exists between flowers (plants in general) and the sun, and between subjects and their king. Wither's book of emblems has one making exactly such a parallel. The icon shows flowers turning to the sun; the epigram says that:

> Thus fares it with a *Nation,* and their *King,*
> 'Twixt whom there is a native Sympathy.
> His *Presence,* and his *Favours,* like the *Spring,*
> Doe make them sweetly thrive, and fructify.[48]

Exactly the same parallel was presented on stage through purely visual and theatrical means of expression. The accompanying verses function as the epigram to the emblem's icon. A three-dimensional, theatrical emblem is created. The particular occasion for the presentation of the cycle was only a pretext to talk about much wider and more important issues. In fact, the actual marriage of Frances Howard and the earl of Somerset is relevant only because it alludes—by analogy—to other unions of this world. The garden is England's paradise and it is also like the biblical garden promised to God's redeemed people (Isaiah 58:11).

Masque Cycle II

Note, too, that there are numerous similarities between particular elements of the cycle. In Campion's masque, for instance, the knights become golden pillars and then come back to human shape by the power of the golden bough—handed over by the queen. In *The Masque of Flowers,* in turn, young men are transformed into flowers and then brought back to human shape by the power of the sun, by King James. In both cases, the young men are masquers and dance with the ladies of the court. In the *Irish Masque* a series of transformations shows the progress from "barbarism" to civility. The challenge of two cupids finds its extension and solution in the "real" world, in the knightly tilt. The last masque provides a comical antimasque that originates from yet another challenge—that of winter and spring. The same antimasque shows the antiworld, where vices bring people to damnation.

In addition, a number of motifs continue and develop throughout the whole cycle. The apocalyptic imagery with which the cycle begins finds its conclusion in the direct claim that Britain under James is fit to become the seat for the Fifth Monarchy. The coming of the spring is prophesied early in the cycle, and it actually happens in the last masque. The garden that appears is an emblematic representation of Britain (and, perhaps, the whole world) under James's rule. The king himself is the sun that brings life to that garden. Thus, the whole cycle creates many levels of meanings by alluding to other works, and even to other systems such as emblem books, garden architecture, and the Bible,[49] and, of course, to other masques and entertainments. The latter factor is of particular importance, for it proves that most of the masques, if not all of them, are variations of the same "theme." For instance, King James's miraculous power to bring order and harmony to the world in chaos, to the elements in confusion, was fully recognized during the welcoming celebrations of 1604. The last arch prepared for the royal entry was called the *New World* because it had a globe in the middle, surrounded by the four elements. Thomas Dekker writes in his description that "upon the approach of his Majestie, [the four elements] went round in a proportionable and even circle." In a speech written by Thomas Middleton, Zeal addressed James at the arch, observing that the globe has been set in proper motion by the presence of the new king:

> But see, the vertue of a Regall eye,
> Th'attractive wonder of man's Majestie,
> Our globe is drawne in right line agen

> . . . .
> The elements, Earth, Water, Ayre, and Fire,
> Which ever clipt a naturall desire
> To combat each other, being at first
> Created enemies to fight their worst,
> See at the peacefull presence of their King,
> How quietly they movde without their sting.[50]

Similarly, the image of the king as the Sun shining over Britain and bringing peace and eternal spring to this "happy island" appears in earlier masques. A typical example is Silenus in Ben Jonson's *Oberon* (1611), who says that King James is "the matter of vertue" and also a "god" over all other kings. Moreover,

> 'Tis he, that stayes the time from turning old,
> And keepes the age up in a heap of gold.
> That in his owne true circle, still doth runne;
> And holds his course, as certain as the Sunne.
> He makes it euer day, and euer spring,
> Where he doth shine, and quickens every thing
> Like a new nature: so, that true to call
> Him, by his title, is to say, He's all.
>
> (F2, 195)

And in *The Vision of Delight* (1616) Phant'sie asks the others to "Behold a King / Whose presence maketh this perpetual *Spring*." Also the tilt lies within a long courtly tradition. King James, after all, impersonates the supreme virtues of chivalry, being himself the direct descendant of King Arthur. The manifestation of these virtues during a tilt was an important part of courtly behavior.

While continuing an established tradition, the cycle develops new motifs (such as Britain being the seat for the Fifth Monarchy) that enrich the masque "canon." In this way one cycle is always related to other cycles, which always share a number of features. Some of their structural elements, for instance, are recurrent. There has to be a pompous courtly event, full of ceremony and theatricality, such as a wedding of importance, a prince's investiture, an important political event such as a signing of a treaty or an ambassador's visit and so on. This provides the occasion for devising a cycle of related events that must include one or more masques or plays, dances, a tilt, and—quite frequently—some public celebrations such as a progress through the city or by the river, a sea battle, and fireworks. In other words, each of these cycles fulfills the features of what Roy Strong calls the Renaissance "festival."[51] The particular elements of the cycle form a logical sequence and their unity is additionally secured by their intertextual character, which may perhaps be labeled their "interreferentiality."

Conclusion

My most important goal was to show that masques may be approached from at least several angles. Each of these approaches is equally valid, although it does not claim to be ultimate and decisive. In the beginning of this discussion I drew a distinction between several types of masques. In chronological order one may distinguish the dramatic masque, which later could become incorporated into the masque-in-performance (the second type), and the literary masque preserved either in manuscript or in print. Since hardly any dramatic masques have survived to the present, the focus of this book has been on the remaining two types.

Following the above distinction, it appears possible to view the literary masque as a new (albeit transitory) genre developed in the first half of the seventeenth century. From this perspective the masque is an amalgam of poetic and narrative elements with the distinctive feature of the genre being a focus on theatrical performance. The literary masque, a text about court theater, requires a reader who is acquainted with the new theater techniques of the period. The masque attempts to evoke an imaginary spectacle in the reader's mind, but at the same time carefully controls the selection of the elements of this "performance" and their possible interpretation(s). It constructs the performance with strictly literary means, unlike the masque-in-performance, which relies on a much more complex system of theater signs. The effect of this is an imaginary performance substantially different from the actual spectacle at court.

The fundamental difference, then, between drama and the literary masque is that the former attempts to create a performance of itself on a real stage, whereas the latter tries to create an imaginary performance in the reader's mind. Moreover, drama by definition anticipates its transposition into a different system of signs (theater), whereas the literary masque does not foresee such a possibility. Moreover, when the dramatic masque is transposed into the masque-in-performance, it loses its autonomy and becomes one of many elements of the theatrical text. This also

Conclusion

implies that the literary element in the masque-in-performance creates meanings only in relation to other elements of the production. In other words, it has only a partial effect on the ultimate outcome of the production. The literary masque, on the other hand, creates meanings independently of other systems; in this sense it is an autonomous work of art. It is not interpreted by anyone before it reaches the reader (the literary element of the masque-in-performance is always interpreted by whoever directs the whole). It is filtered only through the imagination and intellect of the reader. The author of the literary masque reaches the reader directly, as is the case with all literary works that are read by an individual (reading a literary work to somebody would inevitably include an element of interpretation).

The masque-in-performance in turn may be seen as a theatrical equivalent of a book of emblems. In a sequence of "openings" the "book" unfolds its pages on the illusionistic stage, which functions as the emblem icon. The verbal elements of the performance function as the emblem motto. Interestingly, the masque emblems show striking resemblance to the Stuart ideology in general and to James I's own writings. The masque-in-performance may also be treated as part of yet another complex system of signs—that is, as part of courtly behavior. In the first half of the seventeenth-century the latter was characterized by conspicuous theatricality. Individual courtiers acted the roles they assumed, and an individual's behavior at court often revealed the features of a work of art. The theatricality of court life inevitably led to theatrical forms of artistic expression, of which the masque-in-performance was the ultimate achievement. It may therefore be treated as a peculiar manifestation of courtly behavior ("peculiar" largely because it reveals the distinctive features of a ritual).

The masque-in-performance and to a lesser extent the literary masque reveal the tendency to form cycles of masques and also to become part of whole sequences of courtly events. This trend may be treated as the masque's distinctive feature; in itself it proves the masque's close relationship to other forms of courtly behavior. The masque-in-performance creates its full meaning only within its immediate court context. As my discussion of the two exemplary cycles attempted to show, when treated in isolation individual masques are deprived of their original richness and often fail to create coherent meanings. Moreover, a Stuart masque cannot be "staged" outside its original place and time as a typical theatrical performance can. It cannot be staged without the participation of the original performers and "spectators," if one is to keep to the traditional distinction, which actually does not apply to the masque. This is yet another feature that makes the masque unique among theatrical spectacles and brings it closer to the courtly ritual (this applies to the continental masques as well).

The masque-in-performance may also be considered as the fullest single manifestation of early Stuart culture. In actual productions it fused together all the arts—poetry, painting, music, architecture, sculpture, dancing, and acting—each created by the leading talents of the period. Its appearance was made possible only by the royal patronage (I do not know of a single instance of somebody writing a masque for its own sake); with the disappearance of this patronage the masque ceased to exist (the Commonwealth and Restoration "masques" are spectacles of an entirely different nature). From James's accession in 1603 to the outbreak of the Civil War, the masque-in-performance served an important ideological function at the Stuart court. Basically it presented in an allegorical and emblematic form the doctrine of Divine Right, the fundamental component of Stuart ideology, expounded in James's *Basilikon Doron*. The masque-in-performance presented an image of the monarch and of court that had little to do with reality. This image, however, is not a distinctive feature of the masque. The discrepancy between the real nature of people and systems in power and the image they try to create in the media is inseparably linked to the history of humanity and there are no signs that this should change in the near future, if ever at all.

Notes

Chapter 1. The Literary Masque

1. Which, of course, is a procedure as equally preposterous as if one labeled contemporary British literature "Thatcherite." In the case of the masques, however, there is some justification for the use of the qualifier "Stuart": most of the masques were directly sponsored by members of the royal family.
2. *Stuart Masque and the Renaissance Stage* (New York: Harcourt, Brace and Co., 1938).
3. Introduction to *The Court Masque,* ed. David Lindley (Manchester: Manchester University Press, 1984), 1.
4. *PQ* 22 (1943): 28.
5. First published in *ELH* 22 (1955): 108–24. I have used a later edition of this article, in *Ben Jonson: A Collection of Critical Essays* (Englewood Cliffs, N.J.: Prentice-Hall, 1963), 160–74.
6. Ibid., 160.
7. (Cambridge: Harvard University Press, 1965), 65.
8. *Inigo Jones: The Theatre of the Stuart Court,* 2 vols. (Berkeley and Los Angeles: University of California Press, 1973), 19.
9. MS J.a.1, ff. 168–74b.
10. Robert Cecil Papers, 164.36, f. 268b.
11. Royal MS. 17. B.xxxi; an example of this can be found right after the first song of the Tritons, when in the manuscript we read: "Wch ended, and the Musique ceassinge Oceanus provokes *Niger* as followeth," a stage direction that does not appear in the quarto, where there are no stage directions at all. This makes the manuscript a dramatic text, something that the Q edition is not.
12. *The Masque of Beauty,* F1 (1616), 910.
13. *Hymenaei* (London, 1606), sig. D3r-v.
14. (London, 1580), 65.
15. Ibid., 70–70b.
16. *The Masque of Queens* (Folio, 1616), 946.
17. Quoted from the 1631 edition, sig. C3.
18. Quoted from the 1638 edition, 1.
19. Q (1622) sig. B4v. Note that the order of names on title pages of the printed masques was significant to the people responsible for the invention. This was, in fact, one of the causes of the ongoing conflict between Ben Jonson and Inigo Jones. As we learn from a contemporary source, in 1632 the poetic script for a masque was commisioned to Aurelian Townshend, "Ben Jonson being for this time discarded, by reason of the predominant power of his antagonist, Inigo Jones, who this twelvemonth was angry with him for putting his own name before his in the title-page, which Ben Jonson made the subject of a bitter satire or two against Inigo" (Mr. Pory to Sir Thomas Puckering, 12 January 1632; quoted

from Thomas Birch, *The Court and Times of Charles the First* [London, 1848], 2:158–59).

20. *Britannia Triumphans: Inigo Jones, Rubens and Whitehall Palace* (London: Thames & Hudson, 1980), 15.

21. *The Golden Age Restor'd: The Culture of the Stuart Court, 1603–1642* (Manchester: Manchester University Press, 1981), 45.

22. See the discussion of the masque in my *Dangerous Matter: English Drama and Politics in 1623/24* (Cambridge: Cambridge University Press, 1986). Interestingly, Ben Jonson complained to William Drummond that the king's tutor, Buchanan, "had corrupte his [James's] eare when young, and learned him sing verses when he sould have read them" (*Notes of Ben Jonson's Conversations with William Drummond of Hawthornden* [London, 1842]), 34–35.

23. See the performance by Orazio Busino, *Calendar of State Papers, Venetian, London, 1909,* 15:111–14.

24. Quoted from Chambers, *The Elizabethan Stage* (Oxford: Clarendon Press, 1924), 1:172n.

25. Quoted from Sarah P. Sutherland, *Masques in Jacobean Tragedy* (New York: AMS Press, 1983), 121, n. 25.

26. (London, 1607), sig. C2v.

27. See Andrzej Zgorzelski, *Dramat: Między literaturą a teatrem* (Drama: Between literature and theater) (Gdańsk: Gdańskie Towarzystwo Naukowe, 1983), 226–30.

28. Sig. B.

29. His *Hymenaei* is a good example; for instance, on sig. Cv there are only seven lines of verse and the whole page is filled with notes.

30. (London, 1610), sig. E.

31. As Paula Johnson pointed out, "The relative literary merits of masque and pageant books are . . . less striking . . . than the common impulse to turn ephemeral entertainment into enduring text . . . the booklets share with another new phenomenon, the earliest "newspapers," an implicit assumption that the printed report validates the event" ("Jacobean Ephemera and the Immortal Word," *Renaissance Drama* 8 [1977]: 158). One has to remember, of course, that the earliest "newsbooks" appeared in England in the early 1620s—long after the first masques had appeared in print.

32. "The Jonsonian Masque as a Literary Form," 165.

33. See, for instance, Stephen Orgel's Yale edition of Jonson's masques.

34. Some of the printed pageant books are also about "fictitious" events, for they describe, for instance, royal entries that never took place (as the one prepared for and canceled in 1604). Paula Johnson observed that "the divergence of text from event in its own time, let alone now, makes evaluations of a given show's "dramatic unity" radically fallacious. We might try to judge a *text's* dramatic unity . . . but the texts, as the other evidence proves, are far more independent of the actual performances than are the scripts of plays, or even of masques. They are a combination of script, schema, and report, written according to developing customs and the changing styles" ("Jacobean Epherema," 160).

35. *The Jonsonian Masque,* 106.

36. (London, 1637).

37. *Hymenaei* (1606), sig. A3.

38. "On Linguistic Aspects of Translation," in *On Translation,* ed. Reuben A. Brower (Cambridge: Harvard University Press, 1959), 233.

39. This was written in 1594 and first published in 1596; I have used E. M. W. Tillyard's edition (London: Chatto & Windus, 1945).

Notes

40. Timothy Murray, *Theatrical Legitimation: Allegories of Genius in Seventeenth-Century England and France* (Oxford: Oxford University Press, 1987), 84.
41. Quoted from *Drammaticke Poems: Written by Samvell Daniell* (London, 1623), 409-10.
42. Quoted from John Nichols, *The Progresses, Processions, and Magnificent Festivities, of King James the First* . . . (London, 1828), 3:291.
43. Note "a," sig. Bv.
44. Ibid., sig. D3v.
45. F1 (1616), 987.
46. Sig. Br–v.
47. See sig. C–C3.
48. See *Theatrical Legitimation*, 83–93.
49. Ibid., 87.
50. Ibid., 87–89.
51. Carleton was the author of this report; see Nichols, *Progresses, Processions, and Festivities*, 1:472–73.
52. See John Russell Brown's introduction to his edition of *The Spring's Glory*, in *A Book of Masques in Honour of Allardyce Nicoll* (Cambridge: Cambridge University Press, 1967), 320 in particular.
53. As, for instance, Nabbes's *Microcosmus: A Morall Maske* (London, 1637), which is in fact—and in spite of its title—a full-length play.
54. In his "address to the reader" Heywood praises Inigo Jones's contribution to the splendor of production: "who to every Act, nay almost to every Sceane by his excellent Inventions, gave an extraordinary Luster; upon every occasion changing the stage, to the admiration of all the Spectators." See also Raymond C. Shady's essay "Thomas Heywood's Masque at Court," in *The Elizabethan Theatre VII*, ed. George Hibbard (Hamden, Conn.: Archon Books for the University of Waterloo, 1980), 147–66.
55. *The Jonsonian Masque*, 128.
56. Quoted from the folio edition (1640), 83.
57. See John P. Cuts, "Seventeenth-Century Illustrations of Three Masques by Jonson," *Comparative Drama* 6 (1972): 126.
58. I am grateful to Peter Blaney for pointing out to me the significance of black letter.
59. *The Jonsonian Masque*, 125.
60. Quoted from Nichols, *Progresses, Processions, and Festivities*, 3:295.

Chapter 2. The Emblematic Masque

1. Introduction to *The Court Masque*, ed. Lindley, 1.
2. See discussion of this concept in George R. Kernodle, *From Art to Theatre* (Chicago: University of Chicago Press, 1947), 47.
3. See Samuel Y. Edgerton, Jr., *The Renaissance Rediscovery of Linear Perspective* (New York: Basic Books, 1975), 74–75.
4. See, for instance, Marjorie Hope Nicholson, *The Breaking of the Circle: Studies in the Effect of the "New Science"* (New York: Columbia University Press, 1960), passim.
5. *Poems*, ed. W. C. Ward (London, 1894), 2:263.
6. *Minerva Britanna, or a Garden of Heroical Deuises, furnished, and adorned with Emblems and Impresa's of sundry natures* . . . (London, 1612), sig. Dd1.
7. "Universal Analogy and the Culture of the Renaissance," *Journal of the History of Ideas* 15 (1954): 304.

8. H. James Jensen, *The Muses' Concord* (Bloomington and London: Indiana University Press, 1976), 3.
9. Ibid., 19.
10. Cf. ibid., 50–55.
11. As was often the case with masques "invented" by Inigo Jones.
12. *Art and Power: Renaissance Festivals 1450–1650* (Berkeley and Los Angeles: University of California Press, 1984), 40–41.
13. See an interesting discussion of this problem in Dobrochna Ratajczak, "Teatralność i sceniczność" (Theatricality and stageability) in *Miejsce wspólne: Szkice o komunikacji literackiej i artystycznej,* ed. E. Balcerzan and S. Wysłouch (Warsaw: Polska Akademia Nauk, 1985), 66.
14. This was first printed "from the manuscript," now apparently lost, in Peter Cunningham, *Inigo Jones and Ben Jonson* (London: The Shakespeare Society, 1853), 131–42.
15. Several examples are: *The Masque of Augurs:* "Then he advanced with them to the King" (F2, 2:87), "After which *Apollo* went up to the King and sung" (ibid., 91); *The Fortunate Isles:* "Proteus, Portunus, and Saron come forth, and goe up singing to the *State*" (ibid., 139); *Love's Triumph Through Callipolis:* "Here hee goes up to the State" (Q1, 1631, sig. A3v); *The Lord's Masque:* "Sixteen pages, like fiery spirits . . . come forth below dancing a lively measure."
16. The distinction between the stage and the proscenium is, of course, of a later date than the period under discussion.
17. First published in London in 1938; the quoted passage comes from the New York edition (B. Blom, 1963), 35.
18. *Inigo Jones*, 16–17.
19. Nicoll, *Stuart Masque*, 35.
20. Cf. Claudio Guillén's "On the Concept and Metaphor of Perspective," *Comparatists at Work*, ed. Stephen G. Nichols, Jr., and Richard B. Vowles (Waltham, Mass.: Blaisdell Publishing Co., 1968), 26–90; 32–34 in particular.
21. Hence the masque's similarity to liturgical drama. For some interesting comments see Rainer Warning, "On the Alterity of Medieval Religious Drama," *New Literary History* 10 (1970): 267. As David Woodman observes, "the ceremony that drew the audience into the revels resembled a magical ritual, both audience and masquers entering into a celebration through which nature was controlled and villainous enchanters subdued" *(White Magic and English Renaissance Drama* [Rutherford, N.J.: Fairleigh Dickinson University Press, 1973], 88).
22. "The Reformation of the Masque," in *The Court Masque*, ed. Lindley, 97.
23. *Ben Jonson and the Language of Prose Comedy* (Cambridge: Harvard University Press, 1960), 244.
24. Graham Parry goes as far as to draw an analogy between the masque and the holy mass:

> One might draw an analogy with the Mass: the rituals of the ceremony, the formulae, the instruments employed, even the vestments of the celebrants bear witness to certain truths and have a symbolic significance which is only partially understood by those who attend. The central purpose is clear; the rituals are powerful and suggestive, beyond the level of rationality; the meaning of the symbolism can be known in detail by those who desire, but a limited understanding of the theological significance of the words, actions and instruments does not impair the efficacy of the ceremony. The religious analogy is not inappropriate, for both mass and masque solemnly and ceremonially reveal a mystery about the higher powers that operate in the world." *(The Golden Age Restor'd,* 44).

Notes

This of course is an extremely simplified view of the sacrament of the mass and may only be treated as a far-fetched simile.

25. Keir Elam, *The Semiotics of Theatre and Drama* (London and New York: Methuen, 1980), 102–9.

26. Ibid., 109.

27. (New York, 1982), 112.

28. *The Jonsonian Masque*, 14.

29. This is also the case of those masques in which elements of "drama" are introduced.

30. *Music in the Theatre of Ben Jonson* (Oxford: Clarendon Press, 1980), 241. This is an excellent book but unfortunately it has not found the recognition that it deserves.

31. This masque was first published by Rudolf Brotanek in *Die Englische Maskenspiel* (Vienna and Leipzig: W. Braumüller, 1902), 328–37.

32. I am using the second folio edition, 2:86.

33. This was first published in London in 1609.

34. The emblem showing the sleeping Hercules surrounded by Pigmees was very well known in England at that time.

35. *The Essays of Covnsels, Civill and Morall* (London, 1625), 225.

36. *Criticism and Compliment: The Politics of Literature in the England of Charles I* (Cambridge: Cambridge University Press, 1987), 199.

37. (London, 1580), 20b. For an interesting discussion of the function of music in the masques see Chan, *Music in The Theatre of Ben Jonson,* and John C. Meagher, *Method and Meaning in Jonson's Masques* (Notre Dame, Ind.: University of Notre Dame Press, 1966), 57–80.

38. This is *The Vision of Delight* (1617), which begins with a scene showing a street in perspective; "Delight is seene to come as afarre off, accompanied with *Grace, Love, Harmonie, Revell, Sport, Laughter."*

39. *Inigo Jones,* 11.

40. See the discussion of this problem in Nicoll, *Stuart Masque,* 36–38. More recently Joseph Loewenstein has argued that the function of the proscenium "is not to conduce between audience and stage, but to render the distinction between the two realms ceremonial. . . . Neither precisely barrier nor passageway, the proscenium celebrates the boundary between the phenomenal world of the play and that of its audience, so that the two spaces persistently verge on each other" (*Responsive Readings: Versions of Echo in Pastoral, Epic, and the Jonsonian Masque* [New Haven and London: Yale University Press, 1984], 122).

41. This was first published in a quarto edition in 1623, a unique copy of which is in private collection; I have used the second folio edition.

42. Cupid characteristically addresses also the Masquers and the Ladies, urging them to love and dance.

43. F2, 2:87.

44. (London, 1619), sig. C3. In his excellent book, John C. Meagher pointed out that "Jonson's masquers are not the highest powers represented in the masques; they are something more than ordinary mortals, but they are clearly subordinated to a god or a demigod. . . . In their subordination, the masquers are exalted, because they are presented in some form of participation in the glory of the superior powers. Sometimes the masquers are the votaries of the presiding gods. . . . In other cases, the masquers are direct representatives of the gods they serve, expressions of their power" (*Method and Meaning,* 49).

45. *The Jonsonian Masque,* 118.

46. *The Masque of Heroes,* sig. C3.

47. *Loves Triumph* (London, 1631), sig. A2.
48. Note "a," F1, 985.
49. Quoted from Nichols, *Progresses, Processions, and Festivities*, 3:258.
50. Max Jammer, *Concepts of Space: The History of Theories of Space in Physics*, 2d ed. (Cambridge: Harvard University Press, 1969), 40; Meagher, *Method and Meaning*, 124.
51. Quoted from Elam, *Semiotics of Theatre and Drama*, 68.
52. Discussing Ben Jonson's masques, Mary Chan observed that "In his development of the court masque Jonson draws together all the arts to create an image or emblem of the macrocosm itself" (*Music in the Theatre of Ben Jonson*, 137). She also makes an interesting point that the "audience" was in fact part of the emblem that a masque created (229).
53. Elam, *Semiotics of Theatre and Drama*, 30.
54. Quoted from ibid.
55. Many of the emblematic designs for the masques were commonplace in seventeenth-century England.
56. Orgel and Strong, *Inigo Jones*, 1:21.
57. *From Ritual to Theatre*, 81–82.
58. Elam discusses this phenomenon in a similar context; *Semiotics of Theatre and Drama*, 68.
59. "On Linguistic Aspects of Translation," 233.
60. Q1, sig. B3v–B4v.
61. *Art and Power,* 155.
62. *Stuart Masque,* 155.
63. *Changeable Scenery: Its Origin and Development in the British Theatre* (London: Faber and Faber, 1952), 34.
64. (London: Chatto & Windus, 1948), 96–97.
65. Margery Corbett and Ronald Lightbrown, *The Comely Frontispiece: The Emblematic Title-Page in England 1550–1660* (London: Routledge and Kegan Paul, 1979), 4–5.
66. *Inigo Jones*, 19.
67. (London, 1614), sig A4.
68. Corbett and Lightbrown, *The Comely Frontispiece*, 6.
69. Ibid., 35.
70. Ibid.
71. Roy Strong noted in his *Britannia Triumphans* the general similarity of the masque allegory to the Whitehall ceiling as painted by Rubens; he also gives several examples of direct iconographic relationship between particular masque designs and the murals (see, for instance, 15).
72. This was staged in 1617 and published in the second folio of Jonson's *Workes* (London, 1640).
73. Corbett and Lightbrown, *The Comely Frontispiece*, 47.
74. Other examples may be readily provided; see, for instance, *Tempe Restord* and *The Triumph of Peace*.
75. *Albions Trivmph: Personated in a Maske at Court. By the Kings Maiestie and his Lords* . . . (London, 1631[=32]), sig. A2v–A3. The design for the proscenium arch has been preserved and was reproduced by Orgel and Strong, *Inigo Jones*, 2:458–59.
76. "The Quarrel between Ben Jonson and Inigo Jones," in *The Renaissance Imagination*, ed. Stephen Orgel (Berkeley and Los Angeles: University of California Press, 1975), 88.

77. Leonard Barkan, in "Imperialist Arts of Inigo Jones," observed that "The definition of architecture is clearly all embracing: art and nature, theory and practice, heaven and earth, real and ideal. But what may be even more significant is the direct association of architecture with an imperial vision of the British monarchy. *Albion's Triumph* as a whole expresses monarchist imperialism by constant diverse allusions to imperial Rome. . . . These buildings are specific emblems of imperial power. Jones, having glorified himself and architecture, now demonstrates that the glory of an imperial realm is inextricable from its architecture. The monarch and the architect are engaged in similar and mutually interdependent arts . . ." (*Renaissance Drama*, n.s., 7 [1976]: 279).

78. It may be noted that in emblem books the icons were sometimes accompanied by dialogue, as in F. Quarles, *Emblems* (London, 1635), sig. G2v–G4.

79. Corbett and Lightbrown, *The Comely Frontispiece*, 47. Peacham's collection was entitled *Basilikon doron in emblemata versum*.

80. *Britannia Triumphans*, 45ff.

81. Freeman, *English Emblem Books*, 73.

82. "The Interpretation of Jonson's Courtly Spectacles," *PMLA* 61 (1946): 462. In a recent book Leah S. Marcus points out the similarity of language in Hercules' speeches (*Pleasure Reconciled to Virtue*) to King James's *Basilikon Doron*—see *The Politics of Mirth* (Chicago and London: University of Chicago Press, 1986), 124.

83. *The Symbolic Persons in the Masques of Ben Jonson* (Durham, N.C.: Duke University Press, 1948), 26.

84. Nicolson, *The Breaking of the Circle*, 59.

85. *Sermons*, ed. L. P. Smith (Oxford: Clarendon Press, 1920), 67.

86. *Emblems*, sig. A3.

87. "The Poetic Emblem," *Neophilologus* 54 (October 1970): 388.

88. See Strong, *Britannia Triumphans*, passim.

89. See Robert J. Clements, *Picta Poesis: Literature and Humanist Theory in Renaissance Emblem Books* (Rome: Edizioni di storia e letteratura, 1960), 68ff.

90. For Neoplatonic views of human and divine movements, see Paul Oskar Kristeller, *The Philosophy of Marsilio Ficino* (1943; reprint, Gloucester, Mass.: P. Smith, 1964), 387.

91. Orgel and Strong, *Inigo Jones*, 7.

92. Yuri Lotman and Boris Uspensky observed in their essay "On the Semiotic Mechanism of Culture," "it is clear that the very fact of emphasis on expression, of strictly ritualized forms of behavior, is usually a consequence either of seeing a one-to-one correlation (rather than an arbitrary one) between the level of expression and the level of content" (*New Literary History* 9 [1978]: 217).

93. Ibid.

94. *The Jonsonian Masque*, 123.

95. With the exception of those texts that in their printed form try to free themselves from the spectacle and become autonomous literary texts.

96. Lotman and Uspensky, "Semiotic Mechanism of Culture," 218.

97. This was published in London in 1615; the subtitle is significant to the point I am making: *A Dialogue shewing that our Souereigne Lord King Iames, being immediate vnder God . . . Doth rightfully claime . . . the Oath of Allegeance*.

98. *The Survival of the Pagan Gods: The Mythological Tradition and Its Place in the Renaissance Humanism and Art* (New York: Pantheon Books, 1953), 260–61.

99. "The Poetic Emblem," 385.

Chapter 3. The Masque of Behavior

1. Greenblatt, *Renaissance Self-Fashioning: From More to Shakespeare* (Chicago and London: University of Chicago Press, 1980), 162.
2. "Aesthetic Constituents in the Courtly Culture of Renaissance England," *New Literary History* 19 (Spring 1983): 599.
3. Greenblatt, *Renaissance Self-Fashioning*, 4.
4. Ibid., 165.
5. *Poetry and Courtliness in Renaissance England* (Princeton: Princeton University Press, 1978), 71.
6. *From Ritual to Theatre: The Human Seriousness of Play* (New York: Performing Arts Journal Publication, 1982), 79.
7. Ibid., 80.
8. Ibid., 81.
9. "Interpretation at Court: Courtesy and the Performer-Audience Dialectic," *New Literary History* 14 (1983): 625.
10. See the discussion of everyday life in Russia by Yuri M. Lotman, "The Poetics of Everyday Behaviour in Eighteenth-Century Russian Culture" in *The Semiotics of Russian Cultural History*, ed. A. D. Nakhimovsky and A. S. Nakhimovsky (Ithaca, N.Y.: Cornell University Press, 1985), 80–81.
11. James could spend as much as a third of the year hunting. It is not surprising therefore, that an echo for that "passion" appears in the masques.
12. I am using the plural because there were several banqueting houses.
13. Busino's description of the performance of Ben Jonson's *Pleasure Reconciled to Virtue* (1618), printed in translation in *Calendar of State Papers, Venetian*, 15:112.
14. Quoted from Nichols, *Progresses, Processions, and Festivities*, 2:74.
15. Quoted from J. Q. Adams, ed., *The Dramatic Records of Sir Henry Herbert, Master of the Revels, 1623–1673* (New Haven: Yale University Press, 1917), 56.
16. In *The Baroque: Literature and Culture in Seventeenth-Century Europe* (London: Methuen, 1978), 25. Skrine also adds that "on one level it was, no doubt, the stiffness and forced unnaturalness of court life and courtly behavior that led many people to seek relief in the delights offered by disguise: there are similarities here to the relaxation many aristocratic people found in pastoral play and poetry" (26).
17. Ralph Winwood, *Memorials of Affairs of State in the Reigns of Q. Elizabeth and K. James I* (London, 1725), 2:44.
18. (London, 1603), sig. H2.
19. A modern translation of Giovanni Battista Gabaleoni's letter, dated 8 January 1614 (29 December 1613, o.s.); quoted from John Orrell, "The Agent of Savoy at *The Somerset Masque*," *ELH* 28 (1977): 301–5.
20. Petr Bogatyrev, "Forms and Functions of Folk Threatre," in *Semiotics of Art: Prague School Contributions*, ed. Ladislav Matejka and Irwin R. Titunik (Cambridge: MIT Press, 1976), 55.
21. *The Political Works of James I*, ed. C. H. McIlwain (Cambridge: Harvard University Press, 1918).
22. Nichols, *Progresses, Processions, and Festivities*, 2:646–47.
23. *A Relation of the Royall, Magnificent, and Sumptuous Entertainment Given to the High and Mighty Princesse Queene Anne, at the Renowned Citie of Bristoll* (London, 1613).
24. Quoted from Nichols, *Progresses, Processions, and Festivities*, 2:667–68.
25. Lotman, *Poetics of Everyday Behaviour*, 85.
26. *The Survival of Pagan Gods*, 24.

Notes

27. Ibid., 26.
28. Ibid., 33.
29. *Jacobean Pageant or the Court of King James I* (Cambridge: Harvard University Press, 1963), 162.
30. Quoted from ibid.
31. See Roy Strong, *Henry, Prince of Wales and England's Lost Renaissance* (New York: Thames and Hudson, 1986), 158.
32. Ibid., 158–59.
33. Ibid. Strong identified an Inigo Jones design as the one that made Lord Campton a Shepherd Knight (il. 76).
34. This was the name Prince Henry frequently used; an anagram of this reads "Miles a Deo," or God's knight. It is worth mentioning that Meliadus, "the lord of the isles," appears in the extant *Barriers* by Ben Jonson, which leads one to suspect that he may have been the author of the "Challenge." It is known that Jonson did write a challenge of that kind in 1613/14 as part of celebrations of the Somerset marriage; see chap. 6 in this volume for details.
35. Charles Cornwallis, *The Life and Death of Ovr Late most Incomparable and Heroique Prince, Henry Prince of Wales* (London, 1641), 12–14. Cornwallis, as treasurer to the Prince, was an eyewitness to the events he described.
36. Nichols, *Progresses, Processions, and Festivities*, 2:49–50.
37. Ibid.
38. Quoted from ibid., 2:489–90.
39. *Criticism and Compliment*, 179–80.

Chapter 4. Masque Cycles and Courtly "Festivals"

1. Roy Strong, *Henry, Prince of Wales and England's Lost Renaissance* (New York: Thames and Hudson, 1986), 139.
2. Quoted from Nichols, *Progresses, Processions, and Festivities*, 1:291; see also n. 1.
3. Quoted from ibid., 1:301–2.
4. See Gertrude Marian Sibley, *The Lost Plays and Masques 1500–1642* (Ithaca, N.Y.: Cornell University Press, 1933), 188.
5. See *Jacobean and Caroline Revels Accounts, 1603–1642*, Malone Society Collections, no. 13 (Oxford: Malone Society, 1986), 3.
6. During the same occasion other festivities took place as well, including running at the ring. See F. P. Wilson, ed., *Dramatic Records in the Declared Accounts of the Office of Works, 1560–1640*, Malone Society Collections, no. 10 (London: Malone Society, 1977), 19.
7. Quoted from Nichols, *Progresses, Processions, and Festivities*, 2:90–91.
8. Quoted from Winwood, *Memorials*, 2:43.
9. *Jacobean and Caroline Revels Accounts, 1603–1642*, 8–9.
10. The Revels Accounts has the following entry: "Twelfe, Night The Princes Mask performed by Gentelmen of his High"; and in a marginal note: "This day the King: & prince, wth diuer of his Nobelmen did run att ye Ring for a prize."
11. Quoted from Nichols, *Progresses, Processions, and Festivities*, 1:330.
12. Birch, *Court and Times of Charles I*, 1:312; see also *Dramatic Records*, Malone Society Collections, no. 10, 38–39.
13. *Calendar State Papers, Venetian, 1625–26*, 345–46.
14. Quoted from Nichols, *Progresses, Processions, and Festivities*, 2:358.
15. *Henry, Prince of Wales and England's Lost Renaissance*, 139.
16. Ibid.

17. Published in London in 1610.

18. As David M. Bergeron has first noticed, Anthony Munday was paid forty-seven shillings "for devising of two speeches to be delivered to the Prince" and four pounds, six shillings, and four pence "for his paines and labour taken . . . for divers necessaries concerning the same preparation" (*English Civic Pageantry 1558–1642* [Columbia: University of South Carolina Press, 1971], 94).

19. Amphion is later identified as "the Genuis of Wales" [C4].

20. Compare the appropriate passage from King James's Bible [Gen. 28:12]: "And he [Jacob] dreamed, and behold a ladder set up on the earth, and the top of it reached to heaven: and behold the angels of God ascending and discending on it"; with Munday's "Jaacobs Ladder, reaching from Earth to Heaven. Whereon, their [the citizens' of London] hourelie, holie and deuoute desires (like to so many blessed Angelles) are continually ascending and descending."

21. (London, 1610), sig. A4v–B.

22. As John Pitcher has observed, "when Henry landed at Whitehall, late in the afternoon, to a salute of guns and tumultuous cheering, he had been acknowledged by two of the estates, the People and the City. Parliament and the Court would follow a few days later" (" 'In those figures which they seeme': Samuel Daniel's *Tethys' Festival*," in *The Court Masque*, ed. Lindley, 35). The sea monsters were played by Richard Burbage and John Rice.

23. The sermon was printed in a separate booklet, *The Creation of the Prince. A Sermon Preached in the Colledge of Westminster, on Trinity Sunday, the day before the Creation of the most Illustrioous* PRINCE *of Wales* (London, 1610).

24. "The Scene itself was a Port . . . within this Port were many Ships, small and great, seaming to lie at Anchor, some neerer, and some further off, according to perspective: beyond all appeared the Horison . . . which seemed to mooue with a gentle gale, and many Sayles, lying some to come into the Port, and others passing out" [sig. E3].

25. In " 'In those figures which they seeme,' " 35.

26. *Calendar of State Papers, Venetian, 1610–13*, 12:507.

27. Quoted from Nichols, *Progresses, Processions, and Festivities*, 2:361–62.

Chapter 5. Masque Cycle I

1. The complexities of the masque authorship are discussed in chap. 1 of this book.

2. *Finetti Philoxenis: Som[e] Choice Observations of Sr John Finett Knight . . .* (London, 1656), 8.

3. Elias Ashmode, *The Institutions, Laws & Ceremonies of the most Noble Order of the Garter* (London, 1672), 265. On extraordinary occasions the assembly of Knights Companions was sometimes held in the Windsor Castle, as was the case in 1613. The Saint George chapel, the official sanctuary of the order, was at Windsor. Note too that the image of Saint George slaying the dragon was adopted as part of the order's insignia.

4. (London, 1613), sig. C2.

5. Ibid., sig. C.

6. *Rosicrucian Enlightenment* (London and Boston: Routledge and Kegan Paul, 1972), 3–4.

7. *History of Fireworks* (London: Harrap, 1949), 34–35.

8. Ibid., 35.

9. The full title of this piece is *Heaven's Blessing and Earth's Joy; or, A True*

Notes

Relation of the Supposed Sea-Fights and Fire-Woerkes as Were Accomplished Before the Royall Celebration of the All-Beloved Marriage of the Two Peerlesse Paragons of Christiandome, Frederick and Elizabeth (London, 1613); this is reproduced in Nichols, *Progresses, Processions, and Festivities*, 2:527–35.

10. Yates also noted that "Coming between the investiture and the wedding it [the show of fireworks] was already intended as an allegory of the Elector Palatine as St. George, patron of the Order of the Garter, clearing the world of evil enchantments" (*Rosicrucian Enlightenment*, 4).

11. This was originally written in Latin; anonymously translated into English, the poem appeared in print in London in 1613.

12. Cf. Religion's speech, up to stanza 65 in part 1.

13. Nichols, *Progresses, Processions, and Festivities*, 2:529.

14. Ibid.

15. Reproduced in ibid., 2:536–52.

16. Ibid., 2:540–41.

17. As John King, the bishop of London, wrote in his sermon to be preached on the Tuesday after the marriage: "The meaning is, that God must be present at the ioyning of man and woman, that they must marry in Domino, in the Lord . . ." (*Vitis Palatina: A Sermon Appointed to be preached at Whitehall vpon Tuesday after the marriage of the Ladie Elizabeth her Grace* [London, 1614], sig. C3).

18. Quoted from Nichols, *Progresses, Processions, and Festivities*, 2:541.

19. A ground plan of the hall is extant and was reproduced, among others, by Per Palme in *Triumph of Peace* (London: Thames and Hudson, 1957), 116.

20. Orgel and Strong, *Inigo Jones*, 1:241.

21. Ibid., 1:253.

22. For full documentation see *Dramatic Records, Malone Society Collections*, no. 10, 24.

23. John Chamberlain, *Letters*, ed. N. E. McClure (Philadelphia: American Philosophical Society, 1939), 1:425.

24. *Inigo Jones*, 1:241.

25. Ibid.

26. In the commentary to the accounts of the Office of Works, R. F. Hill noted that the "new banqueting house" was a temporary building, specially built for these festivities at a cost of £648.18.5, and that the building "was not used for any of the marriage masques" (*Dramatic Records, Malone Society Collections*, no. 10, xvii and 24).

27. *Survey of London* (London: London County Council, 1930), 13:61.

28. *The Earl of Strafford's Letters and Dispatches* (Dublin, 1740), 2:140.

29. Ibid., 2:130.

30. Quoted from Nichols, *Progresses, Processions, and Festivities*, 2:548.

31. *Calendar of State Papers, Venetian, 1610–13*, 12:499.

32. Sir Ralph Winwood, *Memorials of Affairs of State* (London, 1725), 3:435 (Chamberlain to Winwood, 23 February 1613).

33. Chamberlain, *Letters*, 1:428.

34. In *A Book of Masques in Honour of Allardyce Nicoll* (Cambridge: Cambridge University Press, 1987), 98.

35. Ibid., 98.

36. *The Works of Francis Bacon*, ed. Basil Montague (Philadelphia, 1853), 1:295.

37. Ibid., 1:305.

38. Remember that a "Pyramid" of fire was the last "act" of fireworks.

39. This particular emblem is called "Gloria de Prencipi" (Glory of the Princes).

40. Sir Edward Phelips (1560?–1614) was the Speaker of the House of Commons (also in 1610) and Master of the Rolls. He had also been chancelor to Prince Henry.

41. Costuming the players is similar to the "show" with the captured "Turks," discussed above.

42. The investiture could, however, take place outside England by proxy.

43. (London, 1672).

44. Ibid., 2–3.

45. This detail has been noticed by D. J. Gordon in his well-known essay "Chapman's *Memorable Masque*," in *The Renaissance Imagination*, ed. Orgel, 194–202.

46. "Chapman's *Memorable Masque*," 198–99.

47. Ibid., 198.

48. Ibid.

49. Ibid.

50. For a discussion of the complexity of this aspect of the masque see Jack E. Reese, "Unity in Chapman's *Masque of the Middle Temple and Lincoln's Inn*," *SEL* 4 (1984): 291–305.

51. In Gordon, "Chapman's *Memorable Masque*," 201.

52. All these direct references to the king leave no doubt that he is one of the important characters in the masque. He plays the role of the spectator.

53. There seems to be a distant contrast as this point with the "fallen tree" in the stage set, from which "baboons" appeared for their antimasque. The symbolism of a fallen tree needs no explanation.

54. Reese, "Unity," 294; Gordon, in his interpretation of the masque, claimed that Chapman's America is reminiscent of Guiana rather than Virginia. The worship of sun is not Virginian at all, neither is the gold. Gordon concludes: "And this [Guiana] of course brings us to Ralegh. It was Ralegh who discovered Guiana for the English . . . from the Tower he had been attempting to revive interest in an expedition to Guiana, and in 1612 he had offered to send Keymis there again, offering to fit out vessels at his own expense. . . . We know of Chapman's connexions with the Ralegh circle, and I cannot doubt that the Colonizing projects and the political ideas of the Ralegh circle are presented in this masque . . . [this] had from the beginning been also part of an anti-Spanish policy, a Protestant anti-Catholic policy . . . ." ("Chapman's *Memorable Masque*," 202). This, I think, is a typical example of reading into the text things that may only have been loose associations of contemporaries. Besides, seeing the masque only as a reflection of somebody's colonizing projects would narrow its scope immensely.

55. Reese, "Unity," 295.

56. In Bacon's *The Wisdome of the Ancients* Pan is identified with nature.

57. The text survives in two different versions: the Q1 of 1613 and the Folio of 1647 (in Beaumont and Fletcher's *Comedies and Tragedies*).

58. Chamberlain to Alicia Carleton, 18 February 1613 (Chamberlain, *Letters*, 1:425–26).

59. It is explained earlier in the text that this is quite appropriate for the "device," for rivers get water from springs and rain.

60. Which is of course an echo of Chapman's masque.

61. This arrangement is strikingly similar to the one in *The Lords Masque*, where the stage is also divided horizontally into a lower and an upper region. First the lower region is uncovered, and later the masquers are discovered by a falling curtain.

Notes

62. Nichols, *Progresses, Processions and Festivities*, 2:549.
63. Ibid.
64. Chamberlain to Carleton, 25 February 1613 (*Calendar State Papers, Domestic, 1611–18*, 9:172).
65. Chamberlain to Sir Dudley Carleton, 25 February 1613 (*Letters*, 1:431).
66. In a recent article David Norbrook has noted that the whole idea of the masque may have originated before Prince Henry's death, for "Francis Beaumont's masque for the Inner Temple and Gray's Inn presented festivities held on Mount Olympus, which seems to have been particularly associated with Henry by his panegyrists" ("'The Masque of Truth': Court Entertainments and International Protestant Politics in the Early Stuart Period," *Seventeenth Century* 1 [July 1986]: 91–92).
67. Ibid.
68. Jocquet derived most of his text from an English pamphlet which, however, mentions Beaumont's masque. This means that Jocquet must have used a different source for his summary. See ibid., 82.
69. Ibid., 82–83.
70. Ibid., 83.
71. Ibid., 90–91. I do not agree with David Norbrook, however, that this motif makes the masque unique among Stuart works. As I show below, the cycle of masques presented at the marriage of the earl of Somerset develops this apocalyptic motif into an elaborate ideological statement.
72. This representation in turn derives from Ripa, fig. 311 (1709 ed.).

Chapter 6. Masque Cycle II

1. As, for instance, in Peacham, *Minerva Britanna*, 158.
2. Ibid., 182.
3. The first of the quoted references comes from a letter, written in Spanish by Ferdinand de Boischot. The letter has been preserved in the Vienna Archives and was first reproduced by Willem Schrickx, *Foreign Envoys* (Wetteren, Belgium: Universe, 1986), 325–28. I would like to thank Eileen McWilliam for translating the letter. The reference to the "devils" comes from Giovanni Battista Gabaleoni's letter dated 8 January 1614 (29 December 1613, o.s.), reproduced by John Orrell. The appropriate passage reads as follows: "The show was begun with a speech made by four men dressed poorly, which, to judge by the tenor of their voices, would have been more suitable to a funeral than to the joys of a wedding. When that was over a masque of twelve devils was begun" (John Orrell, "The Agent of Savoy at *The Somerset Masque*, *ELH* 28 [1977]: 304). Quite contrary to Orrell's comments (cf. 303), Gabaleoni correctly understood the appearance of the squires as seeming funereal. And, of course, he is right again (also contrary to Orrell's opinion) when he takes the antimasquers for devils.
4. Ibid., 326.
5. See, for instance, Geffrey Whitney, *A Choice of Emblems and Other Devices* (Leyden, 1586), 119; Peacham, *Minerva Britanna*, 5, 146.
6. *The Heroical Devices of M. Claudius Paradin*, transl. P. S. (London, 1591; reprint, Delmar, N.Y.: Scholars' Facsimiles & Reprints, 1984), 137.
7. (London, 1635), 42. This was an English version of Gabriel Rollenhagen's *Nucleus Emblematum Selectissimarum* (Cologne, 1611).
8. Whitney, *A Choice of Emblems*, 96.
9. P.S., *Heroical Devices*, 17.

10. *The Fifth Monarchy Men* (Totowa, N.J.: Rowman and Littlefield, 1972), 21.

11. Ibid., 31. See also James's own *A Fruitfull Meditation* (1603 ed.)., sig. A4v, B3v. On 14 February 1609 Chamberlain wrote to Carleton mentioning that "the Pope hath written to the French king, complaining that our king misuseth him continually in table-talk, and calls him *Antichrist* at every word" (quoted from Birch, *The Court and Times of James the First*, 1:87–88). For a discussion of James's apocalyptic thought see Paul Christianson, *Reformers and Babylon* (Toronto: University of Toronto Press, 1978), 94–97.

12. The phrase "Ancient of daies" designates the judge in the eschatological sense; see *The Interpreter's Dictionary of the Bible* (New York: Abingdon Press, 1962), 1:126.

13. Spring appears as a character in the last masque of the cycle, *The Masque of Flowers*.

14. Chamberlain, *Letters*, 1:498.

15. Barnaby Rich, *A New Description of Ireland* (London, 1610), 38.

16. Ibid., 34–36.

17. *The Works of Francis Bacon*, ed. Basil Montagu (Philadelphia, 1853), 2:285.

18. Ibid., 477.

19. John Davies, *A Discoverie of the State of Ireland: with the true Causes why that Kingdom was neuer entirely Subdued, nor brought vnder Obedience of the Crowne of ENGLAND, vntil the Beginning of his Maiesties most happie Raigne* (London, 1613), 259. For a brief but interesting outline of the situation in Ireland around 1613 see Linda Levy Peck's *Northampton: Patronage and Policy at the Court of James I* (London: Allen and Unwin, 1982), 89–94.

20. Davies, *Discoverie*, 264.

21. Ibid., 272.

22. Ibid., 282.

23. Chamberlain to Carleton, 5 January 1614: "The Marriage still continues in gallantry and triumph. . . . The lofty Maskers were so well liked at Court the last week, that they are appointed to perform it again on Monday; yet this Device, which was a mimical imitation of the Irish, was not so pleasing to many, which think it no time, as the case stands, to exasperate that nation by making it ridiculous." As is apparent from Chamberlain's comments, some of the spectators did not understand the broader implication of the masque.

24. Bogatyrev, "Semiotics in the Folk Theatre," 42.

25. Rich, *New Description of Ireland*, sig. B2.

26. Ibid., 116. Many people in Ireland were offended by Rich's book; he defended his basic ideas in *A Trve and Kinde Excvse Written in Defense of that Booke, intituled A Newe Description of Irelande*, published in London in 1612.

27. Nichols, *Progresses, Processions, and Festivities*, 2:732.

28. Chambers, *The Elizabethan Stage*, 3:442–43.

29. Nichols, *Progresses, Processions, and Festivities*, 2:733–34. In an earlier letter, dated 23 December 1613, Chamberlain informed Carleton that "Francis Bacon prepares a masque to honour this marriage, which will stand him in above £2000" (quoted from Birch, *The Court and Life of James the First*, 1:282).

30. Published in London in 1614.

31. Quoted from *Regales Aphorismi: Or, a Royal Chain of Golden Sentences, Divine, Moral, and Politicall, as at severall times, and on several occasions they were delivered by king JAMES* (London, 1650), 77–79. Another contemporary, Godfrey Goodman, mentions in his *Fall of Man* (1616) the use of tobacco and drunkenness as evidences of the general decline of society and an indication of humanity's fall;

Notes

see Victor Harris, *All Coherence Gone* (Chicago: University of Chicago Press, 1949), 41.

32. In the masque the firmament on stage is not the source of light: it is "night" there; however, the glittering lights in the garden must be the reflection of the sun, or of James.

33. Francis Bacon, *Of Gardens*, in *Essays*, vol. 6 of *The Works of Francis Bacon*, ed. J. Spedding and L. R. Ellis (London, 1858), 485–92; the quoted passage comes from 489–90.

34. Ibid., 486.

35. Roy Strong, *The Renaissance Garden in England* (London: Thames and Hudson, 1979), 113.

36. Ibid., 115.

37. Published in Paris in 1624; see "Problesme VI." His first book, *La Perspective* (1612), was dedicated to Prince Henry.

38. Wither, *A Collection of Emblemes*, 218.

39. (Paris, 1633), 5.

40. Bacon, *Of Gardens*, 485.

41. Quoted from Katharine R. Firth, *The Apocalyptic Tradition in Reformation Britain 1530–1645* (Oxford: Oxford University Press, 1979), 167.

42. Quoted from ibid., 186.

43. D. Maxey, *Five Sermons Preached before the King* (London, 1614); the quoted passage comes from the third sermon, "The Churches Sleepe," 84–85.

44. Ibid., 88.

45. Sampson Price, *A Heavenly Proclamation to Fly Romish Babylon* (London, 1614), 2. This is in fact a sermon preached at Oxford on 21 November 1613.

46. Ibid., 32.

47. London, 1610, p. 18.

48. Wither, *A Collection of Emblemes*, 159.

49. The full title of this work is significant: *The Triumphs of King Iames the First, Of Great Brittaine, France, and Ireland, King; Defender of the Faith. Pvblished vpon his Maiesties aduertisement to all the Kings, Princes, and Potentates of Christendome, and confirmed by the wonderfull Works of GOD, declared in his life*. The quoted passage comes from page 58.

It is interesting to note that in the masque there are echoes, not necessarily direct, of current religious writings. In the latter, the image of a heavenly garden often appears and is usually associated with the state of England, with James being the gardener. For instance, in the anonymous treatise *England's Paradise: Discovered in the Latine prospect of IACOBS blessing* (London, 1612), King James came to England from the north, "as the Angel of the lord, to lead his people," and "Henrie Prince of Wales is our Meridian field, richly planted. . . . His Father *Apollo* the King, hath watered him . . ." (sig. G2). At another place the court is compared to "a mellifluous garden" (G2v).

The author goes on to prove how both the biblical Jacob and the Jacob of England, or James I, are gardening a "blessed field." There are three manifestations of this blessing:

> The first is for scituation, the second for plants, and the third for fruitfull vantages of watering. In the first *Iaacob* is a blessed field, scited in the sunne, the fairest sunne the Sonne of God which always shines. . . .
> The second blessing of *Iaacob* and his brother [James I], is in respect of plants, the most louely plants, the tree of knowledge and the tree of life, both planted in *Iaacob*. . . . Here is the beauty of Paradise. . . . Here the Lord made to grow euery tree pleasant to the

sight and good for meat; the tree of life and the tree of knowledge in the middest of the garden . . . *Loue, Ioy, Peace, Long-suffering, Gentlenesse, Faith, Meekeness, Temperance.* These are plants which our heauenly father hath planted, daily increasing with the increase of God in this garden. . . .

The third blessing of the field, is by the daily watering of the plants. . . . Christ is come into his garden: in the middest of the garden is a fountaine of liuing waters, this maketh the garden blessed. Christ is the well of liuing waters: O blessed fountaine; with thee is the well of life: and this is the happinesse of our Paradise. . . . [H3v–Iv]

50. Quoted from Nichols, *Progresses, Processions, and Festivities,* 1:371.

51. In his recent book *Henry, Prince of Wales and England's Lost Renaissance* (New York: Thames and Hudson, 1986), Strong observed that "The Renaissance festivals in the main embrace three forms: the state entry into a city, the exercise of arms, and forms of spectacle making use of acting, singing, music and dance that took place within a palace" (139).

Bibliography

Masques and Entertainments

Beaumont, Francis. *The Masque of the Inner Temple and Grayes Inne. Presented Before his Maiestie, the Queeenes Maiestie, the Prince, Count Palatine and the Lady Elizabeth their Highnesses, in the Banquetting house at White-hall on Saturday the twentieth day of Februarie 1612* [1613]. London, 1613.

Browne, William. *Circe and Ulysses. The Inner Temple Masque*, MS, Emmanuel College, Cambridge. Published edition by Gwyn Jones. London: Golden Cockerel Press, 1954.

Campion, Thomas. *The Description of A Maske Presented Before the King's Majestie at Whitehall, on Twelfth Night Last, in Honour of the Lord Hayes and His Bride . . . Invented and set forth by Thomas Campion, Doctor of Phisicke.* London, 1607.

———. *The Description of a Maske: Presented in the Banqueting roome at Whitehall, on Saint Stephens night last, At the Mariage of the Right Honourable the Earle of Somerset: And the right noble the Lady Frances Howard. Written by Thomas Campion. Whereunto are annexed divers choyse Ayres composed for this Maske that may be sung with a single voyce to the Lute or Base-Viall.* London, 1614.

———. *A Relation of the Late Royall Entertainment Given by the Right Honorable the Lord Knowles, at Cawsome-House neere Redding: to our most Gracious Queene, Queene Anne, in her Progresse toward the Bathe, vpon the seuen and eight and twentie dayes of Aprill, 1613. Whereunto is annexed the Description, Speeches, and Songs of the Lords Maske, presented in the Banquetting-house on the Marriage night of the High and Mightie,* COVNT PALATINE, *and the Royally descended the Ladie Elizabeth.* London, 1613.

[Carew, Thomas, and Inigo Jones.] *Coelum Britanicum: A Masque at White-Hall in the Banqueting-House, on Shrove-Tuesday-night, The 18. of February, 1633.* London, 1634.

Chapman, George. *The Memorable Maske of the two Honorable Houses or Inns of Court; the Middle Temple, and Lyncolns Inne. As it was performed before the King, at White-Hall on Shroue Munday at night; being the 15. of February. 1613. At the Princely celebration of the most Royall Nuptialls of the Palsgraue, and his thrice gratious Princesse Elizabeth. &. With a description of their whole show; in the manner of their march on horse-backe to the Court from the Maister of the Rolls his house: with all their right Noble consorts, and most showfull attendants. Inuented, and fashioned, with the ground, and speciall structure of the whole worke, By our Kingdomes most Artfull and Ingenious Architect Innigo Iones. Supplied, Aplied, Digested, and Written, By Geo: Chapman.* London, 1613.

Cohayne, Aston. *A Masque Presented at Bretbie in Darbyshire on Twelfth-Night. 1639.* First published in Cohayne's *Chaine of Golden Poems.* London, 1658.

Daniel, Samuel. *Tethys Festival: or The Qvenes Wake. Celebrated at Whitehall, the fifth day of June 1610*. London, 1610. Annexed to *The Order and Solemnitie of the Creation* . . . ; listed below].

———. *The Vision of the Twelve Goddesses, presented in a Maske the eight of January [1604], at Hampton Court. By the Queenes most excellent Maiesty, and her Ladies.* London, 1623.

[Davenant, William.] *The Triumphs of the Prince D'Amour. A Masque Presented by His Highnesse at his Pallace in the Middle Temple, the 24th of Februarie 1635.* London, 1635 [1636].

Davison, Francis. *The Mask of Proteus and the Adamantine Rock.* In *Gesta Grayorum or the History of the High and Mighty Prince Henry Prince of Purpoole Anno Domini 1594* [1595]. Modern edition by Desmond Bland. Liverpool: Liverpool University Press, 1968.

Dekker, Thomas. *The Magnificent Entertainment: Giuen to King Iames, Queene Anne his wife, and Henry Frederick the Prince vpon the day of his Maiesties Trymphant Passage (from the Tower) through his Honourable Citie (and Chamber) of London, being the 15 of March 1603. As well by the English as by the Strangers: with the Speeches and Songes, deliuered in the seueral Pageants.* London, 1604.

The First Antimaske of Mowntebanks. Add. MS. 5956, ff. 74–82b. First published as part of Peter Cunningham's *Inigo Jones and Ben Jonson*, 111–30. London: J. Payne Collier, 1853.

Florimène. The Argument of the Pastoral of Florimène, with the description of scenes and intermedii. Presented by the Queen's majesty's commandment, before the King's majesty in the hall at Whitehall on Saint Thomas' Day, the 21st of December 1635. London, 1636.

Jones, Inigo, and William Davenant. *Lvminalia, or The Festivall of Light. Personated in a Masque at Court, By the Queenes Majestie, and her Ladies. On Shrovetuesday Night, 1637.* London, 1637 [1638].

———. *Salmacida Spolia: A Masque Presented by the King's and Queen's Majesties at Whitehall on Tuesday the 21 day of January 1639* [1640]. London, 1639 [1640].

———. *The Temple of Love. A Masque. Presented by the Qveenes Majesty, and her Ladies, at White-hall on Shrove-Tuesday, 1634.* London, 1634 [1635].

Jones, Inigo, and Ben Jonson. *Pans Anniversarie; or, The Shepherds Holyday. The Scene* ARCADIA. *As it was presented at Court befroe King* JAMES. *1620. The Inventors, Inigo Jones. Ben Jonson*, 118–24. Folio, 1640.

Jonson, Ben. *B. Jon: His Part of King James his Royall and Magnificent Entertainment through his Honourable Cittie of London.* . . . London, 1604.

———. *A Challenge at Tilt*, 995–1000. Folio, 1616.

———. *The Description of the Masque. With the Nuptiall Songs. Celebrating the happy Marriage of Lady Elizabeth Ratcliffe, Daughter to the right Honor: Robert, Earle of Sussex. At Court On the Shroue-Tuesday at night. 1608.* London, 1608.

———. *For the Honour of Wales* [1618], 30–38. Folio, 1640.

———. *The Fortunate Isles, and Their Union. Celebrated in a Masque Design'd for the Court, on the Twelfth night. 1624.* London, 1625.

———. *The Golden Age Restored*, 1010–15. Folio, 1616.

———. *Hymenaei: or the Solemnities of Masque, and Barriers. Magnificantly performed on the eleventh, and twelfth Nights, from Christmas; At Court, To the auspicious celebrating of the Marriage-union, between Robert, Earle of Essex, and the Lady Frances, second Daughter to the most noble Earle of Suffolke.* London, 1606.

Bibliography

———. *The Irish Masque at Covrt, by Gentlemen the Kings Servants*, 1000–4. Folio, 1616.

———. *Love Restored, In a Masque at Court, by Gentlemen the Kings Seruants*, 989–95. Folio, 1616.

———. *Lovers Made Men. A Masque Presented in the House of the Right Honorable the Lord Haye. By diuers of noble qualitie, his friends. For the Entertaynment of Monsieur Le Baron de Tovr, extraordinarie Ambassador for the French King. On Saterday the 22. of February. 1617.* London, 1617.

———. *The Masque of Augurs. With The Several Antimasques. Presented on Twelfe-Night, 1622.* London, 1622.

———. *The Masque of Gypsies* [1621]. MSS Harleian, MS. 4955; Huntington MS. HM 741.

———. *A Masque of Her Maiesties. Love Freed from Ignorance and Folly*, 984–89. Folio, 1616.

———. *The Masque of Owles at Kenelworth. Presented by the Ghost of Captaine Coxe mounted in his Hoby-horse.* 1626, 125–28. Folio, 1640. [Not a masque.]

———. *The Masque of Qveenes Celebrated From the House of Fame: By the most absolute in all State, And Titles. Anne Queene of Great Britaine, & c. With her Honourable Ladies. At White Hall, Febr. 2. 1609.* London, 1609.

———. *Mercurie Vindicated From the Alchymists, at Court, By Gentlemen, the Kings Servants*, 1:217–22. Folio, 1640.

———. *Mocke-maske. The Christmas Shewe before the Kinge. 1615.* Folger MS. J.a.1, ff. 168–74b.

———. *Neptune's Triumph for the Return of Albion.* London, 1624.

———. *Newes From the New World Discover'd in the Moone. A Masque. As It Was Presented at Court Before King Iames.* 1620, 39–46. Folio, 1640.

———. *Oberon, The Fairy Prince. A Masque of Prince Henry*, 975–83. Folio, 1616.

———. *Pleasure Reconciled to Virtue* [1618], 22–29. Folio, 1640.

———. *The Qveenes Masque. The first, of Blacknesse: Personated at the Court, at White-Hall, on the Twelu'th night, 1605.* London, 1608.

———. *The Second Masque Which was of Beavtie; Was presented in the same Court, at White-Hall, on the Sunday night after the Twelfth Night. 1608.* London, 1608.

———. *The Speeches at Prince Henries Barriers*, 965–74. Folio, 1616.

———. *Time Vindicated to Himself and to His Honors. In the presentation at Covrt on Twelfth night.* London, 1623.

———. *The Vision of Delight*, 15–22. Folio, 1616.

———. *The Vision of Delight Presented at Covrt in Christmas, 1617*, 2:16–21. Folio, 1640.

Jonson, Ben, and Inigo Jones. *Chloridia. Rites to Cloris and Her Nymphs. Personated in a Masque, at Court. By the Queenes Maiesty and her Ladies. At Shroue-tide.* London, 1630 [1631].

———. *Loves Triumph Throvgh Callipolis. Performed in a Masque at Court. 1630. By his Maiestie with the Lords, and Gentlemen assisting. The Inventors. Ben. Ionson. Jnigo Iones.* London, 1630 [1631].

The King and Qveenes Entertainment at Richmond. After Their Departure from Oxford: In a Masque, presented by the most Illustrious Prince, Prince Charles Sept. 12. 1636. Oxford, 1636.

[Kynaston, F.?] *Corona Minervae. Or a Masque Presented before Prince Charles His Highnesse, The Duke of York his Brother, and the Lady Mary his Sister, the 27th of February, at the Colledge of the Mvseum Minervae.* London, 1635 [1636].

Marston, John. *The Noble Lorde & Lady of Huntingdons Entertainment of theire right Noble Mother Alice: Countesse Dowager of Darby the first night of her honors arrivall att the house of Ashby.* Modern edition by A. H. Bullen. *The Works of John Marston,* 3:383–404. London, 1887.

The Maske of Flowers. Presented By the Gentlemen of Graies-Inne, at the Court of Whitehall, in the Banquetting House, vpon Twelfe night, 1613. . . . London, 1614.

The Mask of Four Seasons [1634?]. First published by Peter Cunningham. In *Inigo Jones and Ben Jonson,* 143–48. London: The Shakespeare Society, 1853.

A Masque at Coleoverton [1618?]. First published by Rudolf Brotanek. In *Die Englischen Maskenspiele,* 328–37. Vienna and Leipzig: W. Braumüller, 1902.

Masque in 5 Acts [1643?]. Egerton MS. 1994, ff. 212–23.

The Masque of the Twelve Months. First published by Peter Cunningham. In *Inigo Jones and Ben Jonson,* 131–42. London: The Shakespeare Society, 1853.

Middleton, Thomas. *The Inner-Temple Masque. Or Masque of Heroes. Presented (as an entertainment fro many worthy Ladies:) By Gentlenmen of the same Ancient and Noble Hovse.* London, 1619.

Middleton, Thomas, and William Rowley. *A Courtly Masque. The Deuice called, The World tost at Tennis. As it hath beene diuers times Presented to the Contentment of many Noble and Worthy Spectators: By the* PRINCE *his seruants. Inuented and set downe,* BY *Tho: Middleton & William Rowley Gent.* London, 1620.

Shirley, James. *The Trivmph of Peace. A Masque, presented by the Four Honourable Houses, or Innes of Court. Before the King and Queenes Majesties, in the Banquetting-house at White Hall, February the third, 1633. Inuented and Written,* BY *James Shirley.* London, 1633 [1634].

The Theatre of Apollo where Fires of Joy are raised: secred to the euer happie and aeternall memory of our Soveraygne the Great Apollo, and his most Roiall Ofspring. Before prepared to be offered to the sacred Maiesty of our deceased Souereigne King Iames. And now presented to the Roiall handes of our Gracious ord, King Charles, heir to the Kingdomes, vertues, and glories of his Father [1624/25]. MSS Royal, MS. 18A. LXX.

Townshend, Aurelian. *The Anti-Masques* [1635?]. Huntington MS 136016.

Townshend, Aurelian, and Inigo Jones. *Albions Trivmph. Personated in a Maske at Court. By the Kings Maiestie and his Lords. The Sunday after Twelfe Night.* London, 1630 [1631].

———. *Tempe Restord. A Masque Presented by the Qveene, and fourteene Ladies, to the Kings Maiestie at Whitehall on Shrove-Tuesday. 1631.* London, 1631 [1632].

Webster, John. *Monuments of Honour . . . Celebrated in the Honourable City of London . . . Expressing in a Magnificent Tryumph, all the Pageants, Chariots of Glory, Temple of Honor, besides a specious and goodly Sea Tryumph.* London, 1624.

White, Robert. *Cupid's Banishment* [1617]. First published by John Nichols. In *The Progresses, Processions, and Magnificent Festivities, of King James the First, His Royal Consort, Family and Court,* 3:283–96. London, 1828.

Books and Articles

Adams, J. Q., ed. *The Dramatic Records of Sir Henry Herbert, Master of the Revels, 1623–1673.* New Haven and London: Yale University Press, 1917.

Bibliography

Akrigg, G. P. V. *Jacobean Pageant or the Court of James 1.* Cambridge: Harvard University Press, 1963.

Alciatus, Andreas. *Emblems in Translation.* Edited by Peter M. Doly and Simon Cuttler. 2 vols. Toronto: University of Toronto Press, 1985.

Altieri, Joanne. "Responses to a Waning Mythology in Carew's Political Poetry." *SEL* 26 (1986): 107–24.

———. *The Theatre of Praise: The Panegyric Tradition in Seventeenth-Century English Drama.* Newark: University of Delaware Press. London and Toronto: Associated University Presses, 1986.

Arnheim, Rudolf. *Art and Visual Perception: A Psychology of the Creative Eye—The New Version.* Berkeley and Los Angeles: University of California Press, 1974.

Astington, John H. "The King and Queenes Entertainment at Richmond." *Records of Early English Drama* 12 (1987): 12–18.

Ashmode, Elias. *The Institutions, Laws & Ceremonies of the most Noble Order of the Garter.* London, 1672.

Babington, John. *Pyrotechnia or, A Discovrse of Artificiall Fire-works.* London, 1635.

Bacon, Francis. *Works.* Edited by J. Spedding and R. L. Ellis. London, 1858.

Barish, Jonas A. *Ben Jonson and the Language of Prose Comedy.* Cambridge: Harvard University Press, 1960.

Barkan, Leonard. "The Imperialist Arts of Inigo Jones. Review Article." *Renaissance Drama*, n.s., 7 (1976): 257–85.

Benesch, Otto. *The Art of the Renaissance in Northern Europe: Its Relation to the Contemporary Spiritual and Intellectual Movements.* London: Phaidon, 1965.

Berger, Thomas L. "Textual Problems in English Renaissance Masques, Pageants, and Entertainments." *RORD* 17 (1974): 13–16.

Bergeron, David M. *English Civic Pageantry 1558–1642.* London: Edward Arnold, 1971.

Birch, Thomas. *The Court and Times of Charles the First.* 2 vols. London, 1848.

———. *The Court and Times of James the First.* 2 vols. London, 1849.

Braunmuller, A. R. *A Seventeenth-Century Letter-Book.* Newark: University of Delaware Press. London and Toronto: Associated University Presses, 1983.

Brightman, Thomas. *A Revelation of the revelation . . . opened clearly with a logicall resolution and exposition etc.* Amsterdam, 1615.

Brock, Alan St H. *History of Fireworks.* London: Harrap, 1949.

Brotanek, Rudolf. *Die Englischen Maskenspiele.* Vienna and Leipzig: W. Braumüller, 1902.

Capp, B. S. *The Fifth Monarchy Men.* London and Totowa, N.J.: Rowman and Littlefield, 1972.

Carlton, Charles. *Charles I. The Personal Monarch.* London: Routledge and Kegan Paul, 1983.

Cartari, V. *The Fovntaine of Ancient Fiction Wherein is liuely depictured the Images and Statues of the gods of the Ancients, with their proper and perticular expositions.* Translated by Richard Linch. London, 1599.

Castiglione, Baldessar. *The Courtier. . . .* London, 1603.

Chambers, E. K. *The Elizabethan Stage.* Oxford: Clarendon Press, 1924.

Chan, Mary. *Music in the Theatre of Ben Jonson.* Oxford: Clarendon Press, 1980.

Christianson, Paul. *Reformers and Babylon.* Toronto: University of Toronto Press, 1978.

Clark, A. M. *Thomas Heywood: Playwright and Miscellanist*. Oxford: B. Blackwell, 1931.

Clements, Robert J. *Picta Poesis: Literary and Humanistic Theory and Renaissance Emblem Books*. Rome: Edizioni di storia e letteratura, 1960.

Corbett, Margery, and Ronald Lightbrown. *The Comely Frontispiece: The Emblematic Title-Page in England 1550–1660*. London: Routledge and Kegan Paul, 1979.

Cornvallis, Charles. *The Life and Death of Ovr Late most Incomparable and Heroique Prince, Henry Prince of Wales*. London, 1641.

The Court Masque. Edited by David Lindley. Manchester: Manchester University Press, 1984.

Creigh, Geoffrey. "Samuel Daniel's Masque 'The Vision of Twelve Goddesses.'" *Essays and Studies* 24 (1971): 22–35.

Cunningham, Dolora. "The Jonsonian Masque as a Literary Form." *ELH* 22 (1955): 108–24.

Cutts, John P. "Seventeenth-Century Illustrations of Three Masques by Jonson." *Comparative Drama* 6 (1972): 125–34.

Daly, Peter M. *Literature in the Light of Emblem: Structural Parallels between the Emblem and Literature in the Sixteenth and Seventeenth Centuries*. Toronto: University of Toronto Press, 1979.

———. "The Poetic Emblem." *Neophilologus* 54 (October 1970): 381–97.

Daniel, Samuel. *Hymens Trivmph. A Pastorall Tragicomaedie*. London, 1615.

Davies, John. *Discoverie of the State of Ireland: with the true causes why that Kingdom was neuer entirely Subdued, nor brought vnder Obedience of the Crowne of* ENGLAND, *vntill the Beginning of his Maiesties most happie Raigne*. London, 1613.

———. *Orchestra, or A Poem of Dancing*. London, 1596.

Demaray, John G. *Milton and the Masque Tradition: The Early Poems, "Arcades," and Comus*. Cambridge: Harvard University Press, 1968.

A Dialogue shewing that our Souereigne Lord King Iames, being immediate vnder God . . . Doth rightfully claime . . . the Oath of Allegeance. London, 1615.

Diehl, Huston. *An Index of Icons in English Emblem Books 1500–1700*. Norman and London: University of Oklahoma Press, 1986.

A Direction for the Plantation in Vlster. London, 1610.

Donne, John. *Sermons*. Edited by L. P. Smith. Oxford: Clarendon Press, 1920.

Dramatic Records in the Declared Accounts of the Office of Works 1560–1640, Malone Society Collections, no. 10. Oxford: Malone Society, 1977.

Dundas, Judith. "The Truth of Spectacle: A Meditation on Clouds." *Comparative Drama* 14 (1980–81): 332–45.

Dunlap, Rhodes. "King James's Own Masque." *PQ* 41 (1962): 249–56.

The Earl of Strafford's Letters and Dispatches. Dublin, 1740.

Edgerton, Samuel Y., Jr. *The Renaissance Rediscovery of Linear Perspective*. New York: Basic Books, 1975.

Elam, Keir. *The Semiotics of Theatre and Drama*. London and New York: Methuen, 1980.

Elyot, Thomas. *The Boke, Named the Governour*. London, 1580.

Englands Paradise. Discovered in the Latine prospect of IACOBS *blessing*. London, 1612.

Finett, John. *Finetti Philoxenis*. London, 1656.

Bibliography

Firth, Katharine R. *The Apocalyptic Tradition in Reformation Britain 1530–1645.* Oxford: Oxford University Press, 1979.

Franchis, M. Joannes Maria de. *Of the Most Auspicatious Marriage: Betwixt, the High and Mightie Prince Frederick . . . and the most Illustrious Princesse . . . in III Boc˙s.* London, 1613.

Freeman, Rosemary. *English Emblem Books.* London: Chatto and Windus, 1948.

Furniss, W. Todd. "Ben Jonson's Masques." In *Three Studies in the Renaissance: Sidney, Jonson, Milton,* 89–179. New Haven: Yale University Press, 1958.

Gascoigne, George. *Complete Works.* Edited by J. W. Cunliffe. Cambridge: Cambridge University Press, 1907–10.

Gent, Lucy. *Picture and Poetry 1560–1620.* Leamington Spa, Warwickshire: James Hall, 1981.

Gilbert, Allen H. *The Symbolic Persons in the Masques of Ben Jonson.* Durham, N.C.: Duke University Press, 1948.

Gilman, Ernest B. *The Curious Perspective: Literary and Pictorial Wit in the Seventeenth Century.* New Haven and London: Yale University Press, 1978.

Goldberg, Jonathan. *James I and the Politics of Literature.* Baltimore and London: Johns Hopkins University Press, 1983.

Gombrich, E. H. *Art and Illusion: A Study of the Psychology of Pictorial Representation.* New York: Pantheon Books, 1960.

Gordon, D. J. "Chapman's *Memorable Masque.*" In *The Renaissance Imagination,* edited by Stephen Orgel. Berkeley and Los Angeles: University of California Press, 1975.

Gossett, Suzanne S. "The Term 'Masque' in Shakespeare and Fletcher, and *The Coxcomb.*" *SEL* 14 (1974): 285–95.

Greenblatt, Stephen. *Renaissance Self-Fashioning: From More to Shakespeare.* Chicago and London: University of Chicago Press, 1980.

Greg, W. W. *A Bibliography of the English Printed Drama to the Restoration.* 2 vols. Oxford: Bibliographical Society at the University Press, 1939.

———. *Jonson's Masque of Gipsies in the Burley, Belvoir, and Windsor Versions, an attempt at reconstructing.* London: Oxford University Press, for the British Academy, 1952.

Guibbory, Achsah. *The Map of Time: Seventeenth-Century English Literature and Ideas of Pattern in History.* Urbana and Chicago: University of Illinois Press, 1986.

Guillén, Claudio. "On the Concept and Metaphor of Perspective." In *Comparatists at Work,* edited by Stephen G. Nichols, Jr. and Richard B. Vowles, 28–90. Waltham, Mass., Toronto, and London: Blaisdell Publishing Co., 1968.

Harris, John [Stephen Orgel and Roy Strong,] *The King's Arcadia: Inigo Jones and the Stuart Court.* Exhibition catalogue. London: Arts Council of Great Britain, 1973.

Harris, Victor. *All Coherence Gone.* Chicago: University of Chicago Press, 1949.

Hawkins, Henry. *Parthenia Sacra, or, the Mysterious and delicious Garden of the Sacred Parthenes.* Paris, 1633.

Herford, C. H. [and Percy and Evelyn M. Simpson], eds. *Ben Jonson.* 10 vols. Oxford: Clarendon Press, 1925.

Heywood, Thomas. *Loves Mistresse: or The Queenes Masque.* London, 1636.

———. *Pleasant Dialogves and Dramma, Selected out of Lucian, Erasmus, Textor, Ovid, & c. With sundry Emblems extracted from the most elegant Iacobus Catsius. . . .* London, 1637.

Howes, Edmond. *The Annales, or General Chronicle of England, begun first by maister Iohn Stow, and after him continued and augmented . . . by Edmond Howes.* London, 1614 [1615].

Howard-Hill, T. H. "Towards a Jonson Concordance: A Discussion of Texts and Problems." *RORD* 15–16 (1972–73): 17–32.

Jacobean and Caroline Revels Accounts, 1603–1642, Malone Society Collections, no. 13. Oxford: Malone Society, 1986.

Jakobson, Roman. "On Linguistic Aspects of Translation." In *On Translation,* edited by Reuben A. Brower, 232–39. Cambridge: Harvard University Press, 1959.

Jammer, Max. *Concepts of Space: The History of Space in Physics.* 2d ed. Cambridge: Harvard University Press, 1969.

Javitch, Daniel. *Poetry and Courtliness in Renaissance England.* Princeton: Princeton University Press, 1978.

Jay, Bruce Louis. "The Role of Verse and the Dynamics of Form in Jonson's Masques." *Etudes Anglaises* 29 (1976): 129–43.

Jones, W. J. *The Elizabethan Court of Chancery.* Oxford: Clarendon Press, 1967.

Jensen, H. James. *The Muses' Concord.* Bloomington: Indiana University Press, 1976.

Johnson, Paula. "Jacobean Ephemera and the Immortal Word." *Renaissance Drama* 8 (1977): 151–71.

Kelly, Joseph John. "Ben Jonson's Politics." *Renaissance and Reformation,* n.s., 7 (1983): 192–215.

Kernodle, George R. *From Art to Theatre: Form and Convention in the Renaissance.* Chicago: University of Chicago Press, 1947.

King, John. *Vitis Palatina: A Sermon Appointed to be preached at Whitehall vpon Tuesday after the marriage of the Ladie Elizabeth her Grace.* London, 1614.

Kipling, Gordon. "Triumphal Drama: Form in English Civil Pageantry." *Renaissance Drama* 8 (1977): 37–56.

Knight, William Alexander. *Doomes-day, or, The Great Day of the Lords Ivdgement.* London, 1614.

Kogan, Stephen. *The Hieroglyphic King: Wisdom and Idolatry in the Seventeenth-Century Masque.* London and Toronto: Associated University Presses, 1986.

Kristeller, Paul Oskar. *The Philosophy of Marsilio Ficino.* 1943. Reprint. Gloucester, Mass.: P. Smith, 1964.

Larkin, James F., and Paul L. Hughes. *Stuart Royal Proclamations.* Vol. 1, *Royal Proclamations of King James I 1603–1625.* Oxford: Clarendon Press, 1973.

Lemmi, Charles W. *The Classical Deities in Bacon: A Study in Mythological Symbolism* (Baltimore: Johns Hopkins University Press, 1933).

L'Estrange, Hamon. *The Reign of King Charles.* London, 1655.

Limon, Jerzy. *Dangerous Matter: English Drama and Politics in 1623/24.* Cambridge: Cambridge University Press, 1986.

Loewenstein, Joseph. *Responsive Readings: Versions of Echo in Pastoral, Epic, and the Jonsonian Masque.* New Haven and London: Yale University Press, 1984.

Bibliography

Londons Love, To the Royal Prince Henrie, Meeting Him on the River Thames, at his returne from Richmonde, With a Worthie Fleete of Her Cittizens, on Thursday the last of May. 1610. With a Breife Reporte of the water Fight, and Fire workes. London, 1610.

Lotman, Yuri. "The Poetics of Everyday Behaviour in Eighteenth-Century Russian Culture." In *The Semiotics of Russian Cultural History*, edited by A. D. Nakhimovsky and A. S. Nakhimovsky, 67–94. Ithaca and London: Cornell University Press, 1985.

Lotman, Yuri, and A. M. Piatigorsky. "Text and Function." *New Literary History* 9 (1978): 233–44.

Lotman, Yuri, and B. A. Uspensky. "On the Semiotic Mechanism of Culture." *New Literary History* 9 (1978): 211–32.

McKerrow, R. B., ed. *A Dictionary of Printers and Booksellers in England . . . 1557–1640*. London: Bibliographical Society, 1910.

McKerrow, R. B., and E. S. Fergusson. *Title-page Borders used in England and Scotland*. London: Bibliographical Society at the Oxford University Press, 1932.

The Magnificent Marriage of the Two Great Princes. London, 1613.

Marcus, Leah S. *The Politics of Mirth*. Chicago and London: University of Chicago Press, 1986.

Maxey, D. *Five Sermons Preached before the King*. London, 1614.

Mazzeo, Joseph A. "Universal Analogy and the Culture of the Renaissance." *Journal of the History of Ideas* 15 (1954): 299–304.

Meagher, John C. *Method and Meaning in Jonson's Masques*. Notre Dame and London: University of Notre Dame Press, 1966.

[Mocket, Richard?] *God and the King: or, a Dialogue shewing that our Soueraigne Lord King Iames, being immediate vnder God . . . Doth rightfully claime . . . the Oath of Allegeance*. London, 1615. ["Imprinted by his Majesties special privilege and command."]

Munday, Anthony. *The Trivmphs of re-vnited Britania. Performed . . . on 29. of October. 1605*. London, n.d.

Murray, Timothy. *Theatrical Legitimation: Allegories of Genius in Seventeenth-Century England and France*. New York: Oxford University Press, 1987.

Nabbes, Thomas. *Microcosmus. A Moral Maske. . . .* London, 1637.

———. *The Springs Glorie. Vindicating Love by temperance against the tenent, Sine Cerere & Baccho friget Venus. Moralized in a Maske. With other Poems, Epigrams, Elegies, and Epithalamiums of the Authors*. London, 1638.

New Poems by James I of England. Edited by Allan F. Westcott. New York: Columbia University Press, 1911.

Newton, Richard C. "Jonson and the (re-) Invention of the Book." In *Classic and Cavalier: Essays on Jonson and the Sons of Ben*, edited by Claude J. Summers and Ted-Larry Pebworth, 31–55. Pittsburgh, Pa.: University of Pittsburgh Press, 1982.

Nichols, John. *The Progresses, Processions, and Magnificent Festivities, of King James the First, His Royal Consort, Family and Court*. 4 vols. London, 1828.

Nicoll, Allardyce. *Stuart Masque and the Renaissance Stage*. 1938. Reprint. New York: B. Blom, 1963.

———. "The Symposium at Stockholm, 1960." *Theatre Notebook* 18 (1964): 103–6.

Nicolson, Marjorie. *The Breaking of the Circle: Studies in the Effect of the "New Science."* In *Upon Seventeenth-Century Poetry.* New York: Columbia University Press, 1960.

——. "The 'New Astronomy' and English Literary Imagination." *SP* 32 (1935): 428–60.

——. *A World in the Moon: A Study of the Changing Attitude Toward the Moon in the Seventeenth and Eighteenth Centuries.* Vol. 17, Smith College Studies in Modern Languages. Northampton, Mass.: Departments of Modern Languages of Smith College, 1936.

Nixon, A. *Great Brittaines Generall Ioyes. Londons Glorious Triumphs.* London, 1613.

Norbrook, David. " 'The Masque of Truth': Court Entertainments and International Protestant Politics in the Early Stuart Period." *Seventeenth Century* 1 (July 1986): 81–110.

Orbison, Tucker, ed. *The Middle Temple Documents Relating to George Chapman's The Memorable Masque.* Malone Society Collections, no. 12. Oxford: Oxford University Press, 1983.

The Order and Solemnitie of the Creation of the High and mightie Prince Henrie, Eldest Sonne to our sacred Souereigne, Prince of Wales, Duke of Cornewall, Earle of Chester, &c. As it was celebrated in the Parliament House, on Monday the fourth of Iunne last past. Together with the Ceremonies of the Knights of the Bath, and with other matters of speciall regard, incident to the same. Whereunto is annexed the Royall Maske, presented by the Queene and her Ladies, on Wednesday at night following. London, 1610.

Orgel, Stephen. *The Jonsonian Masque.* Cambridge: Harvard University Presses, 1965.

Orgel, Stephen, and Roy Strong. *Inigo Jones: The Theatre of the Stuart Court.* 2 vols. Berkeley and Los Angeles: University of California Press, 1973.

Orrell, John. "The Agent of Savoy at *The Somerset Masque.*" *ELH* 28 (1977): 301–5.

Palme, Per. *Triumph of Peace.* London: Thames and Hudson, 1957.

Parry, Graham. *The Golden Age Restor'd: The Culture of the Stuart Court, 1603–1642.* Manchester: Manchester University Press, 1981.

Peacham, Henry. *Minerva Britanna, or a Garden of Heroicall Deuises, furnished, and adorned with Emblems and Impresa's of sundry natures. . . .* London, 1612.

——. *The Period of Mourning . . . In Memorie of the late Prince. Together With Nuptiall Hymnes, in Honour of this Happy Marriage . . . Also the manner of the Solemnization of the Marriage at White-Hall, on the 14. of February. . . .* London, 1613.

Peck, Linda Levy. *Northampton: Patronage and Policy at the Court of James I.* London: Allen and Unwin, 1982.

Perkins, William. *The Workes of That Famovs and Worthy Minister of Christ in the Vniversity of Cambridge. Mr. William Perkins.* 3 vols. London, 1612–13.

Petowe, Henry. *Englands Caesar. His Maiesties most Royal Coronation. Together with the manner of the solemne shewes prepared for the honour of his entry into the Cittie of London. Eliza, her Coronation in Heauen. And Londons sorrow for her visitation.* London, 1603.

Pitcher, John. " 'In those figures which they seeme': Samuel Daniel's *Thetys' Festival.*" In *The Court Masque*, edited by David Lindley, 33–47. Manchester: Manchester University Press, 1984.

Plett, Heinrich F. 'Aesthetic Constituents in the Courtly Culture of Renaissance England." *New Literary History* 14 (Spring 1983): 597–621.

Praz, Mario. *Mnemosyne: The Parallel Between Literature and the Visual Arts.* London: Princeton University Press, 1970.

———. *Studies in Seventeenth-Century Imagery.* 2d ed. Rome: Edizioni di storia e letteratura, 1964.

Prescott, Anne Lake. "The Stuart Masque and Pantagruel's Dreams." *ELH* 51 (1984): 407–30.

Prest, Wilfrid R. *The Inns of Court under Elizabeth I and the Early Stuarts 1590–1640.* Totowa, N.J.: Rowman and Littlefield, 1972.

Price, Daniel. *The Creation of the Prince. A Sermon Preached in the Colledge of Westminster, on Trinity Sunday, the day before the Creation of the most Illustrious PRINCE of Wales.* London, 1610.

Price, Sampson. *A Heavenly Proclamation to Fly Romish Babylon.* London, 1614.

P.S. *The Heroicall Deuices.* London, 1591.

Ratajczak, Dobrochna. *Przestrzeń w dramacie i dramat w przestrzeni teatru* (Space in drama and drama in theater space). Poznań: Wydawnictwo UAM, 1985.

———. "Teatralność i sceniczność" (Theatricality and stageability). In *Miejsca wspólne: Szkice o komunikacji literackiej i artystycznej,* edited by E. Balcerzan and Seweryna Wysłouch, 63–85. Warsaw: Polska Akademia Nauk, 1985.

Reynolds, George F. "The Dramatic Quality of Jonson's Masques." *PQ* 22 (1943): 23–28.

Reese, Jack E. "Unity in Chapman's *Masque of the Middle Temple and Lincoln's Inn.*" *SEL* 4 (1984): 291–305.

Regales Aphorismi: Or, A Royal Chain of Golden Sentences, Divine, Moral, and Politicall, as at severall times, and on several occasions they were delivered by King JAMES. London, 1650.

Rich, Barnaby. *A New Description of Ireland.* London, 1610.

———. *A Trve and Kinde Excvse Written in Defense of that Booke, intituled A New Description of Irelande.* London, 1612.

Richards, Kenneth R. "Changeable Scenery for Plays on the Caroline Stage." *Theatre Notebook* 23 (1968): 6–20.

Ripa, Cesare. *Iconologia, or Morall Emblems . . . Explained in 326 Figures.* London, 1709. [First Italian edition: Rome, 1593.]

Sayle, R. T. D. *Lord Mayors' Pageants of the Merchant Taylors' Company in the Fifteenth, Sixteenth, and Seventeenth Centuries.* London: Eastern Press, 1931.

Seznec, Jean. *The Survival of the Pagan Gods: The Mythological Tradition and Its Place in the Renaissance Humanism and Art.* New York: Pantheon Books, 1953.

Shady, Raymond C. "Thomas Heywood's Masque at Court." In *The Elizabethan Theatre VII,* edited by George Hibbard, 147–66. Hamden, Conn.: University of Waterloo and Archon Books, 1980.

Sharpe, Kevin. *Criticism and Compliment: The Politics of Literature in the England of Charles I.* Cambridge: Cambridge University Press, 1987.

Sibley, Gertrude Marian. *The Lost Plays and Masques 1500–1642.* Ithaca: Cornell University Press, 1933.

Simpson, Perry. "Charles I as a Drama Critic." *Bodleian Quarterly Review* 8 (1936–37): 257–62.

Skrine, Peter N. *The Baroque: Literature and Culture in Seventeenth-Century Europe.* London: Methuen, 1978.
Sommerville, J. P. *Politics and Ideology in England, 1603–1640.* London and New York: Longman, 1986.
Southern, Richard. *Changeable Scenery.* London: Faber and Faber, 1952.
Sparrow, John. *Visible Words: A Study of Inscriptions in and as Books and Works of Art.* London: Cambridge University Press, 1969.
Sternfeld, F. W. "A Song From Campion's *Lord's Masque.*" *Journal of the Warburg and Courtauld Institutes* 20 (1957): 373–75.
Strong, Roy. *Art and Power: Renaissance Festivals 1450–1650.* Woodbridge, Suffolk: Boydell Press, 1984. [First published in 1973.]
———. *Britannia Triumphans: Inigo Jones, Rubens and Whitehall Palace.* London: Thames and Hudson, 1980.
———. *Henry, Prince of Wales and England's Lost Renaissance.* New York: Thames and Hudson, 1986.
———. *The Renaissance Garden in England.* London: Thames and Hudson, 1979.
Survey of London. Vol. 13. London: P. S. King and Son, 1930.
Sutherland, Sarah P. *Masques in Jacobean Tragedy.* New York: AMS Press, 1983.
Talbert, Ernest William. "The Interpretation of Jonson's Courtly Spectacles." *PMLA* 61 (1946): 454–73.
———. "New Light on Ben Jonson's Workmanship." *SP* 40 (1943): 154–85.
Taylor, John. *Heaven's Blessing and Earth's Joy; or, A True Relation of the Supposed Sea-Fights and Fire-Workes as Were Accomplished Before the Royall Celebration of the All-Beloved Marriage of the Two Peerlesse Paragons of Christiandome, Frederick and Elizabeth.* London, 1613.
The Triumphs of King Iames The First, Of Great Brittaine, France, and Ireland, King; Defender of the Faith. Published vpon his Maiesties aduertisement to all the Kings, Princes, and Potentates of Christendome, and confirmed by the wonderfull Works of GOD, *declared in his life.* London, 1610.
Turner, Victor. *From Ritual to Theatre: The Human Seriousness of Play.* New York: Performing Arts Journal Publication, 1982.
Waith, Eugene M. "Things as They Are and the World of Absolutes in Jonson's Plays and Masques." In *The Elizabethan Theatre IV,* edited by George Hibbard, 106–26. Hamden, Conn.: Archon Books, 1974.
Wheeler, C. F. *Classical Mythology in the Plays, Masques, and Poems of Ben Jonson.* Princeton: Princeton University Press, 1938.
Whigham, Frank. "Interpretation at Court: Courtesy and the Performer-Audience Dialectic." *New Literary History* 14 (1983): 623–39.
White, Tristram. *The Martyrdome of Saint George of Cappadocia: Titular Patron of England, and of the most Noble Order of the Garter.* London, 1614.
Whitney, Geffrey. *A Choice of Emblems and Other Devices.* Leyden, 1586.
Wickham, Glynne. *Early English Stages 1300 to 1660.* Vol. 2 pt. 1. London and New York: Columbia University Press, 1963.
Willet, A. *A Treatise of Salomons Mariage.* London, 1612 [1613].
Williams, Ethel Carleton. *Anne of Denmark, Wife of James VI of Scotland: James I of England.* London: Longmans, 1970.

Bibliography

Williams, Mary C. "Merlin and the Prince: The Speeches at Prince Henry's Barriers." *Renaissance Drama*, n.s., 8 (1977): 221–30.

Williamson, J. W. *The Myth of the Conqueror. Prince Henry Stuart: A Study of 17th-Century Personation.* New York: AMS Press, 1978.

Winwood, Ralph. *Memorials of Affairs of State in the Reigns of Q. Elizabeth and K. James I.* 3 vols. London, 1725.

Woodman, David. *White Magic and English Renaissance Drama.* Rutherford-Madison-Teaneck, N.J.: Fairleigh Dickinson University Press, 1973.

Yates, Frances A. *Rosicrucian Enlightenment.* London and Boston: Routledge and Kegan Paul, 1972.

Zgorzelski, Andrzej. *Dramat. Między literaturą a teatrem* (Drama: Between literature and theater). Gdańsk: Gdańskie Towarzystwo Naukowe, 1983.

Index

Akrigg, G. P. V., 100
Albions Triumph (Townshend and Jones), 26, 40, 82–85, 124, 207 n.77
Alchemist, The (Jonson), 124, 176
Anne, Queen, 25, 98–99, 114, 122, 124, 174–75, 180, 187
Antimasque, 47, 57, 61–62, 64–65, 67, 71, 74; as anticulture, 90–91; and folk tradition, 43; in *The Masque of Augurs*, 47; in *The Masque of Flowers*, 187–88, 195; in *The Masque of the Inner Temple and Gray's Inn*, 160–61; in *The Memorable Masque*, 145
Ashmole, Elias, 148
Authorship of masques, problems of, 24–28
Autonomy, of literary text, 18–19, 29, 30, 32, 37, 41, 42, 45, 49

Bacon, Francis, 23, 65, 125, 169, 176; on gardens, 189–90, 192; on Ireland, 181; and *The Masque of Flowers*, 185–86; and *The Masque of the Inner Temple and Gray's Inn*, 136, 157–58
Banqueting House, 47, 81, 83, 85, 95, 96, 99, 103, 115, 116, 123, 133–35, 136, 159
Barish, Jonas A., 63
Barkan, Leonard, 207 n.77
Basilikon Doron (James I), 9, 85, 86, 97, 123, 150, 151, 187, 207 n.82
Beaumont, Francis, 29, 135–36, 157–63, 165–67, 169, 213 n.66
Black letter, 49
Bogatyrev, Petr, 97, 184
Boke, Named the Governor, The (Elyot), 23, 67
Book of Masques (Nabbes), 45
Bretbie Masque (Cohayne), 21
Brightman, Thomas, 192–93
Britannia Triumphs (Jones and Davenant), 26, 124

Browne, William, 74
Bruno, Giordano, 53

Campion, Thomas, 20–21, 25, 26, 30, 32, 40, 81, 98, 113; and Frederick V's marriage cycle, 135–42, 163–66; and Somerset's marriage cycle, 170–78, 180, 195
Capp, B. S., 176
Carew, Thomas, 80, 124
Carleton, Dudley, 100, 114, 117, 185, 214 nn. 11 and 23
Carr, Robert. *See* Somerset, earl of
Cassirer, Ernst, 54–55
Castiglione, Baldessar, 96
Catoptrics, 49
Cecil, Lord Robert, 21,113
Chaine of Golden Poems (Cohayne), 21
Challenge at Tilt (Jonson), 170, 178–80
Chamberlain, John, 28, 102–3, 115; on Frederick V's marriage cycle, 134, 135–36, 137, 158, 163; on Somerset's marriage cycle, 179, 184, 185, 214 nn. 11 and 23
Chan, Mary, 64–65, 206 n.52
Chapman, George, 25, 31, 34, 171; and Frederick V's marriage cycle, 135, 136, 142–57, 165, 169, 212 n.54; Jonson on, 150
Charles I, 17, 63, 86, 112, 115, 123; and *Albions Triumph*, 83, 84; and Banqueting House, 135; as censor, 28; role of in masques, 28, 44
Chloridia (Jonson and Jones), 40, 123
Christian IV (of Denmark), 29, 113, 127
Christmas his Show (Jonson), 20
Circe and Ulysses (Browne), 74
Coelum Britannicum (Carew and Jones), 124
Cohayne, Sir Aston, 21
Colonization: of Virginia, 155, 212 n.54; of Ireland, 182–83, 184–85

Cornwallis, Sir Charles, 101, 102
Costume, 32, 33, 39, 50, 94, 96; in Frederick V's marriage cycle, 147, 165; in Somerset's marriage cycle, 173, 180, 183
Court behavior, theatricality of, 92–104, 178
Cunningham, David, 134
Cunningham, Dolora, 19, 35
Cupid's Banishment (White), 39, 50, 74–75
Cusanus, Nicolas, 53
Cycles, masque, 107–12, 122–24, 163, 170, 195–96. *See also* Frederick V; Somerset, earl of

Daly, Peter M., 87, 90
Dance, 23, 59; in *Cupid's Banishment*, 50; as emblems, 79; in *The Irish Masque*, 180–81, 183; and literary masque, 19, 23, 32, 37; in *The Masque of Augurs*, 47, 48, 49–50; in *The Masque of Beauty*, 29; in *The Masque of Blackness*, 49–50; in *The Masque of Flowers*, 178; in *The Masque of the Inner Temple and Gray's Inn*, 29, 160, 162; meanings of, 23, 50, 88; in *Pleasure Reconciled to Virtue*, 88
Dancing floor, 59–61
Daniel, Samuel, 27, 33–34, 38, 87, 115, 121–22, 178–79
Davenant, William, 26, 80
Davies, Sir John, 37, 182
Davison, Francis, 24–25
de Caus, Salomon, 190–91
de Franchis, M. Joannes Maria, 129–32, 138, 140, 153, 160, 161
Dekker, Thomas, 195
Discovery of the State of Ireland, A (Davies), 182
Divine Right of Kings, 88, 90. *See also Basilikon Doron*
Donne, John, 54, 87
Drummond of Hawthornden, 54

Eco, Umberto, 76
Elam, Keir, 63, 76
Elyot, Sir Thomas, 23, 67
Emblems: books of, 44, 52, 54, 76, 78, 87, 88, 171, 173, 194; and Frederick V's marriage cycle, 140, 141, 168–69;

and James I, 85–86, 123; and Jonson, 78–79, 80, 81–82, 206 n.52; and Somerset's marriage cycle, 171, 172–74, 194
England's Paradise, 215 n.49
Entertainments, royal, 98–99, 113. *See also* Cycles

Festival. *See* Cycles
Fifth Monarchy, 176, 192, 195, 196
Finett, John, 125
Fireworks, 113–14, 115, 122, 127–28, 130, 131–32, 133, 211 n.10
Five Sermons Preached before the King (Maxey), 193
Folk theater, 43, 123, 184
For the Honour of Wales (Jonson), 32
Frederick V: marriage cycle of, 125–69. *See also The Lords Masque, The Masque of the Inner Temple and Gray's Inn, The Memorable Masque*
Freeman, Rosemary, 79

Gardens, 182–83, 184, 188–92, 194, 195, 215 n.49
Gascoigne, George, 24
Gilbert, Allen H., 86
God and the King (James I), 90
Gordon, D. J., 82–83, 84, 86, 149–50, 151, 212 n.54
Great Brittaines Generall Ioyes (Nixon), 126
Greenblatt, Stephen, 92, 93

Haddington Masque (Jonson), 86
Harington, Sir John, 29–30, 96
Hawkins, Henry, 192
Heavenly Proclamation to Fly Romish Babylon (Price), 193–94
Heaven's Blessing and Earth's Joy (Taylor), 127–28, 132
Henry, Prince of Wales: investiture of, 116–22, 180, 210 n.22, 213 n.66
Heroical Devices, The (P. S.), 173–74
Heywood, Thomas, 36, 45, 114, 203 n.54
Howard, Frances, 170, 177. *See* Somerset, earl of
Hue and Cry After Cupid (Jonson), 115
Hymenaei (Jonson), 39, 78, 86, 114
Hymen's Triumph (Daniel), 178, 179

Index

Iconologia (Ripa), 52, 141
Ideology, Stuart, 52, 63, 89, 107, 123; and Frederick V's marriage cycle, 149, 167–68
Invention, of masques, 25–28, 55–56, 89, 116, 201 n.1
Irish Masque, The (Jonson), 170, 180–85, 195

Jakobson, Roman, 37, 78
James I, 29, 62, 90, 122, 127, 180; as actor, 99–100, 122, 133, 212 n.52; on alcohol, 187–88; and Bible, 193, 195, 215 n.49; and Frederick V's marriage cycle, 125, 168; as "gardener," 182–83, 184, 215 n.49; influence of death on masques, 122–23; and *Haddington Masque*, 86; and *The Irish Masque*, 180, 181–84, 185; and *The Lords Masque*, 164; and *The Masque of Augurs*, 50, 86; and *The Masque of Flowers*, 186, 187–88, 189, 191–96; and *The Masque of the Inner Temple and Gray's Inn*, 161–63; and *The Masque of Truth*, 167–68; and *The Memorable Masque*, 146–47, 150–55, 165; and millenarianism, 176, 193–96; and *Oberon*, 196; and *Pleasure Reconciled to Virtue*, 87; role of, in masque, 44–45, 59, 64, 68, 71–72, 85–86; and *The Somerset Masque*, 172, 174–78; as source of light, 71–72, 74–75, 151–54, 164, 184, 187, 191, 195, 196, 215 n.32; and *Tethys Festival*, 121; and *Time Vindicated*, 57; and tobacco campaign, 187, 188; and *The Vision of Delight*, 196. See also *Basilikon Doron*
Jammer, Max, 75
Javitch, Daniel, 93
Jensen, H. James, 55
Jocquet, D., 166–67
Johnson, Paula, 202 nn. 31 and 34
Jones, Inigo, 17, 40–41, 56, 68, 69; and architecture, 207 n.77; and Banqueting House, 134; and Jonson, 25, 91, 112, 201 n.19; and literary masque, 32–33, 40; and masque as emblem book, 78, 80, 123; and problems of authorship, 25–28
Jonson, Ben, 17, 18, 31–32, 36, 43, 57, 74, 150, 176; and allegory, 39–40; and antimasque, 64, 65, 74; artistic autonomy of, 28–29, 116; and cycles, 114–16; and dance, 23, 49–50; and emblem books, 78–79, 80, 81, 206 n.52; on invention, 25, 116; and Jones, 25, 91, 112, 201 n.19; literary innovation of, 32, 35–37, 41–42, 45, 46; masquers in, 73–74, 205 n.44; and music, 39, 62, 202 n.22; pre- and postperformance texts in, 20, 21, 34–35, 39; and problems of authorship, 25–28; and royal entertainments, 98–99, 113; and Somerset's marriage cycle, 170, 178–85; and typography, 42, 49, 51

Life of Prince Henry (Cornwallis), 101, 102
Lindley, David, 18, 52
Loewenstein, Joseph, 205 n.40
Lord Hayes Masque (Campion), 20–21, 26, 30, 32, 40, 73, 80; (Jonson), 81–82
The Lords Masque (Campion), 62, 125, 135–42, 159, 163–65, 166, 169, 212 n.61
Lotman, Yuri, 76, 99, 100
Lotman, Yuri, and Boris Uspensky, 89, 90, 207 n.92
Love Freed From Ignorance and Folly (Jonson), 39–40, 43, 74, 115
Love Restored (Jonson), 64, 73, 115
Lovers Made Men (Jonson), 81
Love's Mistress: or The Queenes Masque (Heywood), 45
Loves Triumph Through Callipolis (Jonson and Jones), 69, 123
Luminalia (Jones and Davenant), 25–26, 124

Magnificent Marriage of the Two Great Princes, 132–35
Marcus, Leah S., 207 n.82
Mask of Proteus and the Adamantine Rock, The (Davison), 24–25
Masque, Caroline, 40, 122, 123–24
Masque, dramatic, 20–21, 24, 25, 28
Masque, literary: allegory in, 35, 38–39, 41, 51; basic elements of, 37–38, 50; as descriptions, 31–41, 42; dialogue in, 31, 33–34; distinct from

dramatic masque, 20–21, 24; distinct from masque-in-performance, 19, 27–28, 42; evolution of, 50; and staging, 20–21, 30, 38–39, 44; interpretation in, 47, 48; postperformance texts in, 18, 21, 25, 34, 43; preperformance texts in, 18, 20–21, 24, 25, 28–29, 33. *See also* Autonomy, of literary text
Masque at Kenilworth, The (Gascoigne), 24
Masque cycles. *See* Cycles, masque
Masque-in-performance: architectural settings of, 82–84, 207 n.77; audience in, 63–64, 68, 88, 96, 206 n.52; authorship of, 26–27; basic elements of, 36, 38, 67, 71, 90; censorship in, 28, 112; dance in, 59–60; distinct from literary masque, 19, 27–28, 42; as emblem book, 44, 76, 78–82, 85–91; king's role in, 64, 68, 71–72, 75, 85, 86, 94; new philosophy in, 53–54; ostension in, 76; and ritual, 62–67, 76, 77; seating order in, 63–64, 96–97; semiotics of, 89; stage space organization in, 58–60, 67, 68, 205 n.40; uniqueness of, 23, 30–31, 36; and visual arts, 77–78
Masque of Amazons, The, 28
Masque of Augurs, The (Jonson), 26, 46–50, 57, 65, 69, 86
Masque of Beauty, The (Jonson), 29, 46, 67, 80
Masque of Blackness, The (Jonson), 21, 22, 46, 49–50, 74, 114, 115
Masque of Cupid, The (Middleton), 170, 185
Masque of Flowers, The (anon.), 43, 80, 170, 177, 185–95
Masque of Heroes, The (Middleton), 72, 73
Masque of Queens, The (Jonson), 21, 27, 31, 39, 62, 65
Masque of Scots, The (lost), 113
Masque of the Inner Temple and Gray's Inn, The (Beaumont), 29, 126, 135–36, 157–63, 165–67, 213 n.66
Masque of the Knights of India and China, The (lost), 113
Masque of Truth, The (lost), 166–69
Masque of Twelve Months, The, 59

Masquers, 72–74, 88, 165, 184, 205 n.44
Maxey, D., 193
Mazzeo, Joseph A., 55
Meagher, John C., 75, 205 n.44
Memorable Masque, The (Chapman), 25, 31, 34; biblical references in, 153–54; in Frederick V's marriage cycle, 126, 135, 136, 142–57, 165, 166, 171, 180, 212 n.54
Mercury Vindicated (Jonson), 74
Microcosm: A Moral Maske (Nabbes), 54
Middleton, Thomas, 72, 73, 115, 170, 185, 195–96
Millenarianism, 91, 168, 176, 193–94
Minerva Britanna (Peacham), 54, 149, 168–69
Munday, Anthony, 117–18, 121, 122, 210 nn. 18 and 20
Murray, Timothy, 37, 41–42
Music: in masque-in-performance, 61–62, 67; in *The Irish Masque*, 180–81, 183; and literary masque, 19, 23–24, 32, 39; in *The Lords Masque*, 138, 164; and *The Masque of Queens*, 39; in *The Memorable Masque*, 151–52
Mythological characters, 52, 57, 71, 85, 99, 113, 118–19, 137

Nabbes, Thomas, 44, 54
Neoplatonism, 55–56, 61, 65, 67
Neptune's Triumph (Jonson), 28, 44
New Description of Ireland (Rich), 181, 184–85
News From the New World Discovered (Jonson), 75, 87
Nicoll, Allardyce, 17, 60, 78
Nichols, John, 101–2
Nixon, A., 126
Norbrook, David, 63, 166–69, 213 nn. 66 and 71

Oberon (Jonson), 35, 80, 115, 196
Of the Most Auspicatious Marriage (de Franchis), 129–32, 138, 140, 153, 160
Orchestra, or a Poem of Dancing (Davies), 37
Orgel, Stephen, 19, 35–36, 46, 49–50, 64, 73, 89
Orgel, Stephen, and Roy Strong, 20, 60, 68, 80, 88, 134
Orrel, John, 213 n.3

Index

Panofsky, Erwin, 53
Pans Anniversarie (Jones and Jonson), 26, 62, 63, 74
Parry, Graham, 27–28, 204 n.24
Peacham, Henry, 54, 85, 140, 149, 168–69
The Penates (Jonson), 98–99
Pitcher, John, 121–22
Pleasant Dialogues and Drammas (Heywood), 36
Pleasure Reconciled to Virtue (Jonson), 29, 32, 75, 86, 87–88; antimasque in, 65; dance in, 79; grammatical tenses in, 21, 31–32
Plett, Heinrich F., 93
Poetry, 37, 41–42, 43, 55
Price, Sampson, 193–94
Progresses, 95, 100, 143, 147–48, 157
Proscenium arch, 27, 59, 79–81, 82, 84–85, 205 n.40

Quarles, Francis, 87
Queens Masque, The (Jonson), 46

Ralegh, Sir Walter, 93, 193, 212 n.54
Reese, Jack E., 155
Relation of the Late Royall Entertainment, A (Campion), 98, 136–37
Revelation of the revelation, A (Brightman), 192–93
Reynolds, George F., 18
Rich, Barnaby, 181, 184–85
Ripa, Cesare, 52, 141
Ritual: and courtly behavior, 92–93, 95, 120; masque-in-performance as, 62, 63–64, 67, 74, 76, 77, 93–94
Rubens, Peter Paul, 85, 135

Salmacida Spolia (Davenant), 26
Scenery: in *Albions Triumph*, 82–84; in *The Irish Masque*, 184; in literary masque, 40, 50; in *The Lord Hay's Masque*, 30; in *The Lords Masque*, 137; in *The Masque of Flowers*, 188–89; in *The Memorable Masque*, 143–45; in *The Somerset Masque*, 170–71
Sea battles, 100, 108, 115, 122, 132–33, 135
Semiotics. *See* Sign-systems
Seznec, Jean, 90, 99
Shapiro, I. A., 137

Sharpe, Kevin, 65, 103–4
Shirley, James, 26, 27, 32–33, 40, 72, 124
Sign-systems, 53; and courtly behavior, 52, 92, 94–95; and cycles, 108; and dance, 50; and fireworks, 114; transformations in, 21, 23, 37, 78
Skrine, Peter N., 96, 208 n.16
Somerset, earl of: marriage cycle of, 170–97. *See also Challenge at Tilt, The Irish Masque, The Masque of Cupid, The Masque of Flowers*
Somerset Masque, The (Campion), 81, 170–78, 195, 213 n.3
Southern, Richard, 79
Spheres, of masque universe, 57–63, 65, 67, 69, 74, 84, 95
Spring's Glory, The (Nabbes), 44–45
Stage: directions of, 21, 31–32; "frontispiece" of, 79–80, 81, 82, 85; illusionistic, 19, 30, 40, 43, 52, 53, 57–61, 67, 77; perspective, 53, 60, 67–69, 71, 77
Strong, Roy, 27, 62, 78, 85, 190, 206 n.71; on cycles (festivals), 56, 108, 117, 197, 216 n.51

Talbert, Ernest William, 86
Taylor, John, 127–28, 132
Tempe Restord (Townshend and Jones), 25, 40, 56, 80, 124
Tethys Festival (Daniel), 27, 33–34, 38, 60, 121–22
Tilts, 100–101, 102, 115, 122, 161, 162–63, 178–80
Time Vindicated (Jonson), 57, 69, 124
Townshend, Aurelian, 25, 40, 56, 80, 82, 83, 124
Triumphs of King Iames the First, The, 194
Triumph of Peace, The (Shirley), 26, 27, 32–33, 40, 72, 124
Triumphs of the Prince D'Amour, The (Davenant), 80
Turner, Victor, 64, 77, 93–94

Universal analogy, 54–55, 74
Uspensky, Boris, and Yuri Lotman, 89, 90, 207 n.92

Vision of Delight, The (Jonson), 196

Vision of the Twelve Goddesses, The (Daniel), 33–34, 38, 87, 113

Whigham, Frank, 94
White, Robert, 74–75
Whitney, Geffrey, 171, 173
Wisdom of the Ancients, The (Bacon), 138
Wither, George, 173, 194
Wood, Anthony à, 98
Woodman, David, 204 n.21
Workes (Jonson), 18, 20, 34–35, 180
World-as-book, concept of, 86–89

Yates, Frances A., 126–27, 211 n.10

Zgorzelski, Andrzej, 30

WITHDRAWN from the Alma College Library